Ambiguities of Domination

Ambiguities of Domination

Politics, Rhetoric, and Symbols in Contemporary Syria

Lisa Wedeen

The University of Chicago Press
Chicago and London

The University of Chicago Press, Chicago 60637
The University of Chicago Press, Ltd., London
© 1999 by The University of Chicago
All rights reserved. Published 1999
15 14 13 12 11   6 7 8 9 10

ISBN-13: 978-0-226-87787-7 (cloth)
ISBN-13: 978-0-226-87788-4 (paper)
ISBN-10: 0-226-87787-6 (cloth)
ISBN-10: 0-226-87788-4 (paper)

Library of Congress Cataloging-in-Publication Data
Wedeen, Lisa.
    Ambiguities of domination : politics, rhetoric, and symbols in
contemporary Syria / Lisa Wedeen.
        p. cm.
    Includes bibliographical references and index.
    ISBN 0-226-87787-6 (alk. paper)
    ISBN 0-226-87788-4 (pbk. : alk. paper)
    1. Symbolism in politics—Syria. 2. Rhetoric—Political aspects—
Syria. 3. Syria—Politics and government—1971- 4. Assad, Hafez,
1928-   5. Political culture—Syria. 6. Public opinion—Syria. I. Title.
DS98.4. W43   1999
320.95691—dc21
                                                                98-46430
                                                                      CIP

Contents

Acknowledgments

This work would not have been possible without the assistance of many Syrians whose names must go unmentioned. The hospitality shown to me by my hosts made my years of field work remarkably pleasurable. In particular, I thank my longtime friends who shared their experiences, introduced me to their friends, and encouraged me in my intellectual concerns. Syrians taught me what I know about Syria. They helped me to think about power and official rhetoric in ways that allowed me to question some of the abiding assumptions and underlying concepts of social science. Although official interviews were an important part of this learning process, it was really the events of everyday life, the periods of "hanging" out—of drinking coffee, studying at the university, teaching exercise classes, making olives, babysitting, hosting salon-like gatherings in my home, going to films, shopping for groceries, riding the bus with friends to visit relatives in faraway places—that produced the chance encounters and enduring connections that animate this book.

Many people have earned my gratitude for their intellectual support. Hanna Pitkin's love for and precision with language has had a lasting impact on the way in which I think and write about the world. For her careful, critical readings of many drafts, I am particularly appreciative. Laura Green's invaluable comments on several versions of the book reinforce my admiration for her acuity, wit, and eloquence. I would also like to thank my colleagues at the University of Chicago who helped me to transform the dissertation into a book. Specifically, the members of the Wilder House

Editorial Board and audiences at many workshops offered insightful suggestions that helped to make the metamorphosis possible. For incisive readings of all or parts of the book at various stages of its development, I am indebted to Lila Abu-Lughod, Andrew Apter, Nadia Abu el-Haj, Lauren Berlant, Robin Derby, Gaston Alonso Donate, James Fearon, Debbie Gould, John Mark Hansen, Gary Herrigel, Ken Jowitt, David Laitin, Ira Lapidus, Zachary Lockman, Volker Perthes, Karen Pilkington, Moishe Postone, Michael Rogin, Lynn Sanders, William H. Sewell Jr., and Robert Vitalis. Joseph Logan was a fine research assistant. Engseng Ho's erudition made the process of reviewing transliterations more delightful than it otherwise would have been.

Earlier versions of chapter 3 were presented at the 1995 annual meeting of the American Political Science Association, at the Massachusetts Institute of Technology, the University of California at Berkeley, the University of Chicago, New York University, and Wesleyan University. I am grateful to those audiences for their comments. I would especially like to thank the anonymous reviewers at Comparative Studies in Society and History for their critical readings. James Schaefer's editorial assistance and permission to reprint a slightly different version of chapter 3 here are appreciated.

I would also like to thank the staffs at the Asad library and at the Institut Français d'Études Arabes de Damas for their assistance. In France, the staffs at the Institut du Monde Arabe, at the Ministère des Affaires Étrangères, and at the Ministère de la Défense in the Chateau de Vincennes were also helpful. Two years of field research were funded by the Fulbright Commission. Summer funding in 1996 was provided by Wesleyan University.

Recognition is also due the anonymous readers at the University of Chicago Press for their wise comments and criticisms. Executive editor John Tryneski's support for the project and his professionalism have made this book possible. Leslie Keros and Bob Caceres deserve credit for their fine work as well.

For their constancy and companionship over many years, I would like to thank, sometimes for a second time, Betsy Andrews, Kateri Carmola, Gaston Alonso Donate, Laura Green, Rick Hooper, Susan Lehman, Carol Lloyd, and Karen Pilkington. My parents, Harvey Wedeen and Helen Kwalwasser Wedeen, helped me remember to keep working. My son Zack often urged me to stop and come out and play. This book is dedicated to Don Reneau, the reader of countless drafts over many years, for his curiosity, erudition, tolerance, and occasional sense of humor.

A Note on Transliteration

The transliteration method used in this book attempts to combine accuracy with technical simplicity. It is based primarily on the system adopted by the *International Journal of Middle East Studies*. However, diacritical marks indicating long vowels and emphatic consonants are dropped. Widely recognized Anglicized variants of places are spelled according to convention. Most names are spelled according to *IJMES* rules with the exception of those in which the letter "g" is pronounced in English: Bourguiba and Gamal ʿAbd al-Nasir.

FIGURE 1   The banner below the bust of Syrian President Hafiz al-Asad
bears the Islamic *shahada* or standard testimonial of faith: "There is no god
but God; Muhammad is His Messenger" (*La ilaha illa Allah; Muhammad
Rasul Allah*).

One

Believing in Spectacles

INTRODUCTION

In official Syrian political discourse, President Hafiz al-Asad is regularly depicted as omnipresent and omniscient. In newspaper photographs he appears as the "father," the "combatant," the "first teacher," the "savior of Lebanon," the "leader forever," or the "gallant knight," a transparent reference to the modern-day Salah al-Din, after the original, who wrested Jerusalem from enemy control in 1187. At regional summit meetings he "shows complete understanding of all issues." Religious iconography and slogans attesting to his immortality bedeck the walls of buildings, the windows of taxi cabs, and the doors of restaurants. If only by dint of repetition, everyone is fluent in this symbolic vocabulary of the Syrian state, which has become a hallmark of Asad's regime.

There is no reason to doubt that those members of the political and cultural elite who conceive and deliver these panegyrics to Asad's greatness in fact respect his leadership qualities. He is widely known both within and beyond the Middle East for his political savvy, especially in matters of foreign policy. But surely no one in modern Syria, neither those who orchestrate official praise nor those who are forced to consume it, believes that Asad is the country's "premier pharmacist," that he "knows all things about all issues," or that he actually garners 99.2 percent of the vote in elections. Neither the haloed images sanctifying his mother nor paintings of Asad framed by the sun are likely to inspire belief in his literal holiness. As one prominent scholar of Syria writes: "Enthusiasm may not go very deep; even party members cannot be forced 1 to believe the slogans they chant. . . . Lack of inner conviction is acceptable as long as every single party member and official is prepared to demonstrate publicly his/her commitment to party and President."[1] In fact, the main product of the cult of Hafiz al-Asad seems to be a general atmosphere of skeptical ambivalence that attends the practice of politics in Syria. "When [Asad] does make a public appearance," writes a Middle East Watch representative, "the delirious masses such as those that used to greet Egyptian president 'Abd al-Nasir are not present. Even the casual visitor to Syria can tell that Asad is not the object of universal adulation."[2]

It is easy to adduce examples of the distanced, irreverent attitude Syrians adopt in relation to the cult and its propaganda. Daily state-controlled newspapers in Syria are widely considered to be functional tablecloths, rather than respected records of current events. One such paper, *al-Thawra* (The revolution), allegedly experienced a 35 percent drop in sales after it temporarily suspended its independent-minded cartoonist and political satirist.[3] Television comedies and feature-length films often poke fun at official discourse, and underground jokes about the cult abound. People from different social classes and from diverse religious backgrounds privately grumble about the sheer financial extravagance of the cult. Spectacles such as opening festivals, referendum celebrations, and state holiday rituals are orchestrated and attendance is generally enforced by regime officials. (For example, party members have been known to order the university gates closed to keep students from leaving the campus; then they marshal students onto buses and transport them to festivities honoring the president.) This is not to say that no one would go to spectacles if the state did not compel attendance, but state authorities are sufficiently anxious about the matter to devise strategies ensuring a good turnout. One journalist estimated that at the opening ceremony of the 1996 "Festival of Basil," which was named after Asad's oldest son and sponsored by the Ministry of Culture, over 75 percent of those attending were military conscripts or members of the Ba'th Party's "popular" organizations.[4]

Syrians of all sorts, at one time or another, have been compelled to bend their talents to the service of state propaganda. Youth are ritualistically enlisted to assemble at rallies orchestrated by "popular" organizations;[5] individual poets, university professors, artists, and playwrights are periodically called upon to help produce the public spectacles and to maintain Asad's cult; the federation of peasants and workers and the professional syndicates of journalists, lawyers, teachers, and doctors, among others, are all required at one time or another to conjure up slogans and imagery representing their idealized connection to party and president. Often citizens respond by finding a way to avoid trouble without feeling deeply compromised. For example, one artist ordered to create a poster chose to copy a painting that hangs in Asad's office. The painting depicts the battle of Hittin in which Salah al-Din defeated the Crusaders and reclaimed Jerusalem for the Arabs. Over the battle scene, the artist superimposed a large photograph of Asad's face, adding the caption: "from Hittin to Tishrin." *Tishrin* (October) is universally understood to refer to the October 1973 war, so the poster, which was widely distributed during Asad's 1991 referendum, seems to identify Asad's October War with Salah al-Din's legendary military victory. The artist claims that his point, however, was to draw people's attention to the *contrast* between Salah al-Din's triumph and Asad's "victory." The artist found a way to subvert (or at least to persuade himself that he was subverting) the state's symbols without causing himself trouble with the authorities.[6] He walked a fine line that many Syrians recognize as expertly as they practice what is required of them by the cult. Even members of the regime who are directly responsible for disseminating propaganda and ideology sometimes acknowledge the disparity between the slogans they produce and the political convictions they hold.[7] As one independent member of Parliament said privately, "What the regime says is 180 degrees from the truth: they make a workers' union against the workers, a women's union against women, a Parliament against democracy. . . . No one believes the things they say, and everyone knows that no one believes them."[8]

In Syria, in other words, it is impossible *not* to experience the difference between what social scientists, following Max Weber, might conceive as a charismatic, loyalty-producing regime and its anxiety-inducing simulacrum. There is a shabbiness to Asad's cult, even a cynicism about it, that is as apparent as its laudatory slogans and sempiternal images are ubiquitous. If its purpose is to create charisma and induce popular belief, then Asad's cult of personality does not seem to be working. Yet the Syrian leadership considers the cult worthy of considerable expenditures of both time and money.

Accounts of Syrian politics fail to address the question of why the state continues to devote resources to perpetuating the cult and compelling citizens to take part in it; indeed, most of the scholarship tends to ignore the cult and its implications for political life altogether. In the first volume of Raymond Hinnebusch's two-volume study of Syria, for instance, the Syrian state is likened to "a 'Bonapartist' regime—a postrevolutionary authoritarian regime standing 'above' classes and presiding over the formation of a strong new state and the transition from a feudal order to a more modern, complex society."[9] But Hinnebusch fails to mention what Marx, from whom he borrows the term "Bonapartist," takes to be crucial, namely, the ways in which symbols and images publicly represent the leader's power. For Marx, Bonaparte's rule meant that the state could avoid a divisive declaration of its class interests by manipulating symbols, thereby diverting attention from the leader's material aims.[10] "Bonapartism" loses its symbolic dimensions in Hinnebusch's work; he writes as if Asad's cult did not exist. Other scholars who do mention the cult treat it as marginal, worthy of only fleeting attention.[11]

The methods of both the social sciences and the humanities do offer some useful tools for understanding a cult like Asad's, and this chapter will explore some relevant approaches to the significance of symbols for political analyses. Yet while the examples on which I will draw, from comparative politics and the literature on "spectacles" (state rituals, cults, and festivals), are useful and suggestive, they prove remarkably insufficient when applied seriously to the Syrian context. Either Syria is an exception to the explanatory models scholars proffer, or their central concepts are so highly ambiguous that they offer no clear explanation at all. These accounts, furthermore, fail to attend to one phenomenon that fairly leaps to the observer's attention in the Syrian case and that has been theorized abstractly in recent years: the ways in which cult and spectacle both produce political power yet also, paradoxically, invite transgressions. Deficiencies in the available literature imply that a careful investigation of Asad's cult can make a larger contribution beyond Syrian or Middle Eastern Studies. Specifying the nature of and rationale behind symbolic displays in authoritarian countries such as Syria can help to clarify more general concepts such as obedience, complicity, power, and membership.[12]

LEGITIMACY, CHARISMA, AND HEGEMONY

Political scientists have generated neither precise concepts nor an adequate methodology for understanding the role of rhetoric and symbols in producing political power in the absence of belief or emotional commitment. One prominent approach treats politics as basically a matter of material interests and the groups that articulate them, regarding symbolic displays of power and rhetorical practices as epiphenomenal.[13] Applied to Syria, this "materialist" outlook produces studies restricted to the state's power to control material resources, on the one hand, and to construct institutions of enforcement and punishment on the other.[14] Although the question of material and punitive inducements is undeniably important, such approaches fail to analyze the state's attempts to control the symbolic world, that is, to manipulate and manage systems of signification. This literature thereby overlooks the ways in which official rhetoric and images operate as forms of power in their own right, helping to enforce obedience and sustain the conditions under which regimes rule. Materialist studies simply do not explain why the Syrian government expends exorbitant sums of money and scarce material resources on symbolic production, instead of marshalling its limited funds for either increases in punitive enforcement or the positive inducements that goods and services can offer.

A second set of interpretations, which we might call the "ideational" group or the school of political culture, has suggested that rhetoric and symbols determine political outcomes.[15] "Discourse" in the ideational school is an independent variable. Such interpretations tend to suggest that "successful" rhetoric and symbols produce "legitimacy," "charisma," or "hegemony" for the regime, enabling political leaders to win support for themselves and their policies by fostering collective ethnic, national, or class identifications. The problem with these treatments is that they fail to distinguish between public dissimulation of loyalty or belief, on the one hand, and real loyalty or belief, on the other.[16] That all Syrians are capable of reproducing the regime's formulaic slogans tells us mainly that the regime is capable of enforcing obedience on the level of outward behavior. Interviews with men and women from diverse generational, religious, sectarian, and class backgrounds, combined with other types of evidence drawn from two-and-one-half years of fieldwork, suggest that Asad's cult does not produce popularity, establish his moral right to rule, or even work with those sorts of goals in mind.

It is impossible to get into policymakers' heads and come away with exact knowledge of why they do what they do. In countries like Syria it may be difficult even to get access to the relevant party circulars. But state action in the symbolic sphere is legible in the effects it produces, and these effects are both demonstrable and politically significant. By identifying them, it becomes possible to understand how a noncharismatic authoritarian regime uses rhetoric and symbols to produce political power, thus helping to ensure its own survival. That Asad has been in power since 1970 suggests the effectiveness of such a strategy.

This book argues that Asad's cult is a strategy of domination based on compliance rather than legitimacy.[17] The regime produces compliance through enforced participation in rituals of obeisance that are transparently phony both to those who orchestrate them and to those who consume them.[18] Asad's cult operates as a disciplinary device, generating a politics of public dissimulation in which citizens act *as if* they revere their leader. A politics of "as if," while it may appear irrational or even foolish at first glance, actually proves politically effective. It produces guidelines for acceptable speech and behavior; it defines and generalizes a specific type of national membership; it occasions the enforcement of obedience; it induces complicity by creating practices in which citizens are themselves "accomplices," upholding the norms constitutive of Asad's domination; it isolates Syrians from one another; and it clutters public space with monotonous slogans and empty gestures, which tire the minds and bodies of producers and consumers alike.

This argument is not meant to suggest that there are no ways in which the Syrian regime enjoys "legitimacy" or that the rhetoric never articulates any deeply held beliefs. Sometimes the rhetoric is patently absurd; sometimes it blends consensual understandings with obviously false statements, appropriating meanings and converting heroic acts into acts committed for Asad. And sometimes, too, the official discourse represents widely shared convictions about political life, albeit in stark Manichaean terms that simplify the range of complex, differentiated visions expressed by Syrians in private. At least three widely shared beliefs of political life find some expression in contemporary official discourse: first, the regime defends Syrians against Israeli threats; second, the Golan Heights, land seized by Israel in the 1967 War, must be returned to Syria; third, Asad's rule has produced unprecedented stability in Syria, which is desirable.[19] The example of the Lebanese civil war is a chilling reminder of the consequences of not living under a strong state. Asad's cult clearly does more than call attention to consensually acknowledged achievements and aspirations of the regime. The particular role it plays in Syrian political life also suggests that the regime can do without legitimacy and that the regime's investment in rhetoric and symbols need not produce it to be valuable politically.[20]

Legitimacy, as Samuel Huntington has acknowledged, is a "mushy" concept, yet it nevertheless continues to be widely employed by social scientists, even those who acknowledge its "mushiness."[21] John H. Schaar has argued that lexical usage centers on an appeal to a higher authority, such as divine law, the law of nature, custom, or constitutions, external to the claimant making the appeal. Social scientific understandings of the word revolve around belief and opinion. For most authors, "successful" spectacles are those in which legitimacy is gained either by appeal to an external, consensually acknowledged authority or by making the represented figure popular.[22]

To sanction Asad's leadership, Syrian rhetoric routinely invokes the external authorities of religion and Syria's modern constitution. Neither of these purported "higher" sanctioning authorities, however, can possibly be regarded as higher by the Syrian populace. For instance, no constitutional provision actually overrides or even limits Asad's power. And Syrians live in the contemporary world where appeals to sacred authority possess less resonance than they did in sixteenth-century Europe (an exemplary period for the scholarship on legitimacy and Western "cults of personality"), when ideologues in emerging Western states were justifying their respective monarchs' right to rule. The many practicing religious Syrians, in fact, comprise precisely the group that is least likely to believe the cult's claims. The greatest political opposition to Asad's regime thus far has been from organized religious Muslims, who resent the privileges conferred on Asad's clansmen and do not consider the ʿAlawi sect (to which Asad and his elite cohort belong) to be Islamic at all.[23] Religious Muslims are likely to be deeply offended by the cult, rather than enamored of Asad.[24]

Revolutionary regimes will call on the "higher" principles of the revolution to justify, even sanctify, the regime's leaders. Syria's regime, however, is not revolutionary, despite rhetorical pretensions to the contrary. In the 1960s, the Baʿth party's leadership had visions of social and political transformation. Baʿthists were inspired by Arab nationalist calls for a single Arab nation free of colonial control, by Leninist understandings of economic justice and progress, and by fascism's "worship of the people."[25] The Baʿth party under Asad's predecessors destroyed the political power of many of Syria's wealthiest families and fostered a new elite. This new elite tended to be drawn from the country's minority populations, especially from the ʿAlawi sect, and to come from rural lower- and middle-class backgrounds. Under Salah Jadid, Asad's immediate predecessor, the state invested in projects aimed at industrializing Syria and transforming the countryside through land reform.[26] But Jadid surrendered to Asad a country beleaguered by sectarian rivalries, military conspiracies, and class conflicts. Asad moderated the revolutionary ideology that Jadid had articulated and re-established relations with the Sunni bourgeoisie. He promised Syrians the stability conducive to economic investment, policy implementation, and peace of mind. Asad's "Corrective Movement," the term by which his 1970 coup is known, connotes the initiation of reforms rather than any revolutionary break with the past.

In other words, it is not plausible to suppose that spectacles are meant to legitimate Asad's regime by invoking the higher authority of divine or revolutionary inspiration, or of constitutional provisions, if these supposed "higher" authorities are actually less authoritative, palpable, or believable to Syrians than the fact of Asad's dominance. Such rhetorical fictions function poorly if they are meant to "legitimate" power in the lexical understanding of the word.

Seymour Martin Lipset, drawing on Weber, proposes an alternative understanding of legitimacy: "the capacity of the system to engender and maintain the belief that the existing political institutions are the most appropriate ones for the society."[27] This contemporary social scientific use of the term, which revolves around Western liberal understandings of popular opinion or consensual belief, raises awkward questions if applied to the Syrian case. Do spectacles "engender and maintain the belief" that Asad's rule is the "most appropriate" for society? Do Syrian spectacles make Asad popular? It is, in fact, difficult to assess Asad's popularity or the ways in which people might consider his rule "most appropriate." The practice of holding elections in which Asad stands unopposed implies that the regime doubts its own popularity. Opposition to the regime, especially but not exclusively from Islamicist groups, also suggests that the regime is or has been unpopular among significant parts of the population.[28] Such observations do not indicate that Asad lacks all support. Asad's constituency has included influential members of the Sunni and Christian bourgeoisie, the "nouveaux riches" city dwellers, primarily but not exclusively ʿAlawis originating in the provinces, and wealthy peasants who have benefited from the regime's policies while continuing to reside in the countryside.[29] This support, however, can be attributed to Asad's ability to offer material gains, such as state services, perquisites, and political privileges, rather than to the rhetoric's ability to cultivate belief or popularity among key groups.

To my knowledge, there is no explicit scholarly account of how cults and their attendant spectacles might actually make a leader popular or seem "most appropriate." Scholars do, however, suggest that invoking culturally and historically resonant symbols can help to "legitimate" a particular regime. If by "legitimacy" they mean popularity or appropriateness, then they are saying the regime tries to associate itself in people's minds with culturally resonant symbols, which are already emotionally meaningful to the population in a favorable way. This way of seeing the relationship between symbolism and legitimacy tends to prove platitudinous or even tautological, however, unless an independent way of identifying culturally resonant symbols is provided. A culturally resonant symbol becomes one invoked by a successful regime, or regimes invoke these symbols because they resonate.

In Syria, the Asad regime appropriates symbols that otherwise might be subject to competing interpretations. Insofar as these symbols are historically and culturally meaningful for people, they may link Asad to "memories" of collective glory, like the battle of Hittin. As the Syrian artist who designed a poster for the 1991 referendum suggested, however, invoking the battle of Hittin might as easily call to mind the *contrasts* between Asad's regime and the legends of Salah al-Din. Folkloric symbols, in particular, may stimulate pride in a constructed, glorious past, that is, a history before colonial humiliation and Western hegemony. However, such symbols may also call attention to the deficiencies of the current regime by comparison with this past. "Culturally resonant symbols" are less easy to control than may be allowed by the theorists who invoke them.

Even if a political cult fails to produce belief in its outlandish claims, it may nevertheless create an emotional connection between leaders and followers. Scholars have used fascism as perhaps the most dramatic example of the power of symbols to reaffirm and cultivate an emotional connection between leaders and followers.[30] Fascism's appeal, therefore, might be said to reside in its "legitimacy," in its emotion-charged popularity among the masses, and in its appeal to the external authority of the sanctity of "the people," in whose name the leader rules. The emotional bond between leaders and followers is made immediate and concrete through the enactment of spectacles. The case of Nazi Germany suggests the success of symbols in the cultivation of fascist politics. Even here, however, it is difficult to know for certain whether individuals are emotionally committed, for the system of fear that fascism creates means that people will act loyally, even if they do not feel loyal.[31]

Studies of fascism and of Leninism have emphasized both the coercive practices of the state and the dissemination of "propaganda."[32] But few link the system of coercion that mandates participation to the production of a cult that advertises allegiance. In the literature one may find accounts of enforcement and bribery and of propaganda to induce belief (and thereby compliance), but there is no explanation for the practice of enforcing rituals that are obviously not believable and seem patently incapable of evoking emotional commitment. According to conventional understandings of legitimacy, then, the Asad cult is simply absurd. Why then does the regime persist in so blatant an absurdity? The inability to explain the persistence of Asad's cult suggests that the cult has a different "payoff" than those suggested by our conventional accounts of legitimacy.

Anthropologists and other cultural theorists sometimes invoke the Gramscian concept of "hegemony" to indicate the importance of ideas, signs, and images in producing dominant understandings that are taken for granted and perceived as natural and commonsensical.[33] Stuart Hall's formulation exemplifies the way in which Gramsci's definition has come to be interpreted in contemporary social theory:

> Ruling or dominant conceptions of the world [may] not directly prescribe the mental content of . . . the heads of the dominated classes. But the circle of dominant ideas *does* accumulate the symbolic power to map or classify the world for others; its classifications do acquire not only the constraining power of dominance over other modes of thought, but also the inertial authority of habit and instinct. It becomes the horizon of the taken-for-granted: what the world is and how it works, for all practical purposes. Ruling ideas may dominate other conceptions of the social world by setting the limit to what will appear as rational, reasonable, credible, indeed sayable or thinkable, within the given vocabularies of motive and action available to us.[34]

It is Hall's characterization of hegemony as the "horizon of the taken-for-granted" that anthropologists Jean and John Comaroff invoke "to refer to that order of signs and practices, relations and distinctions, images and epistemologies—drawn from a historically situated cultural field—that come to be taken for granted as the natural and received shape of the world and everything that inhabits it." Paraphrasing Pierre Bourdieu, the Comaroffs argue that hegemony "consists of things that go without saying because, being axiomatic, they come without saying; things that, being presumptively shared, are not normally the subject of explication or argument."[35]

This understanding of hegemony, although helpful in suggesting ways in which images and ideas are implicated in producing power, fails to capture the dynamics of official rhetoric in Syria, which consistently includes statements whose explicit content cannot possibly be, and indeed is not, "taken for granted" or perceived as "axiomatic." On the contrary, countless examples of contestation, to be discussed at length in chapter 4, suggest that Syrians recognize the cult as manifestly incredible, that its claims in no way "reign as common sense"; nor do its practices seem "natural."

Although the outlandish claims of the cult cannot produce "hegemony," however, the argument pursued here is that the practices and language of the cult do cultivate Asad's *power* in ways that *are* "taken for granted." In other words, while the literal statements of the cult are frequently clearly preposterous, the dominance to which they refer (and which they also help produce) is implicit in the regime's demands of public dissimulation and in people's conformity to them. The term "hegemony" does not have the precision to specify the dominance-producing aspects of claims that are themselves transparently unconvincing. The concept also fails to capture the ways in which people are differentially related to and critical of Asad's cult.

This book therefore offers what Louis Althusser and others might call a "materialist" approach to rhetoric and symbols.[36] It focuses on the observable, material effects of the cult and on the everyday practices of domination and transgression the cult produces through its system of representations.[37] For Althusser and Hall, there is a dialectical relationship between practices and ideology in which practices produce ideological representations, and ideology is material because it is "inscribed in practices."[38] In the case of Syria, the idea being reproduced in the specific practice of uttering patently spurious statements or tired slogans is not the one expressly articulated—Asad is in no meaningful literal sense the "premier pharmacist." Rather, Asad is powerful because his regime can compel people to say the ridiculous and to avow the absurd.

ON SPECTACLES AS MODES OF REPRESENTATION

The term "spectacle" is broad, and its use in the literature tends to encompass a number of different but related practices: festivals, royal rituals, mass demonstrations, and more.[39] At their best, analyses of visible symbolic displays of power treat spectacles both as systems of signification that publicly represent a regime's understanding of dominance and community and as functional strategies to enforce dominance and construct community. In other words, spectacles are taken simultaneously to represent dominance and to operate as a means of dominating.[40]

Treatments of spectacles as texts reveal them to be compelling pictures of the tensions, fears, and hopes that define a particular political epoch. Spectacles dramatize the aspirations of the regime, but also promote images designed to convey certain ideas to spectators. Clifford Geertz, for instance, argues that the rituals of state power in nineteenth-century Bali represented the Balinese conception of cosmic order and also the image of discipline to be imitated by spectators.[41] According to Frances A. Yates, royal iconography in Elizabethan England and in sixteenth-century France stressed the "idea of monarchy" and registered the religious tensions characteristic of both countries.[42] The symbols functioned to "fashion through pageantry the imagination of the age"[43] and served as "a vehicle for the expression of [the aristocracy's] hopes and fears."[44] Mona Ozouf claims that spectacles in revolutionary France represented an "imaginary unanimity" that bespoke the revolutionaries' desire to restore order.[45] For James Von Geldern, Bolshevik festivals revealed a "dialogue" between the revolutionaries and spectators in which symbolic meanings were regularly contested.[46]

The literature thus registers the fact that ideologues use spectacles to revise resonant symbols so as to convey current political messages.[47] This symbolic reconstruction may entail creating "traditions" that are in fact quite new, but supposedly have a time-honored, commonly recognized history.[48] Or it may mean constructing an original founding moment that signals a new golden age and an end to the miseries of the past.[49]

Descriptions of the representational dimensions of spectacles contribute to our knowledge of politics and semiotics. But once we begin to inquire into *why* ideologues promote fictions and conjure up myths, why regimes bother to recast space and time, or why they "reinvent" traditions, it is difficult to get beyond problematic and ambiguous answers. Often scholars of spectacle, like political scientists, fall back on inadequately theorized understandings of legitimacy[50] or invoke Durkheimian formulations of "unanimity" and "social bonds" without explaining how spectacles do more than represent (as opposed to generate) these communal bonds or consensus.[51] Even Geertz, who suggests that spectacles put forth an image of what is to be imitated and that regimes orchestrate pageants to produce a mimetic relationship between ruler and ruled, fails to register any discrepancy between the representation of discipline the regime intends and the ways in which such representations are received, negotiated, and reinterpreted by those who consume them.[52] In other words, these works tend to neglect the problem of "reception."

Geertz's treatment of empirical phenomena as "significative systems" remains important, however, because it suggests a reading of Asad's cult that links its content to the disciplinary strategies of public emulation and state dominance Geertz identifies. Geertz's work, situated within a body of literature often termed "interpretive," can be used to identify the tensions inherent in the regime's idealized representations of state dominance and national community.[53] Furthermore, it invites us to think of spectacles not merely as representations of state power, but also as themselves *instances* of that power. As Geertz suggests in his study of political spectacles in nineteenth-century Bali, "the pageants were not mere aesthetic embellishments, celebrations of a domination independently existing: they were the thing itself."[54]

An "interpretive" reading of the Syrian state's iconography and rhetoric suggests that the cult's content expresses the dilemma shared by many postcolonial states: how to build an effective state, which requires the regime to enforce its political dominance, *while* generating support from a broad constituency and cultivating a sense of national membership. By "state" I mean a set of common political institutions capable of monopolizing violence and of distributing some goods and services within a demarcated territory. By "nation" I refer to people's shared, socially constructed sense of "groupness," their sense of belonging to a community and of deriving their identity, at least in part, from membership in the group.[55] It is the historical predicament of the Syrian regime that in order to survive it must negotiate between the conflicting imperatives of state- and nation-building, between exclusive practices to consolidate political power and enforce the regime's dominance, and inclusive policies to generate collective, national identification. The regime does this, in part, by producing a system of signification that exemplifies simultaneously both state dominance and national community.

To provide a context for the different historical trajectory taken by some postcolonial Middle Eastern nation-states, we should compare the experience of some early centralizing European ones. In England and France in the early modern period, an administrative apparatus evolved that gradually centralized power; the "state" came to organize armies, to tax and police its citizens, control food supplies, and organize "technical personnel."[56] Scholars tend not to agree on what a nation is or, consequently, on when it may have gotten underway in Europe, but most do suggest that the state preceded the self-perception of geographically contiguous communities of "nations." According to Eric Hobsbawm, state propaganda on the question of national feeling was uncommon until the 1870s, when political elites formulated the idea of the nation in terms of language and territory in order to give people living under a shared political system a common sense of identity.[57] Liah Greenfeld locates the emergence of nationalism earlier than Hobsbawm, in part because nationalism for Greenfeld seems to be coterminous with citizenship, but she still acknowledges the role of powerful elites in formulating policies that would only later mobilize the masses.[58] Schooling and the creation of national myths regenerated older traditions but also redefined them in terms of the state and society a regime had come to represent.[59] A nation came to be seen as a group of people who perceived their interests as being best served by one state; people could feel that the state was the manifestation of their common will.[60] Other European nationalisms arose within these nation-states but in opposition to them, as did the Irish Fenian movement, or in imitation of them, as in the territories that were to become Italy and Germany. These developing nationalisms fostered a series of quandaries about membership, shared identity, and who was to be incorporated and who positioned outside of each nation-state.[61]

In many areas of the Middle East, nationalism became a politically potent force before artificial borders were carved out of a weakened Ottoman empire.[62] By contrast with Europe, many Middle Eastern nationalisms tended to *precede* the state, and rather than foster state-building, ardently opposed it. Colonial boundaries of states rarely coincided with boundaries of preexisting communities. In countries such as Syria, the particular problems faced by successive regimes stem largely from this incongruity between felt membership and state authority, between "national" identification and political organization.

Ethnic and regional diversities and loyalties to tribe, sect, or locale make the integrative task of many states in the Middle East difficult.[63] Pan-Arab discourse also complicates loyalties by articulating hopes that the artificial boundaries imposed during colonial rule can be replaced by a single Arab nation-state expressive of common culture and history.[64] The Syrian regime, in particular, remains committed to the defense of general Arab interests as it perceives them and to a discourse that underscores Arab unity, even while it builds a circumscribed Syrian nation-state.

Contrasting Western European and Syrian experiences of state- and nation-building clarifies Syria's dilemmas of postcolonial rule. Syria has had to work more quickly to develop a state apparatus capable of delivering goods and basic services in return for allegiance and obedience.[65] The need to manufacture a state-centered national consciousness while developing state institutions has meant that the basis of a shared Syrian identity is fundamentally different from that of Syria's European antecedents.

On the level of representation, Asad's cult registers the paradox between state-formation and nation-building. On the one hand, Asad's cult, like monarchical cults in the West, works to personify the state, to set it above and distance it from society.[66] The cult of Hafiz al-Asad, like former monarchical cults in Europe, can be taken to epitomize the attempt to distinguish between a sacred elite and the profane rest of the population.[67] Power is sanctioned by the ruler's sacred investiture, which functions to identify the mortal body of the leader with the immortal body of the realm.[68] In Weberian terms, individual charisma imbues the office with extraordinary qualities, with the effect that the institutions of the modern state survive the demise of its founders. In the West, charisma became "routinized," and legal-rational states adhering to rules and procedures succeeded those based on personal leadership and personal connections.[69] A cult of Asad as superhuman positions him to perform this state-building function for Syria.

On the other hand, and in keeping with modern notions of equality and national identity, Syria's cult paradoxically narrows the gap between ruler and ruled. In the words of a broadcast on Damascus radio in 1980, "In order to kill the revolution, they will have to kill the people, and this is impossible. They should know that Asad is no one, but one of you. Every citizen in this country is Hafiz al-Asad."[70]

Asad represents not just the extraordinary individual, the authoritative "father," the "knight" who can "lead forever." He is also the average Syrian, a "man of the people," a brother among equals: "Asad is no one, but one of you."[71] Can tropes that function rhetorically to identify an exclusive object of awe be reconciled with the inclusive rhetoric expressing the nation's doctrinal commitment to leveling distinctions in accordance with Baʿthism's socialist dictates? "Every citizen in this country is Hafiz al-Asad." This claim suggests two possible interpretations. All the citizens in Syria together make up Hafiz al-Asad; the leader is a leviathan-like figure whose body is composed of, absorbs, the individual bodies of his citizens.[72] Or, inversely, every citizen absorbs, internalizes, and incorporates Hafiz al-Asad. Hafiz al-Asad's steadfastness (*sumud*) and his willingness to struggle (*nidal*) and to sacrifice (*tadhiya*) are qualities that the ordinary citizen also manifests or can emulate. Being symbolic interpretations, these two readings are not necessarily mutually exclusive. Rather, the leviathan-like image of the leader containing his citizens and the image of citizens internalizing the leader operate simultaneously to represent the connections between ruler and ruled. The symbolic content involves both being included in Asad and imitating him from a distance.

The symbolic system, then, exemplifies both political power and the regime's vision of community. The cult reproduces a solution to the problem of simultaneous state- and nation-building on the symbolic level, while the problem remains intractable in concrete, that is, nonsymbolic, practice. The analysis of significative systems is helpful in representing the particular predicaments of postcolonial rule, which suggest that not all strategies of domination may be equally available to the Syrian regime. An account of state- and nation-building hints at the possibility that an obedience-based strategy may be more adaptive, flexible, and cost effective than the demands a legitimacy-based strategy would impose on the regime, a theme this book will pursue.[73] A semiotic reading of state- and nation-building, however, is unsatisfactory in explaining how symbols and rhetoric actually operate to *produce* power and generate community, especially because such an analysis does not elaborate the actual *effects* of symbolic displays, i.e., the ways in which systems of signification are consumed, upheld, contested, and subverted.

TOWARD A POLITICS OF SPECTACLE

A spate of recent literature, inspired by Michel Foucault's work in both *Discipline and Punish* and the *History of Sexuality, Volume One,* focuses on the disciplinary effects of spectacles and language.[74] More specifically, this literature on historical developments in the West has taken up the significance of the human body for political power.[75] In *Discipline and Punish,* Foucault suggests that European states became increasingly capable of regulating their subjects, devising a "specific technology of power . . . called 'discipline,'" which replaced the practices of overtly punitive public spectacles.[76] The state increasingly depended on its citizens to control themselves. We in the West, according to Foucault, have internalized the patterns of authority and the relations of control originally requiring an external disciplinary figure and external, public bodily punishment. That self-discipline, generalized into what Foucault calls the "carceral society," has transformed state authority.[77] Obedience has been not just internalized in the psyche, but incorporated; discipline displaces punishment and is enforced through an individual's ability to control, regulate, and administer her own behavior.

Syria, however, is a long way from the "carceral society" *Discipline and Punish* claims to discern in Western nations. The highly disciplined requirements of participation in the spectacle do not translate into regimented behavior in daily life. Syrians do not queue in line, for instance, like the British. Nor do they run their bureaucracies with the impersonal efficiency of French and German civil servants. To the extent that it is descriptive, Foucault's is a record of the experience of Western states, where "disciplinary technologies" proliferated over time as punitive practices lost their "spectacular" public prominence. In Syria, by contrast, public executions, though rare, still continue, while disciplinary spectacles take on public prominence. Moreover, Foucault sees the rise of modernity as coinciding with the decline of an externally imposed sovereign power. I want to suggest, as T. Fujitani does in his study of the imperial cult of Japan, that sovereign power can be combined with the panoptic, internalized disciplinary technologies of the West to produce new variants of the modern.[78] Although Foucault's thesis about the "carceral" applies to an understanding of Syria's modernity largely in contrast, his emphasis on bodies, language, and spectacle as loci of modern discipline nevertheless invites us to think about the ways in which the state mobilizes its citizens to demonstrate and embody its power.

Applied to Syria, a broadly construed "Foucaultian" approach suggests the ways in which Asad's cult is *effective:* First, orchestrated spectacles discipline the participants and organize them for the physical enactment of ritual gestures, regimenting their bodies into an order that both symbolizes and prepares for political obedience. Second, spectacles are not only a preparation for but also themselves already instantiations of political power. They dramatize the state's power by providing occasions to enforce obedience, thereby creating a politics of pretense in which all participate but few actually believe. Third, spectacles serve to anchor visually and audibly politically significant ideas and self-conceptions that might otherwise remain fluid and abstract. They ground political thinking in the images and symbols the regime puts forth, framing the ways people see themselves as citizens, much as advertising offers people a frame in which they imagine themselves as consumers.[79] The cult, like advertising, is a mode of ambivalent interpellation, a way of "hailing" spectators that is effective even if its claims are not taken literally. In Syria, spectacles combine the consensual desire for stability with images of Asad's omnipotence. In American advertising, desires for the "good life," for love, comfort, wealth, and efficiency become moored to the acquisition of particular commodities.

The opening ceremony of the Mediterranean Games, hosted by Syria in 1987, provides an example of the ways in which spectacles operate to regiment bodies, occasion mandatory participation, and structure the terms of an official national imagination. Participants, primarily children from the Ba'thist youth organizations (Tala'i' al-Ba'th and Shabibat al-Thawra), were required to train from three to six months prior to the event.[80] During the actual ceremony, which resembled both communist spectacles and the opening of the 1988 Olympics in South Korea, Syrian young men performed gestures analogous to martial exercises preparing soldiers for battle.[81] Real tanks rolled onto the sports field, and soldiers in battle gear engaged in mock skirmishes against an unspecified enemy, presumably Israel. Syrian youths held up placards that combined to create an image of Hafiz al-Asad's face (fig. 2). Then, in an extravaganza blending kitsch with control, the "screen" com-

FIGURE 2   Opening Ceremony of the Mediterranean Games, Lattakia, Syria (1987). Twelve thousand Syrians holding placards form Asad's face.

FIGURE 3   The rebus reads: "We Love Hafiz al-Asad." Opening Ceremony
of the Mediterranean Games, Lattakia (1987).

posed of the combination of placards held by disciplined, coordi-
nated bodies spelled out a declaration of love to Syria's leader in the
form of a rebus: we (in Arabic) love (represented by the heart symbol popular in Western advertising) Asad (represented by his face)
(fig. 3). Spectacles demonstrate the regime's desired representation
of itself—as loved, representative, and popular—but they also
enact the regime's ability to discipline bodies and determine the
iconographic content of public space.

In Syria, regimented bodies are consistently mobilized to perform such gestures of symbolic political order. The training children receive through their membership in organizations modeled
on paramilitary groups may indeed encourage self-discipline (it
may still be too early to gauge the effects of such mechanisms). Insofar as spectacles act as instances of intervention, however, the
body functions in them to *substantiate* rather than legitimate power.
In other words, spectacles make power palpable, publicly visible,
and practical. Bodies serve as the apparent and immediate site upon
which participation is enforced. The spectacle shows that authorities are able to compel citizens to enact the choreographed move-

ments that iconographically configure worship of the leader, representing his power both visibly (in the display) and tangibly (in each participant's body).

These iconographic displays not only serve to regiment bodies and occasion mandatory participation; they also ground collective experiences in the imagery Asad's cult puts forth. Consider the way in which symbols deployed during the gala opening of the Mediterranean Games depicted the community as a nation of internal solidarity and external polarity (figs. 4 and 5). During what was obviously intended to be a particularly instructive moment in the spectacle, Syrian children played on an elaborately designed playground situated in the middle of the stadium field. The backdrop, which was formed by the bodies of twelve thousand other participants holding up placards, exhibited a picture of President Asad surrounded by his nation's children. Ominous music played. The twelve thousand placards next formed a monotone gray backdrop. Then the backdrop changed to black interrupted by a golden lightning bolt, evoking the sense of a menacing, but not yet visible, presence. The backdrop returned to gray. A threatening silhouette of a soldier appeared and was repelled by the first letters of a large, white word. Gradually (in a matter of suspenseful seconds) the word al-salam (peace) displaced the soldier. Actual Syrian military officers emerged on the stadium field and carried the children away, presumably to safety. The image of the enemy soldier linked understandings of solidarity to Asad's image as national patriarch. These sorts of spectacles enforce a kind of political participation by mobilizing men and women to produce the symbolic messages and perform the bodily gestures that glorify Asad. The Syrian regime is able to uphold its fictions, to appropriate consensually meaningful symbols, and to deploy them to dramatize the centrality of Asad's power.

From the point of view of analysis, however, spectacles reveal both the power and the limitations of the regime's project by announcing the gap between enforcing participation and commanding belief. Moreover, images of Asad's sovereign power and national belonging often coincide with moments of incompetence or ambivalence that unsettle this vision of control and glory. In

FIGURE 4   Opening Ceremony of the Mediterranean Games, Lattakia
(1987).

FIGURE 5   Opening Ceremony of the Mediterranean Games, Lattakia
(1987).

spectacles less lavish than the Mediterranean Games, performers with Asad's face imprinted on their parachutes have been known to land outside of the designated stadium; marchers sometimes appear disorganized; and audiences may fail to disguise their boredom. Attendance is generally low at such events. Many attend because they have been mobilized to do so, and spectators tend to talk throughout the speeches glorifying Asad's rule.

Elaborate spectacles are not, of course, daily events, but scenes excerpted from them find repeated representation on television and in newspapers even years after an event has taken place. Less extravagant spectacles than the Mediterranean Games occur annually, and regional offices of the Ba'th Party regularly organize local festivities, mobilizing school children and conscripting poets, artists, actors, and theater directors. The transmission of Asad's cult through spectacles helps replenish the regime's repertoire of symbols while ensuring that citizens throughout Syria remain familiar with and able to reproduce the official hagiography.

Although people may not uniformly believe the cult's claims and although Asad offers no charismatic, revolutionary vision to induce the kind of sustained surrender scholars discern in fascistic regimes, spectacles (even "unsuccessful" ones) nevertheless clutter public space by grounding political ideas and beliefs in the regime's iconography; they structure the images and vocabulary both for complying with the regime and, as we shall see, for contesting it as well. Asad's cult, even when it is not believed, is thus a powerful, albeit ambiguous, mechanism of social control.

METHODS OF RESEARCH

This study is based on archival research in both France and Syria, as well as on extensive field work and open-ended interviews.[82] The primary sources for my analysis of the official rhetoric are the party newspaper, *al-Ba'th*, which I have surveyed for the period from 1969–1992, the official newspapers *al-Thawra* and *Tishrin*, which I read consistently during the years of my field work (1988–89; 1992; summer 1996), and official pamphlets, biographies, and magazines. The analysis of the iconography is further based on orchestrated spectacles I witnessed in person, on video tapes of other events, and on investigation of monuments and poster art in urban and rural regions of Syria. The book also examines underground and tolerated short stories, jokes, cartoons, poems, films, and television comedies, which demonstrate the shared conditions of unbelief in Syria and also illustrate the power of the rhetoric to define the terms in which skepticism and transgression are expressed.

For conceptual orientation, this study borrows techniques from political theory and from "interpretive" anthropology to produce what I call a "political ethnography" of power in contemporary Syria. By insisting on the importance of ethnographic detail I hope to explore the advantages, costs, and political significance of public rituals, while at the same time supplementing those concerns with a symbolic interpretation of the actual content of Asad's cult. This approach helps us to get at the meaning of symbols, rituals, and practices in a way that avoids a simple functionalist interpretation of Asad's cult, as represented in the claim, for example, that Asad's cult was invented to produce political power. We know neither what policy makers were thinking when they contrived the cult, nor whether those aims have changed over time, nor whether the significance of the cult is even substantially under their control. For an exploration of the political significance of Asad's cult, however, the leaders' intentions are not particularly relevant. By investigating the cult's "logic of practice," in Bourdieu's terminology, it is possible to discern the material, real effects Asad's cult has on the lives of ordinary Syrian citizens.

This book draws some of its inspiration from poststructuralist theory. I assume that meanings and human actions are fragile; that "culture" refers to a network of polyvalent practices, texts, and images generating meaning, rather than to a closed, contained system in which essences inhere to or are attached to a particular group; [83] that systems of signification are subject to contestation and renegotiation by people who are both constructed by and also agents in their world; [84] and that power is many-sided, elusive, and diffuse. [85] In addition, this book takes seriously the claim that every act of critique and resistance uses "the tools it condemns and risks falling prey to the practice it exposes." [86] I also want to complicate that assumption, however, by suggesting the ways in which actual experiences of both domination and resistance demonstrate not so much the functional coherence of power, but its ambiguities.[87]

Asad's cult can be imbued with various meanings, and people are related in different ways to its practices. Yet even if one can find a "limit-case" person who believes the cult's most preposterous claims, the point remains that there are people from diverse socioeconomic locations—from the party's popular organizations, the university's dormitories, the cities of Damascus and Aleppo and the countryside outside of Hama and Lattakia—who consider a great many of the cult's statements patently spurious yet are nevertheless exposed to and affected by its disciplinary mechanisms in the ways this book identifies.

The example of Syria thus presents an unusual opportunity to explore the ways in which a state in formation generates political compliance by using political symbols and rhetoric. Although this study is not, strictly speaking, comparative, its insights should have relevance for comparative studies of rhetoric and symbols and of compliance.

There are, oddly, few recent writings on authoritarianism in comparative politics, and they tend to be concerned primarily with the transition from authoritarian to democratic forms of rule.[88] Many contemporary regimes, however, are not democratic in any recognizable sense of that word, and the inattention of current scholarship to the persistence and development of "authoritarian" regimes is puzzling. By "authoritarian" I mean that leaders are intolerant of people or groups perceived as threatening to the regime's monopoly over the institutions of the state, including those state-controlled institutions (the press, radio, television, schools) charged with symbolic production. This study's focus therefore has at least two objectives relevant to the study of comparative politics: first, it seeks to understand how ordinary people live their lives under conditions of authoritarian rule; second, it argues that rhetoric and symbols reduce the need to rely on sheer repression as a mechanism of control.

The recognition that rhetoric and symbols operate as a disciplinary device does not imply that other forms of coercive control are not important. The regime's blatant punitive inducements are, no doubt, considerable. According to Middle East Watch, for example, there were at least 2,700 political prisoners in Syrian jails in 1996.[89] Incarceration and corporal punishment are never, however, the exclusive forms of control upon which regimes rely. Regimes depend not only on the capacity to eliminate would-be opponents but also on strategies that make such punishments unnecessary. Asad's cult, in particular, is a relatively low-cost way of asserting regime dominance. As I argue in chapter 5, symbolic displays of power not only operate in tandem with overt coercive controls, they are themselves a subsystem of coercive control.

I am often asked how Asad's cult compares to other more well-known ones. One preliminary way to identify the specificities of Asad's cult within the context of authoritarian politics is to compare it to regimes that might also be crudely categorized as "authoritarian" and "populist," such as those in the Soviet Union under Stalin and in Iraq under Saddam Husayn.[90] Asad's cult and the spectacles that animate it seem to derive their aesthetic inspiration from the socialist realism of Stalin's cult.[91] Until recently, the Syrian government hired Soviet specialists to help orchestrate spectacles and train participants. Like the art of socialist realism, Syrian political art represents Asad as the embodiment of the "citizen," who is depicted as the archetypal peasant, the worker, even the emancipated woman. A statue of Asad in al-Raqqa (in northeastern Syria) configures his lower body as a triangular base in which the image of the peasant, the woman, and the worker are carved. Syrian youths at rallies, like their former Soviet counterparts, hold placards that combine to make up their leader's face. Like Stalin, Asad is represented as the ultimate father in a political narrative based on the family.[92] Moreover, the Ba'th party's ideological commitments, its organizational strategies, the ways in which it recruits members, channels scarce resources, even the ways in which it has become corrupt, have been appropriately characterized by Raymond Hinnebusch as "quasi-Leninist."[93]

There are, however, also significant differences between these two cults. First, Asad's cult has no physical center of sacred power comparable to Red Square in Moscow.[94] Asad does have a palace but it was, for a long time, unoccupied, leaving his person as the sole focus of contrived sanctity. If he lives there now, he does so with little fanfare or publicity.[95] A second difference is that Stalin's cult was what one might call a second generation cult. Stalin inherited the cult of Lenin and paid extravagant lip service to it. In Syria, there was no state-sponsored cult prior to that of Asad. Only the party, with its aspirations toward "charismatic impersonalism," toward a heroic combat ethos embodied in the impersonal organization of the party, was to be the object of loyalty and adulation.[96] Third, and perhaps most distinctive, Asad shares the iconographic landscape with other heroes. Asad's family members, most specifically his mother (who has been depicted as haloed), his deceased son Basil, his son Bashshar, and his brother Rif'at, a former contender for political power, also appear periodically in the state's symbolic displays.[97] Even Syrian and Lebanese men and women who have sacrificed themselves for the nation get representational play during some of the spectacles the regime choreographs.[98] Stalin's cult also made heroes out of workers and aviators,[99] but it never represented real family members, nor would it have permitted potential rival contenders for power to appear as icons in the metaphorical family of the nation-state.

Syria's cult of Asad might also be compared to Iraq's cult of Saddam Husayn. Although both Iraq and Syria are nominally ruled by Ba'th Parties (of rival wings), coercive and iconic power have become increasingly concentrated in the person of the leader. Both regimes tend to recruit kinsmen for sensitive intelligence and security posts. Both regimes have developed personality cults making exaggerated claims about their leaders. There are, however, critical differences between the two cults.

Iraq has traditionally had significant oil revenues to allot to the state's institutions of symbolic control. Syria, having only minimal oil reserves (though new fields have been discovered), has historically not had as much money as Iraq to spare for symbolic strategies, which may suggest one reason why Syria's statues, posters, and spectacles are less awesome than Iraq's. There are no monuments to compare with the Iraqi "Victory Arch," described graphically in Kanan Makiya's book *The Monument*.[100] The ability of monuments in Iraq to generate awe and to belittle spectators (in the literal sense of making them feel small) has no counterpart in Syria, where most statues of Asad are staid and conventional.

Second, the persistence of tribal associations in Iraq, a direct consequence of the British colonial power's divide-and-rule policy, weakened Iraqi towns, whereas Syrian merchant classes remain entrenched, never having fully lost their commercial and political significance.[101] Syrian cities have had what some scholars consider to be an identifiable "civil society."[102] Societal differences are reflected in the way in which the two cults are designed and the overall reception they generate. Saddam Husayn is often depicted in Arab Bedouin garb; Asad is generally represented in suit and tie.[103] At the same time, the terror that characterizes life in Iraq, according to separate accounts provided by Kanan Makiya and 'Isam al-Khafaji (both exiles), is less pervasive and less frightening in Syria.[104]

Third, Saddam Husayn's cult, like his person, is flamboyant and audacious. Saddam Husayn has over forty palaces; he is physically youthful and vigorous. Asad is emphatically not charismatic; he is not even particularly energetic. His speeches are deliberate and slow. His body is stooped, his voice perennially hoarse, and his movements sluggish. Asad is cautious, a politician known for his cleverness rather than his bravado. His cult therefore inspires less mythologization than Saddam Husayn's.

These contrasts suggest that Asad's regime aspires to lesser levels of control than either Iraq under Saddam Husayn or the Soviet Union under Stalin. Similar to Frederick the Great, who is reported to have said that he did not care what his subjects thought so long as they *did* what he ordered, the Syrian leadership pursues symbolic strategies the effects of which are not to induce charisma or belief, but rather to elicit outward signs of obedience.[105] The relatively "soft" or "nontotalizing" authoritarianism of the Syrian case makes it especially suited to reveal the ways in which cults and their associated spectacles not only discipline participants, but also expose the way state control, on the level of a symbolic strategy, is subject to transgressions.[106] The Syrian case thus presents us with the opportunity to examine how rhetoric and symbols can produce idealized representations of leader and nation-state while also creating alternative spaces of irony and ambivalence.

SUMMARY

Politics is not merely about material interests but also about contests over the symbolic world, over the management and appropriation of meanings. Regimes attempt to control and manipulate the symbolic world, just as they attempt to control material resources or to construct institutions of enforcement and punishment. These appropriations (material, coercive, and symbolic), while mutually reinforcing, are analytically distinct. Operating together, they constitute people's experiences of everyday political life. The cult of Asad remains both effective and powerful, not only to the extent that Syrians submit to its enforcement of civic obedience but also, and perhaps primarily, in that Syrians, patriot and dissident alike, come increasingly to share the common experience of its vocabulary.

Contemporary Syrian political history, conventional scholarship to the contrary, cannot be understood independently of the cult of Hafiz al-Asad. "Authoritarian" politics in Syria generates a mode of compliance previously unspecified in the literature, which I characterize in chapter 5 as "disciplinary-symbolic" power, and which is not adequately contained within the categories familiar to most social scientists. Moreover, since the cult operates to provide a shared orientation in an ethnically, culturally, and politically fragmented polity, the Syrian case requires us to rethink relationships between disciplinary practices and political community wherever such diversity is present. Finally, this study shows how symbols and rhetoric work both to exemplify and to produce political power.

The rest of the book is organized as follows. Chapter 2 examines how the cult's rhetoric both represents relationships of state domination and national membership and also itself operates as a system of control. Asad's cult orients Syrians by providing guidelines for proper public speech and conduct. People are not required to believe the cult's fictions, and they do not, but they are required to act *as if* they did. Chapter 3 explores an exemplary story that demonstrates the ways in which the cult's "politics of *as if*" enforces obedience, induces complicity, and structures the terms of both compliance and resistance. Chapter 4 examines the underground and tolerated television comedies, films, cartoons, and jokes that register Syrian resistance. Together chapters 3 and 4 demonstrate the ambiguities of domination, the ways in which the language and practices the cult encourages can be paradoxically both self-defeating and self-serving, both inviting transgression and delimiting its content. Chapter 5, the final chapter, discusses the implications of Asad's cult for understandings of how regimes generate compliance. It also reviews the ways in which symbols and rhetoric work, not only as occasions for enforcing obedience, but also as the very mechanisms of enforcement.

Two ✆

Killing Politics: Official Rhetoric and Permissible Speech

The power of the Syrian state resides not only in its ability to control material resources and to construct institutions of punishment, but also in its ability to manage the symbolic world, to produce and manipulate what political scientist Achille Mbembe calls "the signification of events."[1] This chapter examines the concrete operation of the cult through its rhetoric, the way the official vocabulary works as a mechanism of political control while representing relationships of state domination and national membership.

The chapter is divided into two parts. The first, "Cluttering Public Space," provides a historical account of the nature of and transformations in the cult's vocabulary. It demonstrates how the cult operates within a larger rhetorical universe.[2] This larger rhetoric shares with the cult a prescriptive "grammar," a coherent system of rules that regulates speech in ways that are comprehensible and facilitate communication.[3] In other words, the cult, like the larger rhetorical universe of which it is a part, has established usages, prohibitions, norms, and constraints that work to specify the form of politically acceptable public conduct. The second part, "Semiotic Content," discusses the cult's invocation of a particular rhetorical device: familial metaphors. The use of familial metaphors is one way in which Asad's cult represents the regime's idealized relationships of domination and national community. The state's ability to appropriate the shared symbols that infuse everyday life with meaning is part of its power to create and sustain national fictions. Familial metaphors, like the formulaic nature of

32

the rhetoric in general, help define the form and content of obedience, at the same time as they operate to generalize membership by generating the shared orientation constitutive of national community.

CLUTTERING PUBLIC SPACE: THE FORMULA

Scholarly attention to the cult has rested content with attempts to identify its origins, as distinct from analyzing its formal characteristics, its political purposes, or its semiotic content. Still, because scholars differ implicitly on what the cult *is,* no two accounts agree even on the date the cult began. Suggested points of origin span more than a decade, from the early seventies to the mid-eighties, signaling key discursive developments in the regime's system of signification. These developments register successive displacements of attention and power away from the Ba'th party onto the person of its leader. Government sources in Damascus contend that Asad himself initiated the cult a few years after his rise to power, over the opposition of George Siddiqni, his Minister of Information from September 1973 to September 1974.[4] Siddiqni is supposed to have objected that the religious sensibilities of the population would be offended by such devices as school notebooks decorated with cameos of Asad. Asad's biographer Patrick Seale claims that Ahmad Iskandar Ahmad, Minister of Information from September 1, 1974 until his death on December 29, 1983, invented the Asad cult to deflect Syrians' attention from economic anxieties and from violence between government forces and the Syrian Muslim Brotherhood that culminated in the massacre of anywhere from 5,000 to 20,000 people at Hama in February 1982.[5] According to Yahya Sadowski, exaggerated homage to Hafiz al-Asad began within the confines of the Ba'th's popular organizations (*al-munazzamat al-sha'biyya*) as part of the party's overall glorification of Ba'thist achievement, and became part of a strategy to rally mass appeal beginning in 1982. In addition to the massacre at Hama and sharply falling oil prices, Sadowski argues, the Israeli invasion of Lebanon on June 4, 1982 threatened to erode Asad's domestic support and challenged his self-assigned role as a leader in the Middle East; the cult was a response to these events.[6] Robert Scott Mason, one of the authors of the *Country Study of Syria* prepared by the Federal Research Division of the Library of Congress, dates the cult from 1985. Mason attributes its emergence to Asad's heart attack and to the subsequent challenge to the regime raised by Asad's brother, Rifʿat al-Asad.[7]

Although adequate conceptualization of the cult does indeed presuppose historical contextualization, it is not helpful to become fixated on a single point of origin. By focusing on the formal operation of the cult and its effects, this chapter shows how Asad's cult emerges as a constituent element in the fabric of political life in contemporary Syria; the cult evolves, waxes and wanes, changes direction, and returns to prior points of emphasis in response to identifiable political crises that challenge the regime's idealized representations of events, conditions, and people.

The proliferation of posters beginning with Asad's coup in November 1970 suggested a new personification of power; the abstract, distant, intangible party became concrete, symbolically proximate, and tangible as Asad came to embody and personify the party and its values. Prior to Asad's assumption of power, it was the Baʿth party that claimed "to embody the will of this [Arab] nation."[8] To the extent that any one Arab leader personified power and political ideals in Syria, it was the pan-Arab hero Egyptian President Gamal ʿAbd al-Nasir, who died one month before Asad seized power.[9] Syria's former *de facto* leader, Salah Jadid, was conspicuous by his absence from press accounts. From November 20, 1970, four days after Asad staged his coup d'état, newspapers reported the emergence of "spontaneous" demonstrations registering the support of the "masses." In Asad's first inauguration of March 12, 1971, at the "mass rallies" organized by the state, thousands of Syrians held pictures of the new leader.

Rhetoric focusing on Asad's individual, exceptional accomplishments and on his role as national patriarch increased over time, as Syrian ideologues responded to stresses by upping the rhetorical ante.[10] During Siddiqni's tenure as Minister of Information, Syria celebrated what was officially styled the "victory" of the October War of 1973. Asad, "the comrade," increasingly became the heroic "combatant." In 1976, Asad's unpopular decision to intervene militarily in Lebanon conflicted with the regime's self-presentation and damaged Asad's Arab nationalist credentials both at home and abroad. Some Syrians have referred to Syrian intervention in and occupation of Lebanon as "Syria's Vietnam." In official rhetoric, however, Asad became the "savior (*munqidh*) of Lebanon" in 1976.

Outlandish declarations of loyalty to Asad increased by the late 1970s and early 1980s, when the poor performance of the Syrian economy and Syrians' perceptions of mismanagement and corruption contributed to growing opposition to the Asad regime.[11] In the aftermath of the regime's crushing defeat of the Muslim Brotherhood at Hama in 1982, for instance, "contracts" or oaths of allegiance to Asad became one way in which members of the "popular organizations" were required to declare their loyalty publicly.[12] These contracts implied that demonstrations of loyalty and obedience were to be exchanged for protection and safety. In the case of Hama, for example, the women and mothers of Hama "contract with the leader to sacrifice everything for the sake of the citizen and of defending him" (*Tuʿahid al-qaʾid ʿala badhl kull shayʾ min ajl al-muwatin wa al-difaʿ ʿanhu*).[13] The themes of contractual obligation continue to find expression in political posters and slogans, such as a picture commemorating the twenty-fifth anniversary of the Corrective Movement in 1995 (fig. 6).[14]

The introduction of sacred imagery into the hitherto secular cult of Hafiz al-Asad followed Asad's illness and his brother Rifʿat's attempt to seize power in 1984, making symbolic Asad immortal at the moment the physical Asad was least so. During the referendum of the following year, he emerged as a hallowed leader who would rule "forever" (*ila al-abad*). Monuments to Asad began to appear, the concrete realization of the impulse toward immortalization. The first statue of Asad in Damascus was erected at the Asad library in 1984, the same year that Rifʿat took advantage of Asad's heart attack and ordered his own Defense Companies to enter Damascus; the statue shows Asad seated with a book opened on his lap, the proverbial scholar. Asad's physical and political recoveries were marked by the reintroduction of loyalty contracts, this time signed in blood. By demanding contracts signed in blood,

FIGURE 6 Postal workers' poster commemorating the twenty-fifth anniversary of "The Corrective Movement." The poster reads: "Yes, we renew the contract [*ʿabd*] of loyalty with the great, historic leader Hafiz al-Asad." The word *ʿabd* could also be translated as "oath" or "pledge," but in the example of the postage stamp it seems to give literal expression to the idea of exchange.

ideologues not only intensified the symbolic demonstration of loyalty, but also offered a paradoxical metonymic referent for the treasonous actions of Asad's blood brother, Rif'at. To sign the contract was to promise a blood loyalty that Asad's blood kin had failed to show.

In addition, the word *bay'a* and the phrase *Baya'nak* (we pledged allegiance to you) became increasingly common in the official rhetoric by the mid-1980s. *Bay'a* denotes an act by which persons acting individually or collectively recognize the authority of a sovereign or leader. Importantly, the word has explicit Islamic connotations and was perceived by many to be a shocking appropriation of religiously charged vocabulary. The *bay'a* of a Caliph, according to the *Encyclopedia of Islam*, "is the act by which one person is proclaimed and recognized as head of the Muslim State." The newly acquired followers of Muhammad practiced the *bay'a*, proclaiming their adherence to Islamic doctrine and acknowledging the pre-established authority of Muhammad. The word implies a submission to authority, but also may suggest, like contracts, a mutual agreement in which the will of the electors is matched by the will or acceptance of the elected person. The binding effect of the *bay'a* is supposed to be "personal and life-long," but the act is made on condition that the leader "remains faithful to divine prescriptions." [15]

Once Asad became god-like, the limits of rhetorical excess seem to have been reached, and the changes in the cult are less pronounced after 1985. Claims to immortality continue, sometimes with remarkable displays of pomp and pretense, sometimes with less highly pitched evocations of loyalty. Books chronicling Asad's achievements proliferate after 1985, as Asad continues to displace the party as the object of discursive attention and political obedience.[16] These books are generally not biographies, nor do they focus on the personality of the leader or on his personal life. Rather, in following a formula that privileges Asad's "ideas," placing them in the acceptable context of consistent Ba'thist ideals, these biographies register both the persisting importance of the party and the way it has been relativized in favor of Asad. Authors and distributors of these biographies are well rewarded for their efforts because every state bureaucracy and school is obliged to buy a copy.[17]

Few bookstores carry them, however, presumably because they do not sell well commercially.

The presidential referendum of December 1991 demonstrated the ways in which the cult, in addition to channeling official rhetoric, can also work to open up a discursive space for popular excesses. Coming in the aftermath of the Gulf War, elections in post-Communist Eastern Europe, the Treaty of Fraternity and Cooperation between Lebanon and Syria ratifying Asad's increased control over Lebanon, and Syria's participation in the peace conference in Madrid, the referendum provided the occasion for unprecedented displays of adulation. One Syrian literary critic privately recalled that a kind of "mass hysteria" gripped Syria's capital.[18] Mona Wasif, Syria's most famous actress, declared to her television audience that it was raining—a welcome occurrence in desert regions—because Syrians were holding a referendum reaffirming their loyalty and allegiance to Hafiz al-Asad.[19] The referendum also advertised the regime's possible dynastic ambitions when posters emerged celebrating Asad as the "father of Basil," in reference to his oldest son. When Basil was killed in a car accident in January 1994, posters with slogans sanctifying his memory appeared alongside pictures of Asad; ideologues also promptly began to elevate the next son, Bashshar, as the successor to his father.

Within the context of a semiotic system that makes increasingly hyperbolic claims about Syria's leader in response to identifiable political stresses, another of the cult's characteristics is its slipperiness. The language possesses a flexibility, an off-again-on-again quality. The symbols the cult invokes tend to disappear and reappear, declining one year only to be revived the next. The blood contracts introduced to indicate loyalty after Rif'at's bid for power were no longer uniformly required in the 1991 elections, in part because the fear of AIDS made parents unwilling to allow their children to prick their fingers.[20] Likewise, the press may one year play up the importance of an official referendum celebrating the promulgation of an "eternal" (*khalid*) document, only to ignore the anniversary of the event a few years later.

The cult's elasticity also allows incompatible claims to exist simultaneously. Asad can be both the "knight of war" and the "man of peace." He can be the country's "premier" pharmacist, teacher, doctor, and lawyer within a single election campaign. The question is: why are the claims about Asad simultaneously hyperbolic, elastic, and often contradictory? The several possible answers demonstrate how the rhetoric's flexibility, i.e., the way it can admit contradictions, is politically functional; they relate not only to the cult per se but to the ways in which the cult operates within Syria's larger rhetorical universe.

First, as Ulrike Freitag suggests in her discussion of Syrian historiography, Ba'thist ideology is intentionally vague in order to help incorporate disparate groups into a nation-state, minimizing conflict and promoting consensus.[21] Although Freitag's analysis makes no reference to the cult, one might argue that the existence of mutually incompatible claims and the continual waxing and waning of the cult's symbols also operate to reduce or hide conflict and to appeal to constituencies with different or even opposing interests. But can claims that require Asad to be the premier scholar, teacher, and pharmacist really be designed to appeal to scholars, teachers, and pharmacists? Slogans that configure Asad as the "knight of war" and the "man of peace" may reassure different groups of Syrians who have conflicting ideas about what would be a just peace settlement in the Middle East. Not all incompatible claims coexisting in the rhetoric, however, necessarily encourage consensus. Moreover, we cannot really know from Freitag's analysis what ideologues intended when formulating the rhetoric or whether those intentions changed over time. We do not even know whether the ideology today succeeds in papering over substantive political differences, although incidents such as the massacre at Hama suggest that it failed to do so at that time. What we do know is that people are required to participate, to echo the formulas, and that Syrians have become fluent in the symbolic imagery of the cult. The language and symbols depict a consensual community, a community without significant political differences.

Second, the diversity of the rhetoric may both demonstrate that Asad surrounds himself with competitive sycophants and encourage this rivalry for his favor by permitting contradictory, incompatible statements to exist concurrently. Competition among sycophants is politically beneficial for a regime insofar as it isolates participants from one another. Competition also organizes work life around the importance of performing regime-related activities, cluttering imaginations with the tasks of contriving panegyrics and concocting the imagery constitutive of Asad's rule. Although this explanation provides us with a potentially rich understanding of why incompatible, hyperbolic claims persist, it fails to account for the patently spurious nature of much of the political discourse: many political regimes and countless places of employment encourage sycophancy without producing the absurd statements characteristic of Syria's official rhetoric. This explanation also confines the functionality of the discourse to its effects on the regime's administrative staff. Such effects, although important, focus exclusively on the producers of the rhetoric, ignoring the impact of the cult on the large population of Syrians who consume it.

Third, it may be that the regime produces counterfactual statements or omits inconvenient truths because the acknowledgment of certain facts is embarrassing to both leaders and ordinary citizens. The vagueness or slipperiness of the rhetoric thus might help to promote internal solidarity *and* to identify external enemies by omitting details that challenge the correctness of the regime or the image of Syria as a country victimized by powerful external others. The grievances and hopes Ba'thism initially articulated as a revolutionary ideology continue to be shared by many Syrians: the outrages of Western colonialism and Zionist occupation seem to require the revitalization of an authentic Arab civilization. Although specific claims might be unbelievable or vague, the overarching vision of national solidarity in the face of powerful external enemies is one shared by most Syrians. The official rhetoric's conflation of consensually held beliefs (e.g., that Zionism is a neocolonial enterprise) with patently absurd propositions (e.g., that Asad will "live forever") may also help citizens justify their compliance to themselves. The rhetoric's consensually shared claims, in any case, help to keep the transparently phony statements from seeming simply comical.

Fourth, the production of spurious claims and of counterfactual statements operates to *communicate* the regime's power by dominating public space and by providing the formulas for acceptable public speech and conduct. Because significant political differences do exist within Syrian society, the rhetoric sometimes works to eliminate potentially contentious facts from public documentation, thereby preserving the regime's monopoly on historical interpretation. The regime's interpretation provides the guidelines for proper public articulations. And the very fact that Syrians look for guidelines helps enforce discipline and caution.

Although each of these four explanations is helpful, the latter two raise fewer serious objections and are more compatible with a view of the cult as an effective disciplinary mechanism. In addition, all four explanations, when taken together, suggest the dynamism of Asad's cult: its power to seize hold of time, to organize the temporality of the national narrative in terms of an intelligible, scripted dramaturgy that monopolizes public space and is eminently reproducible. The editorial in the party's newspaper, *al-Baʿth*, of April 7, 1976, a day commemorating the party's establishment in 1947, exemplifies the formulaic way that the past is represented, new events are assimilated, and future plans adumbrated in all three Syrian daily newspapers, in radio broadcasts, and on television.

Baʿthist party member Fadl al-Ansari writes the editorial disclosing the Baʿth party's raison d'être: it arose to "protect the Arab nation from factionalism, backwardness, and corruption." A list of dates provides an acceptable historical account. There are "victories" that do no violence to the regime's self-conception: the union between Egypt and Syria (1958), the February Revolution in Iraq (1963) and the March 8 Revolution in Syria (1963), when the Baʿth first came to power.[22] There are "conspiracies" that threaten the regime's monopolistic vision: the break up of the union between Syria and Egypt in 1961, and when Salah Jadid, Asad's former rival, came to power in February 23, 1966. The "victories" return Syria to its correct path, while the "conspiracies" generally result from foreign intervention or from the activities of domestic "reactionaries." And then the "Corrective Movement" (known universally among Syrians by its date, November 16) "exploded" or "erupted" (*tafjir*) when Asad seized power. The "Corrective Movement" affirms the reality and importance of the successes that had hitherto eluded the Baʿth. Its glory resides in its achievements, the most important of which was the October War in 1973, marking the beginning of the correct way to deal with the enemy.

The article thus accommodates events and information that cannot be ignored, but it does so without allowing them to alter the overriding "fact" of the regime's invincibility. The elation that had formerly characterized accounts of the October War has gradually diminished; the war is no longer seen as the success that would lead to comprehensive peace, to the "triumph" of Syria over its enemies, to the "victory of the Arab nation" over "conspirators" seeking to undermine it.[23] Al-Ansari does not shy from mentioning circumstances that deflated the hopes experienced in the months following the war. Foremost among them is the "crime" of Sinai Two, the second disengagement agreement between Israel and Egypt, and its devastating effect on the region. According to al-Ansari, it is the "people of Lebanon who are paying the price." Therefore it is "incumbent upon Syria in the face of this conspiracy to save Lebanon." In this instance, the rhetoric both signaled the regime's intentions and also provided citizens in advance with the proper formula for commenting publicly on Asad's unpopular decision to enter Lebanon. Syrian troops crossed the Syrian-Lebanese border in June 1976, two months after the editorial.

This editorial, like countless others, conflates consensual understandings, such as the widespread view that Sinai Two was a bad agreement, with policy positions or interpretations of events that are potentially sources of conflict, such as the need for Syria to "save" Lebanon. The official monopoly on public rhetoric allows the editorialist to use such devices as hyperbole to manage the popular interpretation of historical events. But the use of literary devices also inspires continual maneuvering: because the rhetoric allows no room for failure or uncertainty, inconvenient factual truths have to be assimilated and integrated into the comprehensive vision provided by contemporary Ba'thist rhetoric. There is a formula to which writers, artists, and others adhere. There are prohibitions that are not publicly transgressed. In the official rhetoric, enemies have consistently conspired to destroy the gains of the Ba'th party, but the party will ultimately triumph because it "embraces" history and "embodies" the will of the people; it is led and personified by a warrior hero who makes no wrong decisions and no policy errors. Asad's "Corrective Movement" articulates the aims and aspirations of the party, the nation, and the people.

The official national narrative is coherent and seamless, without the doubts that characterize less orchestrated political life. Official narratives lack detailed accounts of events, presumably because such disclosures would acknowledge a politics that entailed conflict and the possibility of competing interpretations. But in the years 1976–1982, despite the official media's censoring of events and the maintenance of a monopolistic vision without detailed reporting of conflict, the actual violence directed against the regime increased significantly. Newspapers provided some indication of conflict through the ideological campaign waged against the Muslim Brotherhood as "reactionaries," "rightists," and "vermin" threatening to "contaminate" the body politic. Reference to "crimes" and "betrayals" in the Syrian press might conjure up images of bombings or demonstrations Syrians had experienced or heard about, but the rhetoric did not divulge the details, the actual fights between government troops and guerrilla forces. It was as if the mere admission of a substantive challenge to the regime would threaten its interpretive monopoly.

The rhetoric also omits events widely known in Syria to have taken place. The Syrian regime generally does not disseminate bald-faced lies, but it does censor facts, publicize partial truths, and provide implausible images that tax the imagination, such as those of the cult. Hannah Arendt writes about this latter phenomenon in her essays "Truth and Politics" and "Lying in Politics." Arendt criticizes both authoritarian and American, Vietnam-era lies as efforts to "maneuver factual truth out of the world."[24] For Arendt, "consistent lying [in public life] . . . pulls the ground from under our feet and provides no other ground on which to stand."[25] Organized lying *disorients* those who are continually subjected to it and undermines their capacity for action.

Arendt develops the latter point at length in relation to what she problematically calls "totalitarian" regimes.[26] Even regimes with greater aspirations for control than Syria's are not as totalizing as Arendt sometimes suggests. The word *totalitarian,* indeed, erroneously implies that officials can control every aspect of their citizens' thoughts and actions, which even regimes more dependent on coercion and fear than Syria's cannot. The tone of Syrian editorials and headlines is often strident and hyperbolic, and events are often depicted in black-and-white terms—characteristics that apply to rhetorics whose effects are seen to be disorienting.[27] But Syrian rhetoric is, in some respects, also simultaneously *orienting*. Official accounts orient citizens by providing the guidelines for public compliance and dissimulation. The rhetoric specifies the parameters of the permissible, communicating acceptable forms of speech and behavior to citizens.

When facts, such as of a bomb exploding in a government building, are censored, people are left with no way to discuss publicly the events that affect their lives; yet prohibiting public announcements does not prevent people from talking privately among those they trust. The realms of the forbidden, the taboo, and the clandestine expand as the official political realm contracts. Commonplace events become titillating bits of information or gossip to be guarded, cherished, and revealed among friends.

Arendt's formulations may exaggerate the disorienting and totalizing effects of organized "lying," but her analysis does suggest how the rhetoric's formulas also foreclose political action and depoliticize citizens. Authoritarian discourse prevents the emergence of what she identified as the public "personality," a uniquely political self constituted through words and deeds.[28] The rhetoric attempts to destroy the possibilities for public expressions of contingency, frailty, and interpretive ambiguity, thereby fixing meanings and censoring facts in ways that silence or render irrelevant people's understandings of themselves as publicly political persons. As one former employee at the Ministry of Culture put it when asked what he thought the purpose of the official discourse was: "To monopolize public discourse absolutely, to kill politics, to eliminate politics as a means of defending oneself or expressing oneself."[29]

The exclusion of historical events from public representation suggests the regime's power in two significant ways. First, in presenting its interpretation of historical events, the regime broadcasts its freedom to appropriate circumstances for its own uses and to drive competing alternative explanations underground. Second, the regime's ideology, which may not be "hegemonic" according to the Gramscian understandings of the word, nevertheless organizes public conduct and thereby helps to construct what it means to be Syrian—to be Syrian means, in part, to be fluent in the rhetorical formulas. As one Syrian remarked:

> From the moment you leave your house, you ask, what does the regime (*sulta*) want? People repeat what the regime says. The struggle becomes who can praise the government more. People compete. . . . After ten years it becomes its own language. Everyone knows who knows the language better and who is willing to use it. Those who are self-respecting say less, but for everyone the language is like a seatbelt. The language between the government and the people has evolved and persisted for twenty-five years.[30]

A former employee at the Ministry of Culture suggested why this fluency is easy for Syrians to achieve: "Since 1970, there have been only 50–60 sentences. It is a very impoverished discourse, but it *is* internalized."[31] The ability of Syrians to distinguish between political commitments and patently false statements, combined with everyone's fluency in and internalization of the official discourse, suggests the unifying dimensions of a common semiotic lexicon.

The ways in which events at Hama were portrayed exemplifies how the regime uses partial truth-telling, prohibitions against speech, and iconography to provide a consensually understood formula for proper public articulations of conflict. The events at Hama represent perhaps the most significant domestic conflict of Asad's rule. They could not be flatly ignored, and they prompted a public, official explanation that included the usual rhetoric accusing Zionists and Americans of intervening in Syrian internal affairs and marking the Brotherhood as agents of Western imperialism. However, the account went beyond these rhetorical conventions and divulged partial details of what happened. The choice of details reveals how the regime offers a formula for staying safe during especially troubled times, both communicating the official terms of national membership and also interpellating "citizens" in the narrative by occasioning their participation in its reproduction.

Al-Ba'th published a letter from the leader of the Ba'th party at Hama on February 23, 1982, providing an official account of the combat. The letter described how troops stumbled into an ambush while conducting a search on February 2. It acknowledged that the ensuing battles halted economic activity in Hama, that shops were burned, and that women and children were killed.[32] The rhetoric established both the authority of the Ba'th and its victimization at the hands of the enemy: "Our people of Hama woke up on February 3 (Wednesday) to the voice of conspiracy." This voice came from the "enemies of God and of Islam." The Brotherhood fired bullets from the "mosques of God" and in a number of city streets. "And they brutally killed all the citizens who would not open the doors of their homes to them. They killed whom they could of women and children. . . . Their black hatred is like that of mad dogs." But the party and security apparatuses prevailed; the Ba'th defended themselves in the "national and revolutionary spirit emulating the morals of the Arab knight." "The knights of the Ba'th" were able "to defend themselves and their families and the masses of people and the homeland."[33] The letter closed with affirmations of loyalty to Asad and to God. The avowedly secular regime, in the face of the Muslim Brotherhood's challenge, found that it too had to pay lip service to God. God, in turn, sided with the Ba'th.

Below the letter, the newspaper printed other reports from Syria's official organizations. Each organization offered an interpretation that cohered with the others, and helped to define what would be standard and permissible. The peasant federation tied events in Hama to Israel's annexation of the Golan Heights and other such conspiracies. The "men of religion" in Hama rejected the Muslim Brotherhood who killed innocent women and children in the name of religion. The Vanguard Organization of Youth in Hama (Tala'i') condemned American intervention in Syria's internal affairs. The Youth Organization (Shabiba) claimed that the Muslim Brotherhood "sold itself to the devil."[34] On the following day, "the women of Hama" related having experienced "fear" from the "beastly Muslim Brotherhood, which required you [the regime] to kill its members without compassion or mercy because they do not deserve compassion." "The masses of women in Hama," "all the mothers in Hama reject the ugly crimes of the Muslim Brotherhood" and ask Asad to "protect the nation" from its crimes.[35] The professional syndicates and other federations of the Ba'th all rallied around Hafiz al-Asad and pledged their loyalty to him. The newspaper reported the signing of contracts affirming Syrians' public allegiance to Asad.

Such letters and oaths continued on through the days that followed. They demonstrated that members of each organization could repeat the ritual with endless variations on a single theme. Within the broad confines of publicized events, such as the occurrence of violence in Hama, there was still room for establishing the regime's version of reality—a reality that rendered the conflictual coherent and, ultimately, nonproblematic.

Asad himself kept an unusually low profile in February during the disclosure of events, reappearing only when the violence had subsided. The newspapers focused on the events and sought to justify the regime's response by producing images of "treachery." On February 26, pictures of stockpiles of weapons allegedly collected from Muslim Brotherhood hideouts were depicted in the newspapers, presumably to confirm the regime's claims that the Brotherhood was a threat. These images, along with pictures of people reportedly killed by Brotherhood attacks, later appeared in a four-volume series in 1985, representing the regime's version of its relationship with the Muslim Brotherhood.[36]

Only because the cult can wax and wane is it possible for Asad to be (1) the omnipresent leader in charge of events that unify and bring glory to Syrians and (2) absent from and innocent of events that are embarrassing or simply conflictual. On March 8, Asad reappeared in public press accounts. The headlines celebrated the Ba'thist revolution of 1963 which the March 8 holiday commemorates. Over one-and-one-half million people were reported to have rallied in the streets of Damascus to greet Asad. Asad was pictured in the middle of, but elevated above, an adoring crowd. His arms reached out to touch them. Their arms were raised to touch him. On this occasion, Asad addressed the crimes of the Muslim Brotherhood and cautioned Syrians to beware of those "who wear the clothes of Islam" but are not Muslims.

The regime's representation of events at Hama demonstrates the ways in which the official narrative clutters public space and provides a formula for public speech. The regime puts forth the exemplary rhetoric to be imitated and thereby orients would-be commentators. It also communicates its intolerance of alternative symbols, discussions, and language. The rhetoric's flexibility allows definitions to remain slippery, and it uses paradox and hyperbole to construe events in terms of preexisting categories, including assumptions of harmonious unity, Ba'thist control, and Asad's infallibility.

SEMIOTIC CONTENT: THE METAPHORICAL FAMILY

Syrian rhetoric, as we have seen, refers frequently to the struggle against the external enemy, to economic and social "progress," and to the achievements of Asad, the Ba'thist revolution, and the "Corrective Movement." Official rhetoric attributes difficulties and conflict to exogenous, divisive forces while crediting the regime with overcoming problems and disturbances. This symbolic system is matched, however, by an equally powerful invocation of kinship as the ground on which domestic political affairs should be conducted. The cult persistently invokes familial metaphors and produces iconography of Asad's own kin.

Obviously, Syrian ideologues are not alone in likening political relations to familial ones. Political theorists and ideologues in various historical epochs and places have invoked metaphors of the family to define the terms of political membership. Political narratives often displace the emotionally charged, immediately meaningful relationship of family life onto the more impersonal, remote, and abstract relations between rulers and ruled or among citizens. Or conversely, theorists may make the abstract meaningful by analogizing it to people's concrete, lived experiences. Machiavelli praises Brutus, "the father of Roman liberty," who for the sake of his political sons condemned his biological sons and was present at their execution.[37] John Adams asks: "But admitting we are children, have not children a right to complain when their parents are attempting to break their limbs?"[38] Pre-Revolutionary French magistrates sometimes appealed to the King as the "common father" who would show "paternal solicitude, paternal affection and paternal tenderness."[39]

The invocation of these metaphors has different meanings in

different contexts. Adams was justifying the rebellion of the American Colonies by portraying Great Britain and its sovereign as abusive parents, whereas the French magistrates were attempting to mitigate the severity of the monarch's law with the imputed tenderness of the parent. Following the October War of 1973, Syrian ideologues increasingly configured Asad as the national "father" who substitutes for biological fathers killed in battle. On the first anniversary of the 1973 War, for example, a feature article in *al-Ba'th* is explicit in naming Asad "father of all the children of martyrs."[40] The question is, what does this image of Asad as national patriarch mean concretely in postcolonial Syria? The answer depends on our understanding of the historical and semiotic context in which invocations of family metaphors make sense in Syria. Equally revealing, however, is a contrast between the Syrian case and a contemporary Freudian formulation of the significance of family narratives in politics.

Some contemporary scholars of political life adapt Freud's conception of the "family romance" to suggest that political rhetoric and action may be inspired by familial structures and the desires they foster. Freud originally used this phrase to refer to a boy's neurotic fantasy of "getting free from the parents of whom he now has a low opinion and of replacing them by others, who, as a rule, are of higher social standing."[41] Lynn Hunt and Michael Rogin, to name two examples, have extended the idea of the "family romance" beyond the individual psyche to public action and politics.[42] For Hunt, writing on the French Revolution, what she calls "collective unconscious" desires to reinvent one's parents and reconstruct one's filiation meant that citizens imagined themselves as killing their father and ruling as brothers.[43] For Rogin, citizens in the American Revolution sought to replace the tyrannical father, King George, and the monstrous mother, Great Britain, with the benevolent "founding fathers."[44] Rogin and Hunt adduce evidence to suggest that in the French and American Revolutions, people actually fantasized about reinventing their parents; political vocabulary was expressive of this fantasy.

By contrast, in Syria, Asad's designation as "father" does not appear to reflect Syrians' desires to reinvent their parents. The cult's invocation of familial metaphors may or may not be an attempt to enlist feelings of love and desire for Asad, but nothing suggests that large numbers of Syrians actually have these feelings or that the rhetoric signals the externalization of unconscious fantasies. Instead, family metaphors operate in the official narrative to represent the regime's idealized relations of domination and membership and to specify the form of public obedience in Syria. The cult's construction of a national family derives its coherence and intelligibility from the actual relations between the sexes and the practical, lived understandings of gender and power within Syrian families.[45] Asad's cult personifies power, not only by translating the abstract, distant, and intangible party into the concrete, proximate, and tangible leader, but also by situating that power in the gendered and generational constructions of patriarchal family life.

Syrian families, not unusually, tend to be hierarchically organized and stratified on the basis of sex and age: the young are subordinate to the old, women are subordinate to men.[46] Fathers tend to expect obedience and are expected to ensure the family's material well-being.[47] Asad's role as national patriarch positions him symbolically as the dominant figure in a hierarchical national community; citizen-children owe him their obedience. But the invocation of Asad in this role as national father also implies his responsibility to provide for the material needs of Syrian citizen-children. Insofar as Asad personifies state institutions designed to provide goods and services in return for obedience and allegiance, the metaphor of the father operates to underscore that Asad is *like* the family patriarch: similar to but bigger, better, and more powerful than one's own father.[48]

Implicit in the metaphor of the father is also love and connection between ruler and ruled. Under Asad, it is not uncommon to see slogans, bumper stickers, and spectacles invoking "love" or signifying it with a heart to represent public devotion. In contemporary Syria, kinship remains a central organizing institution. In material terms, kinship connections function to mobilize people and resources, while on the symbolic level, kinship conjures up intimate connections, the primacy of male authority, and the unequal reciprocal relations between adults and children.

Connections among actual family members in Syria are expressed concretely in linguistic practices that register what anthropologist Suad Joseph terms "patriarchal connectivity."[49] "Patriarchal connectivity" suggests a "fluidity of boundaries" among family members, describing the way that "persons feel a part of significant others."[50] For example, Syrian parents of all class or religious backgrounds are routinely addressed by the name of their oldest son (e.g. "Mother [or Father] of Basil"), while senior members of the family address younger members as extensions of themselves.[51] In a related and widespread practice, mothers call their children *mama* (mother) and fathers call them *baba* (father).[52] Uncles, aunts, and grandparents similarly refer to their nieces, nephews, and grandchildren as *'ammi* (my paternal uncle) *khali* (my maternal uncle), *'amti* (my paternal aunt), *khalti* (my maternal aunt), *jiddi* (my grandfather), and *sitti* (my grandmother).[53] (There are other words for paternal and maternal nephew, niece, and grandchild, but they are rarely used colloquially.) The regime's imagery and rhetoric cohere with a pattern of social relations in which boundaries among family members are fluid and paternal authority is privileged. The reference to family signifies an idealized formulation of regime connection in which Asad's citizen-children are, like children of an actual Syrian father, extensions of himself.

Nation-building in the Syrian context has been symbolized in the official narrative by extending "patriarchal connectivity" from specific families to a mythic, national family, of which Asad is the male head. The construction of Asad as the national father precedes the October War of 1973, but becomes widespread after it. The increasing use of the term "father" in the aftermath of the war can be seen as related to the specific historical circumstances that called actual fatherhood into question, thereby facilitating the construction of a fantastic, national patriarch. Since the Ba'th "revolution" of March 8, 1963, "the family" had increasingly lost disciplinary and care-taking functions to emergent state institutions, such as the army, factories, hospitals, schools, and prisons. The 1967 War had the effect of transferring additional functions previously performed by Syrian families onto the state. The Federation for the Families of Martyrs was created in the aftermath of the 1967 War to provide for the material well-being of children whose fathers had been killed in battle. By 1973, Asad's figuration as father *personified* these concrete institutional mechanisms set in place in 1967 to subsidize families of martyrs.[54] Asad as the national father substituted for actual dead fathers and represented paternal protection, thereby signifying the acceptability—even advantages—of sacrifice while providing a symbolic assurance that the state would provide for fatherless families.

A children's short story issued by the Ba'th party's Vanguard Organization (Tala'i' al-Ba'th) exemplifies Asad's role as substitute father. The hero is a young orphan who narrates his experience of the October War, his father's death in that war, and his subsequent move to the City of the Sons of Martyrs (his mother died of an illness prior to the war). According to the story, written as a diary in the first person, "a journalist from the newspaper *al-Ba'th* visited me [in 1974] in order to ask me to write on my life in the city [The City of the Sons of Martyrs] and on the care (*ri'aya*) we have received there from the President, the Leader Hafiz al-Asad."[55] Upon settling in at the City, the little boy writes:

> I found my father. . . . No. . . . My father will not come back to life, but the love and affection and care of the President, the leader Hafiz al-Asad for us, we the sons of the martyrs, compensate us for everything. . . . He loves us and visits us during holidays and festivities, and he protects us, and he offers us all that we need to secure our future.[56]

A day later, the boy assures his dead father that he is comfortable and happy in the City. He is excited about the upcoming holiday commemorating martyrs, for on that day "the President, the leader will visit us and he will eat food with us. . . . Papa, I love you and I love Papa Hafiz."[57]

The 1973 War was figured as a Syrian victory and it was the first war fought under Asad's presidential leadership. The previous Arab-Israeli Wars of 1948 and 1967 had been widely experienced as humiliating defeats.[58] In 1948, the combined armies of Egypt, Syria, Jordan, and Palestine could not conquer the Israeli army. The Syrian government had given front-line troops defective and insufficient arms and equipment; arms that had been slated for Syria ended up in Israeli hands, and Syrian officers supplied their troops with substandard provisions.[59] In 1967, in a period of six days, the Israelis defeated the armies of Syria, Egypt, and Jordan. Instead of the much hoped-for reclaiming of territory, Egypt ceded the Sinai and Gaza, Syria lost the Golan Heights, and Jordan surrendered the West Bank and East Jerusalem to Israeli control. In the wake of what was rhetorically termed the "setback" (*al-naksa*), President Nasir resigned. He ultimately withdrew his resignation, but historical accounts are unanimous in suggesting that Nasir lost the ability to inspire general adoration or to unify the Arab intellectual elite at that time. The blunders of the 1948 war prompted a military coup in Syria. The mistakes of the 1967 War contributed to the downfall of Syria's leader, Salah Jadid, and motivated Asad to assume power.[60] The 1967 War also prompted many intellectuals throughout the Arab world to offer pointed criticisms of leaders, official language, and social practices.

The October War of 1973, by contrast, signaled Asad's emergence as both a "father" and victorious "combatant" (*al-munadil*) who could protect the Arab nation and restore its dignity. Initially referring to Asad's substitution for dead fathers and to the state's institutional provisions for these families, the term subsequently came into use to designate Asad's paternal authority in a variety of contexts. He is the "father" of young children and older students in the youth organizations;[61] of soldiers in the military and in the Republican Guard;[62] of martyrs and sports heroes;[63] and of citizens more generally in posters and banners that unmoor fatherhood from the specificities of context or connect Asad's biological paternity with his national one.[64]

Representations of the October War not only emphasized Asad as national patriarch but also stressed his "masculinity" or "manliness" (*rujula*). Newspapers commemorating the war sometimes refer to it as the "war of manliness."[65] Some books documenting Asad's achievements also make explicit reference to his masculinity. Hani Khalil's book, *Hafiz al-Asad: al-idyulujiyya al-thawriyya wa al-fikr al-siyasi* (Hafiz al-Asad: Revolutionary ideology and political thought), for example, is dedicated to "the man of the nation, man of history, man of the Ba'th, to the meaning of steadfastness, and manliness, and heroism, to the knight of war and the man of peace, Hafiz al-Asad."[66] Asad's own speeches invoke "manliness" to refer to male protection and national defense. In a 1989 news-

paper article on the anniversary of the October War, the theme of
male protection took the allegorical form of a knight rescuing a
damsel in distress:

> The Arab nation had awaited her courageous knight to save (liber-
> ate) her from the mire of defeat and submissiveness, and restore her
> self-confidence and the smile of hope to her face. And this cou-
> rageous knight is embodied in the son of the people and in [the
> people's] symbol, the President and the leader, the symbol and the
> combatant Hafiz al-Asad.[67]

Asad's appearance as a brave combatant and the subsequent "triumph" of the October War, the rhetoric suggests, is the remedy for
prior humiliation.

As the damsel-in-distress metaphor implies, constructions of
male protectorship sometimes depend on representing the pan-
Arab nation (*umma*) as a victimized woman.[68] When the Syrian poet Adonis, for example, laments the enslavement of the
nation—*al-ama al-umma*—he invokes the image—*al-ama*—of a
woman enslaved or a concubine.[69] The configuration of the Arab
nation (*umma*) as feminine is linked in contemporary discourse to
the loss of Palestine, which is consistently represented (both discursively and iconographically) as a woman. Palestine is evocative
of different kinds of women: the landscape of Palestine and of the
Arab world more generally operates in literature and in political
discourse as the metaphorical body of a fertile and beloved woman
for whom men long, and for whom they struggle.[70] At a heightened pitch, Palestine is also a raped woman, ravaged by enemies.

The construction of *umma* as an explicitly maternal nation can
be seen in the significance some Ba'th theorists, since the early
pan-Arab days of the party, have attached to the shared etymological root of the words *umm* (mother) and *umma* (nation). Zaki
al-Arsuzi, one of the first ideologues of the party and a mentor for
many of the party's 'Alawis, including Asad, gives expression to
this connection when he remarks: "The terms nation (*umma*) and
mother (*umm*) prove by virtue of their being derived from the same
root that the notion of nation is an extension of one's family—indeed, it is the bond of brotherhood par excellence."[71] Arsuzi continues, "a nation is a womb-like experience" (*rahmaniyya*).[72] It is
difficult to know exactly what "womb-like experience" means, but

FIGURE 7   Asad bowing down in homage to his haloed mother, Naʿisa.

Arsuzi suggests that the nation is the precondition for being, the place where one is nurtured. The nation as womb is the place where life begins. Or, alternatively perhaps *rahmaniyya* means deriving from the womb, i.e., innate, from birth, something one is born in or with, rather than acquires.

A painting hanging at the entrance of Asad's mother's mausoleum (fig. 7) seems to retain these specifically maternal connotations of the pan-Arab nation (*umma*). Asad, the mature man dressed in a suit, is shown bowing down in homage to kiss the hand of his haloed mother, Naʿisa.[73] The painting draws on official references to Asad as the explicitly modern knight, the contemporary Salah al-Din capable of protecting the nation and reclaiming its lost territory. The picture couples mother and son, suggesting that Asad is born of a nation that lives eternally (the halo) despite the mortal, aging body of its incarnation, his actual mother.[74]

An understanding of the nation as connected symbolically to womb and mother and as the precondition for brotherhood may

FIGURE 8   Na'isa al-Asad flanked by her sons, Rif'at and Hafiz.

also be at work in a second painting (fig. 8), this one depicting Asad's mother as winged and flanked by two of her sons (Hafiz and his younger brother, Rif'at). Snapshots of the picture were sold in Asad's home province of Lattakia after Na'isa's death in 1992. The painting is suggestive of Arsuzi's formulation of *rahmaniyya:* the maternal nation gives birth to the brothers who are also the founders of a new Syria.

By rendering abstract concepts of nationalism and fraternity concrete in the embodied images of mother and brothers, however, the painting also draws attention to the spuriousness of the cult's claims and the constraints under which Asad's regime operates. Asad's actual relationships with his brothers have been both necessary to his regime and fraught with conflict. Asad has depended on his brothers for security, and to some extent has had to compromise and share power with them. He has also been militarily challenged by them. During the weeks of convalescence following Asad's heart attack in 1983, Asad's actual brothers, aware of the meaningfulness of political symbols of kinship, appropriated them to announce a new political order. Rif'at had public places in Damascus papered with his own photograph, bearing the caption "the commander," along with photographs of the oldest Asad brother, Jamil, bearing the title "the spiritual father."[75] The interloping brothers split the mythic father Asad into two, the military hero and the spiritual head. Asad eventually regained his health and control of the symbols of power, but only after he had banished Rif'at and divested him of his Defense Companies, which had served as the regime's praetorian guard. Prior to Rif'at's exile, conflicts between him and Asad had often required their mother's mediation. Thus, the picture of Na'isa flanked by her sons suggests the role of the symbolic, winged, eternal mother-nation, who creates the bond between equal men, but also registers the historical, literal mother who had to mediate between her quarreling sons.

The cult is able to appropriate symbols of love and connection that signify affectively meaningful relations, even if the official ideal fails to jibe with people's own lived experiences as members of families. The official narrative also analogizes these familial relationships to gendered understandings of national community. Although Asad's cult is not the first gendered formulation of national belonging—having been preceded by the pan-Arab nation—the rhetoric of the cult in Syria inscribes Asad in the official national narrative in ways that tend also to advertise the ambiguities of his power. The cult represents Asad's power as *shared* with other family members and thereby suggests his periodic reliance on, as well as his dominance over, his kin. This reliance concerns material issues of regime security and symbolic issues, i.e., the ways in which family members generate occasions for reproducing the hyperbolic narratives of Asad's cult. On the occasion of Asad's mother's death in 1992, for example, the Minister of Culture, Dr. Najah al-'Attar, published a poem in the newspaper *Tishrin:* "Our mother who has departed" (*Ummuna allati rahalat*).[76] In the poem, which makes references to pre-Islamic (*al-jahili*) poetry, to the 'Abbasid poet al-Mutanabbi, and to the Qur'an, Na'isa's death provides the opportunity to deliver another panegyric extolling Asad's greatness: "Let everything above earth and under the sky sing for the greatness of this man."[77]

The poem also seems to be an attempt to explain why Asad did not cry during the funeral. Al-'Attar hints that people are disturbed by Asad's lack of emotion, and reasons that his responsibility as a leader means he cannot afford to break down and mourn his mother. In the context of the family narrative, one might argue that Asad's responsibility for the mother-nation prevents him from grieving publicly for his actual mother:

> But the big difference here is that all of us, in a situation like this, we can, when grief explodes, scream: "farewell (my) mother." But he, in his position, paid the ransom of responsibility twice: when he did not cry, and he has the right to cry for the memory of his mother and to experience the relief, and (secondly) when he saw her stretched out in her grave and was unable to scream like us: "farewell (my) mother."[78]

The poem nevertheless invites Asad to mourn while at the same time offering him the condolences of Syria's mothers. The son's personal, concealed grieving is converted into the public, general pain of the community.

> And when you return to your birth place tomorrow or after tomorrow, alas, your mother will not be waiting for you with open arms as she did when you were a baby and young man and a mature man and a leader. And you will find the house of motherhood full of silence and then you will believe that she is gone forever.
>
> I say that the mothers of this country which you built are all your mothers. There is always one mother for each person, whatever his position. But this one man, (Asad) in the exaltation of his position which he deserves, knows how to transform the personal, particular pain into a general pain, and this is what you did and we share it with you from the depth of depths.[79]

The poem also underscores the importance of Asad's filiation, his origins in the womb of his mother. Al-'Attar explicitly makes reference both to the embodied, corporeal, mortality of the man and to his god-like qualities when she writes:

> It is enough that Hafiz al-Asad is the son of Na'isa al-Asad. And it is enough that Na'isa al-Asad is the mother of Hafiz al-Asad. For the glory of the origin is what was made by mighty hands. And your mighty hands made the glory of your mother who has departed. And the womb of this blessed mother made your glory and the glory of your homeland and your people. And I want to ask: did she know,

while you were an embryo inside her belly, what you would become in the days to follow?[80]

The rhetoric and iconography suggest that mothers can stand for the nation, give birth to extraordinary male founders, intervene in quarrels between brothers, and be protected and glorified by their sons. Conspicuous by his absence from this family narrative is any father of the founder-son. The glorified mother thus seems to provide a point of origin that, unlike a father as symbol, does not present competition to the founder-son-father or invite overcoming, and can be less ambivalently sentimentalized.

The postmortem apotheosis of Asad's oldest son, Basil, is similarly instructive: Basil can be unequivocally glorified only after his death. Pictures of the son wearing military fatigues, making the pilgrimage to Mecca, or performing at equestrian matches began to grace the walls of public buildings, shops, and classrooms in January 1994 immediately following his fatal car crash. Cameos of Basil were printed on neckties and featured on some wrist watches at that time. Posters continue to proclaim him the "martyr," the "eternal knight," and Syria's "hope."

The refashioning of Basil's public image began prior to his death, in the late 1980s, when ideologues transformed the playboy who drove fast cars into a potential incorrupt leader. There were also hopes expressed primarily among 'Alawis that Basil, in the event of the president's death, would help to initiate an accommodation between the Sunni bourgeoisie and powerful 'Alawi generals. The regime's dynastic ambitions were publicly articulated in the slogan first made prominent in newspapers, at publicly orchestrated events, and on posters and banners during the 1991 referendum designating Asad "Abu Basil" (the father of Basil). But it is Basil's posthumous ubiquity that proves particularly noteworthy. The glorified dead son may or may not generate genuine emotional allegiance or desire, but as icon he reproduces the manliness and martial qualities of Asad's cult without competing with his father's actual political power. Panegyrics to Basil reaffirm Asad's power without representing an alternative to his rule.

Basil's death diminishes the chances of an Asad dynasty, but his apotheosis has nonetheless facilitated his brother Bashshar's iconographic ascension. By 1996, laminated pictures, buttons, and other paraphernalia regularly showed Asad flanked by his two sons. Sometimes the three are dressed in military fatigues, signifying that the young eye doctor, like his dead brother and aging father, has the requisite military credentials. Unlike Basil before he died, however, Bashshar poses little threat to his father's rule: the younger son has no independent following in the military and was not groomed for succession prior to Basil's accident. According to one Syrian observer of political iconography, Bashshar's recent elevation is "absurd," and "the idea of a twenty-eight year-old orthodontist [*sic*] ruling Syria is laughable."[81] Nevertheless, a mural painted on the walls encircling the home of an Asad family member near Basil's tomb explicitly reasserts the regime's dynastic ambitions in the face of Basil's death: an Arab woman, whose folkloric garb and gender make her synecdochic for the nation, hands the reins of Basil's horse to Bashshar. In the book *Basil fi 'uyun al-Misriyyin* (Basil in the eyes of Egyptians), moreover, a photo depicting men lifting Bashshar up on their shoulders is accompanied by the caption, "the masses carry Doctor Bashshar al-Asad on their shoulders to continue the journey and perseverance of hope."[82]

Asad's image as an extraordinary father figure offers a guide for the public behavior of his national children. One way in which this guide operates is by setting up Asad as the image to be imitated by both men and women. As Asad stands for "struggle" (*nidal*), "steadfastness" (*sumud*), and "sacrifice" (*tadhiya*) in the official narrative, so do his citizen- and soldier-children; as his extensions, they too can struggle, be steadfast, and sacrifice. But what do these abstract values mean concretely? They tend to be martial, oriented toward heroism in battle. If Asad's soldier-children are indeed extensions of him, then their heroic deeds are his as well. This narrative stresses Asad as the progenitor of sons who are enthusiastic volunteers: soldiers die for the higher love of the nation, a nation protected and represented by Asad.

Consistent with policies of what some scholars term "state feminism" or "public patriarchy," women, too, sacrifice themselves for the nation and for its leader.[83] "Daughters" have become part of the rhetoric surrounding national martyrdom, especially after April 9, 1985, when Sana' Muhaydli, a seventeen-year-old Shi'i Lebanese woman from a lower middle-class family, drove a Jeep loaded with dynamite into an Israeli installation in Southern Lebanon and exploded it, killing herself and Israeli soldiers. Muhaydli was the first young woman to perform such an act, and initial reports of her "martyrdom" were restrained. It was after Asad referred to her sacrifice in his opening address to the Federation of Revolutionary Youth[84] that Muhaydli became a familiar icon to most Syrians (from 1985 until 1991).[85] Several other Lebanese women have repeated her sacrifice. They are all termed "Brides of the South."

The displacement of specific family connections onto generalized political affiliations finds expression in the discursive formulations of Muhaydli's sacrifice. Sana' Muhaydli's parents reportedly wrote to Asad:

> Dear President, Father, Lieutenant-General Hafiz al-Asad.... She was our only daughter and now she is your daughter also. She cherished you and loved you before her martyrdom. And her last message was to you and to her father and her mother together. In the resplendent world to which she has departed there is no doubt that she rests easy because her name is on the streets of the dear capital, Damascus, inscribed on the buildings, cherished in the processions . . . we thank you, O foreordained of the resistance and guardian of right and honor.[86]

Although it is difficult to doubt the patriotic commitment of martyrs like Muhaydli, it is harder to believe that Muhaydli and other sacrificed children are in any way directly motivated by an emotional commitment to their metaphorical father. In fact, Muhaydli was closely associated with the Syrian Socialist Nationalist Party (SSNP), a Syrian-Lebanese party that has historically had a conflictual relationship with Syria's ruling Ba'th party, although in the years prior to Muhaydli's act, it had become more identified with policies in Damascus. Of specific interest here, then, is not Muhaydli's devotion to Asad, which was widely recognized to be confabulated by government officials, but rather the investment of the official discourse in remaking her act as evidence of daughterly devotion to Asad.

Sana' Muhaydli's martyrdom inscribes her in the cult of Hafiz al-Asad. Her act occasions the reiteration of statements glorifying

Asad's leadership; her death also reproduces the narratives of sacrifice and of familial loyalty characteristic of Asad's cult. Muhaydli becomes an emblem of sacrifice and womanhood through Asad's recognition and an exemplar for other Syrian women. Other women can orient themselves and identify with her experience, not by literally sacrificing themselves, but by participating and being immersed in a discursive climate that prescribes and celebrates daughterly devotion.

Muhaydli's image exemplifies the ways in which the cult operates both to define obedience to state power and to confer membership in the official, national community. Her example illustrates how the prescriptive "grammar" of the cult works to control the meanings of an act that is popularly understood to be heroic yet which is also potentially destabilizing (because Muhaydli is female and acting independently of Syrian state directives). First, Muhaydli's image serves to announce the regime's power to appropriate meaningful symbols and images, not to cultivate belief or loyalty. The appropriation of Muhaydli registers the regime's attempts to control systems of signification. Second, Muhaydli's iconographic importance stems from her role as exemplar. As icon, Muhaydli specifies the proper conduct of national, metaphorical daughters. She operates, as does the rhetoric more generally, to articulate the form of civic obedience in Syria.

The third way in which the cult works to stabilize meaning is more complex, for it bears on the fact that Muhaydli was a woman and thus exposes the paradoxes in the regime's rhetoric and policy about women.[87] On the one hand, Muhaydli suggests that women *qua* national daughters, like soldier-sons, can emulate Asad. Women, like their male counterparts, can share in Asad's greatness by being *like* him, by being courageous warriors willing to sacrifice their lives for the glory and honor of the nation. On the other hand, Sana' Muhaydli and the women who have followed her example are termed "brides of the south." The appellation reinforces the gendered specificity of women's sacrifice by relating these acts to a fantasy of marriage.[88]

Images of Muhaydli reproduce this paradox. She is depicted in books and in some spectacles as the military combatant dressed in camouflage army fatigues and red beret; she is splattered with blood. Muhaydli is *also* portrayed as an immaculate bride, in a white satin dress and pearls. To some extent, this insistence on Muhaydli's status as bride affirms her purity and chastity. Brides are understood to be chaste; the blood spilled in their defloration on their wedding night affirms their previous purity and announces their adulthood.[89] But the blood Muhaydli spills is the sacrificial blood of the patriotic virgin, not the blood indicative of sexual initiation. In the testament she wrote prior to her suicide, Muhaydli distinguishes between her "marriage" and those of other brides: "I did not leave to marry or to live with any person . . . but I left for an honorable, brave, happy sacrifice."[90]

The death of the bride of the south ensures that she will, in fact, *never* undergo the ritual initiation of an actual bride: "The bride of the south who was married off to the entire homeland (*al-watan*) . . . exploded her chaste body in a red storm above the land of the resisting south."[91] Or, "Sana' the virgin . . . She rose by the wings of sacrifice."[92] Her sacrificial marriage assures that the blood she spills, unlike the blood of the bride, remains pure.[93] Her pure blood ensures the community's honor and the nation's continuance: "From the bright blood of Sana' will emerge the explosion of freedom . . . and from her honorable face radiates the hopes of coming victory . . . and from her pure blessed body flowers the spring of the eternal nation."[94] Marriage, blood, fecundity, purity, and patriotism are merged in this narrative of female self-sacrifice.

Sacrificial blood may also indicate the anxiety aroused by the prospect of female warriors. The blood of martyrdom signifies purity and honor, and for martyred women, therefore, additional assurances of female chastity seem to be required. Blood also invokes blood relations. Muhaydli's spilled blood, like the blood oaths among members of the "popular" organizations, incorporates her into the national family and makes her the daughter of Asad, the nation's father. Furthermore, Muhaydli's example suggests the power of blood as a symbol of national commitment and enduring connection, operating to prove loyalty real. The bodies of martyrs substantiate allegiance by providing concrete, specific examples of national dedication, echoed in the contracts signed in blood. Slogans like "with spirit, with blood, we sacrifice for you, O Hafiz" translate real martyrdom into the signs of a generalized loyalty to Asad.

The official narrative communicates understandings of obedience and community in terms of a chain of filial piety and paternal authority that culminates, and stops, in Asad. The language of the family suggests that citizens (both male and female) should behave *as if* they were children and Asad were their father. They should fear, revere, and honor him with their deference. They should also act as if they loved him and were willing to sacrifice for him. And if called upon publicly, they should not embarrass him or disgrace the community he heads, but rather behave as if they were extensions of him, capable of emulating his qualities and of making him proud. Although these concepts of family are complicated by potentially conflicting significations attached to gender, the iconic significance of "mother" (as nation) and "bride" (as bloody sacrifice) proves flexible enough to bring women as well as men within the specifications of appropriate behavior.

SUMMARY

The symbolic language derives meaning (e.g., signals affective content and is decipherable) in part because it refers to the actual and general experiences of family life in Syria and ascribes mythic kinship roles to actual people, some of whom are Asad's family members. The invocation of family relationships may be more or less resonant to individual Syrians. The rhetoric operates not as a catalogue of Syrians' personal beliefs, however, but chiefly as a formula for public—in a certain, limited sense "civic"—behavior. The formula facilitates obedience; it provides guidelines for politically correct behavior. Identification with and love of Asad need not be felt, but only simulated. Such behavior provides an easy way of obeying and of avoiding trouble. Every Syrian is fluent in the symbolic language because it is impossible to escape it. To be "Syrian" means, in part, to operate within this rhetorical universe.

Examples of discursive fluency can be produced more or less *ad infinitum* in both the self-important tones of official discourse and informally in people's private conversations and jokes. A book publisher and former Ba'thist at a dinner party in Damascus in

1996, for example, in the midst of a discussion about self-respect suddenly declared, "I respect my self . . . and Mr. President" (*bahtarim hali . . . wa al-sayyid al-ra'is*). Everyone began to laugh, understanding that the publisher was poking fun at the ways in which the president seems to be inserted into every domain of life, even the most personal or self-regarding. Then someone enhanced the joke, implying teasingly that the speaker's assertion of self-respect was still too presumptuous: "The President should be before you!"

Whenever I asked interview subjects to recite political slogans or provide phrases from the official discourse, they could invariably produce examples. At soccer games, where it is not uncommon for fans to protest an official's call by hurling bottles in his direction, this fluency could be used to protect transgressive Syrians from punishment. During games I attended, the referee would look up at the stands in an effort to find the bottle-thrower, and on more than one occasion, the fans would shout the slogan "With spirit, with blood, we sacrifice for you, O Hafiz." The slogan operated as armor shielding the offender from further recriminations. A similar use of slogans occurs in this story related to me by a Syrian observer of political life: a young boy went away to the state-sponsored Ba'th party's summer camp for fifteen days. One colonel there continually bullied and cursed the boy. Finally, the colonel hit the boy, and the boy, enraged, hit the colonel back. Rushing to defend him, the boys' campmates began shouting the slogan, "with spirit, with blood, we sacrifice for you, O Hafiz." Their use of the slogan was presumably intended not only to operate almost talismanically, protecting themselves and their campmates from harm, but also to redeploy the official language, to appropriate it for the ordinary citizen against a representative of state power. The next chapter begins to look more closely at the ways in which familiarity with such formulas enable some Syrians to demonstrate their obedience publicly while inviting others to transgress the boundaries of the permissible.

THREE

Acting "As If": The Story of M

The following anecdote was related to me during my fieldwork in
Syria a few days after the event allegedly took place:

> In the spring of 1989 the elite Syrian Presidential Guard discharged of-
> ficer M after breaking some of his bones. A young officer from a lower-
> middle-class 'Alawi family, M had expected his university education to
> secure him power and privilege within the ranks. He was mistaken.
> His commanding officer showed no particular respect for M's accomplish-
> ments, and even prior to the incident that occasioned his beating, his
> friends often heard him crying in his sleep.
>
> One day a high-ranking officer visiting the regiment ordered the sol-
> diers to recount their dreams of the night before. A soldier stepped for-
> ward and announced: "I saw the image of the leader in the sky, and we
> mounted ladders of fire to kiss it." A second soldier followed suit: "I saw
> the leader holding the sun in his hands, and he squeezed it, crushing it
> until it crumbled. Darkness blanketed the face of the earth. And then his
> face illuminated the sky, spreading light and warmth in all directions."
> Soldier followed soldier, each extolling the leader's greatness. When M's
> turn came, he stepped forward, saluted the visiting officer, and said: "I
> saw that my mother is a prostitute in your bedroom." The beating and
> discharge followed. Commenting retrospectively on his act, M explained
> that he had "meant that his country is a whore."[1]

The story of M exists within a climate in which the circulation of
illicit narratives is itself a politically significant and commonplace
fact. Syrian official rhetoric creates a site of important contestation,
the titillating and chilling effects of which are evident not only in
such individual transgressions as M's alleged defiance, but also in   67

countless acts of narration, such as that represented by the story of M itself. The person who told me this story did not witness the actual event, although he believes that it happened as reported. The stylized form of the story recalls a fable, and the bearer of the tale to me has subsequently used it as material for an unpublished—in Syria, unpublishable—short story. It is therefore as a fictional narrative of a purportedly true occurrence that I reproduce it here. Whether the story originates in the actions of M himself or in the imaginations of those telling it, the anecdote typifies an important feature of Syrian political life: the regime's demand that citizens provide external evidence of their allegiance to a cult whose rituals of adulation are manifestly unbelievable.

Set in the selective milieu of an elite military regiment, the story of M nevertheless exemplifies the requirements of public dissimulation the regime also imposes on ordinary "citizens" in the context of daily life. People's participation in the cult may be more or less frequent and arbitrary depending on their socioeconomic location, political history, and age, but exposure to its content and familiarity with the requirements of public dissimulation are so ubiquitous as to be part of the experience of being Syrian. In quasi-mandatory after-school programs organized by the "popular organizations" and during national holidays, school children routinely chant slogans extolling the leader's virtues. On the anniversary of the Corrective Movement, librarians in the Asad Library were told to show up at work and be ready to march, were they to be called upon to do so. Intellectuals often find work as journalists for the regime, reproducing the cult's hagiography. University faculty and students are required to people the "spontaneous" demonstrations or to attend local spectacles; students and professors may also monitor their peers, demanding assurances of outward signs of allegiance to Asad. Private sector employers and commercial shopkeepers, who have more leeway than public sector personnel, also participate in the cult by plastering posters of Asad in their offices, shops, and on their street corners. Ambitious businessmen pepper bids on enticing state contracts with "cultspeak" or by invoking Asad or his sons' names in their project proposals. On at least one occasion, even political prisoners were reportedly compelled to sign loyalty oaths before they could be released.[2]

why is this unusual?

M's story dramatizes experiences such as these, which citizens have both as participants in and as daily consumers of Asad's cult. In this heightened version of a routine encounter, the soldiers enact a politics of "as if" by pretending that they dreamed of Asad's omnipotence. Some of the soldiers may have believed that Asad really is divinely inspired, but surely it is unlikely that any of them happened to have dreamed of the leader the night before. The high-ranking officer proved that he could elicit such fictions from the participants. The participants complied, thereby demonstrating their obedience to the officer and their ability to act as if they had dreamed of Asad. Yet while requiring the soldiers to reveal what would purport to be their innermost selves, the officer conveniently enabled them to narrate the most unverifiable and readily concocted stories.

This chapter therefore poses two related questions: What is the meaning of the soldiers' participation and of M's transgression in the story? And why devise strategies that require people to dissimulate? In other words, why produce a politics that depends on the external and easily falsified trappings of loyalty, rather than on people's actual beliefs? By treating M's story as a meaningful fiction, we can begin to answer these questions, moving beyond the specific example of Syria to explore the general relevance to political and social theory of cognitive states other than belief.

THE RHETORICAL CONTEXT: SWEET DREAMS

In the story, M's comrades draw obediently on an established stock of images, stringing them together to reproduce the political, religious, and popular iconography of the Syrian state. The image of the sun resonates in Syria, as elsewhere, with sempiternal claims of national leadership. The soldier's ascension into the sky to join the leader suggests both the hierarchy of power, with Asad at the top, and the mechanisms of identification by which the leader absorbs his followers into himself. The soldiers' concoctions, in other words, are not difficult to interpret; nor is M's rebellious response, which breaks the spell of sanctification and sycophancy.

Although M's statement also draws upon a stock of set phrases and formulaic imagery, taken in this case from the regime's family narrative, M rearranges the state's symbolism in order to subvert it. His subversion exemplifies possibilities available to Syrian citizens in general, and to Syrian artists required to apply their talents to the cult of Asad, in particular. M's defiant statement addresses the intricate web of patrilineal kin relationships invoked by Asad's cult, in which officers are characteristically figured as elder brothers and all males are sons of the mother-nation. Like state ideologues, M plays off an allusion to the etymological relation between *umma* (nation) and *umm* (mother). His allusion, however, ironically reverses the cult's narrative, constructing an episode of incest in which the younger son witnesses his mother-country having sex for money with his older brother, the senior officer. The senior officer, as son of the corrupt nation and as representative of political power, may thus also be illegitimate. This reading suggests that the officer compounds his illegitimacy by being incestuous, by preying on and debauching his own country. In the story, M's act induces his partial separation from his fellow soldiers, his metaphorical siblings, at the same time it aggressively exposes their pretense. The other soldiers (and the officer) are also "whores" who "sell" their integrity for security or gain; M exposes the charade and names it.

But M also denies himself full compensation for his disobedience, thereby demonstrating concretely the insecurity (for both ideologues and rebels) inherent in the regime's rhetorical interventions. M, after all, chooses not to boycott the ritual but to engage it rebelliously on its own terms. His country, he implies, has sold itself to a corrupt military; Syria has become defiled.[3] Moreover, M says that he "saw" his mother's prostitution, which makes him more than a mere victim of Syria's corruption. He becomes a witness, a voyeuristic spectator to his mother's defilement. Helpless to prevent his mother-country from selling her body to the officer, M nevertheless can and does watch it. His self-announced voyeurism suggests his awareness of his own complicity.

M also registers his complicity in the regime's contamination and in his victimization when he speaks of *his* mother as the prostitute: Syria's corruption directly affects and pains him. M represents his condition as that of the son of a whore, as the product of the prostituting nation. As the son of the mother-nation, M can never be certain that he himself is not, like his metaphorical siblings, a bastard. One interpretation of M's story suggests, therefore, the simultaneous sacrifice of identity (M as bastard) and re-identification with the soldiers (they are all bastards) that his position entails. M does refuse the sycophantic self the regime has designated for the Syrian soldiers, but he nevertheless is unable either to renounce or to change the corrupt mother-nation to whom he remains connected affectively and by origin.

Contemporary Arab literature—of which M's story is, indeed, a minor instance—is replete with indications of predicaments such as M's, depicting the country or landscape as a defiled woman and portraying the Arab man's impotence as emblematic of his post-colonial trauma, his frustration, and sense of weakness. In Egyptian author Naguib Mahfouz's works, the character of the prostitute personifies Egypt's corruption.[4] Ghassan Kanafani's protagonist in *Rijal fi al-shams* (Men in the sun) has lost his genitals in the 1948 Arab-Israeli War. In al-Tayyib Salih's *Mawsim al-hijra ila al-shamal* (Season of migration to the north) the male Sudanese hero inverts the relationship between the explicitly masculine colonizer and the effeminate colonized by compelling British women to commit suicide over him. In this male fantasy of the subaltern's revenge, the Western woman's victimization registers the colonized male's misogyny, but also his enduring weakness; he is, after all, unable to take revenge on the Western white men who initially feminized him. M's "dream" displaces the strength and manliness that Asad's cult works to articulate with the twinned image of a sullied woman and a helpless male. The impotent male is, to some extent, M himself, but it is also Asad. Asad as "knight" and "father" is not only unable to protect the mother-country from corruption, he may also be the agent of corruption.

Dreams, like familial metaphors, offer a charged rhetorical terrain both for producing an idealized representation of the regime and for inviting subversive possibilities. Whether dreams are regarded as divinely inspired messages conveyed to selected ordinary humans or, in common post-Freudian terms, as unconscious, personal expressions of wishes and anxieties that find no outlet in daily life, dreams are suggestive of the private parts of ourselves.

The officer's demand signals that actual dreams may remain private, but the soldiers' public claims must conform to the official national narrative. The officer, as representative of the state, measures the state's possession of the soldiers' willingness to perform by participating in a fantasy of omnipotence, i.e., to act as if they have no untoward anxieties and their deepest wishes are consonant with those idealized by the state. They are to act as if the state can intrude into this most private, inaccessible, potentially transgressive part of themselves; act as if the state's divinity is communicated through the form and content of their dreams; act as if the state can control even that within themselves that they cannot.

Because dreams seem to escape the conscious control of the dreamer, they also often operate in literary and cinematic works as a trope, a site of subterfuge, through which the "dreamer" can simultaneously articulate political criticisms and disavow responsibility for them. Offering a concise formulation of the nonconsensual aspect of dreaming, Roger Caillois writes: "the sleeper has no control over the phantasmagoric, but it is nevertheless a product of his imagination. When it is unfolded before him without his consent, he can hardly believe himself responsible."[5] In M's story, what is nonconsensual is not the dreams recounted, which are fabrications rather than true reports of unconscious narratives, but the context in which the "dreams" must be narrated. In order not to be betrayed by the nonconsensuality of dreams, the soldiers must engage in nonconsensual narration; they are in control of the message—no one requires them to reveal inappropriate dreams—but unless they deliver the message that is expected of them, they lose control of the consequences. M's transgression is his failure to obey the rules of conduct, not his having actually dreamed a "bad" dream.

The "good" dreams purport to show that the Syrian soldiers are bound by love to Asad, the symbolic father and representative of the Syrian nation-state. This bond is registered in two different ways: in the act of complying with the officers' demands and in the nature of the act required. This obedience entails pretending that even dreams have been harnessed to the state's definition of community, a community whose members are united in their glorification of Asad. And, indeed, an in-depth analysis of the regime's rhetoric more generally suggests that people's language, and in some cases their imaginations, are being deployed every day to extol Asad's virtues, to construct ideas of community and sovereignty by devising the narratives and reiterating the formulas that frame the terms of state dominance and national belonging.

OBEDIENCE, COMPLICITY, AND ENFORCEMENT

If the high-ranking officer was not interested in what the soldiers had actually dreamed the previous night, if he was concerned only with how the soldiers would represent their dreams publicly, the question remains: why would a regime devise practices that require such obvious dissimulation? Why promote a politics based on "as if" rather than a politics devoted to fostering loyalty or commanding belief? Slavoj Žižek's definition of obedience suggests a possible answer: "The only real obedience . . . is an 'external' one: obedience out of conviction is not real obedience because it is already 'mediated' through our subjectivity—that is, we are not really obeying the authority, but simply following our judgement, which tells us that the authority deserves to be obeyed in so far as it is good, wise, beneficent." [6] In Žižek's understanding, in other words, obedience differs from good judgment in that obedience requires a self-conscious submission to authority. Stephen Greenblatt argues similarly: "Power manifests itself in the ability to impose one's fictions upon the world. . . . The point is not that anyone is deceived by the charade, but that everyone is forced either to participate in it or to watch it silently." [7] Life is, of course, more complicated than the dichotomous choice Greenblatt offers. There are contexts in *any* regime in which people can treat their participation or the state's demands as irrelevant; there are also ways of being ironic or irreverent, some of them dangerous, as M's example shows, others perhaps permissable outlets.

In the Syrian officer's case, as in the larger public world of official representations, power manifests itself in the regime's ability to impose its fictions upon the world. No one is deceived by the charade, but everyone—even M—is forced to participate in it.

The high-ranking officer's command, in other words, announces the regime's power to elicit demonstrations of "real obedience." And "real obedience" relies on *not believing*.

The soldiers' participation, however, entails more than an outward manifestation of obedience. As each soldier tries to outdo his predecessor with increasingly exaggerated dreams lauding the leader's supernatural feats, he registers not only his obedience, but also his complicity in perpetuating the cult. To be complicit is to allow oneself to be made an accomplice, to become bound up in the actions and practices the regime promotes. As we have seen, M presents himself as aware of his own complicity. And the story construes the soldiers as complicit to the extent that they are entangled in the practices of dissimulation constitutive of the regime's politics of "as if."

Complicity, hegemony, and legitimacy all, in Foucaultian terms, imply the "regulatory power" of norms. But "hegemony" and "legitimacy" presuppose a level of belief or emotional commitment that complicity does not. A comparative look at other contexts, ranging from George Orwell's fantasy of totalitarianism in *1984* to Václav Havel's "post-totalitarian" Czechoslovakia, can help us analyze the political importance of complicity in contexts where patently spurious claims are vigorously enforced. Each of the accounts I shall examine here offers tools for interpreting the story of M, while M's story also suggests some of the problems and limitations of prevailing views.

In "The Power of the Powerless," Václav Havel discusses a gesture of obedience in "post-totalitarian" Czechoslovakia in ways that suggest parallels with the complicity of M's soldiers in "authoritarian" Syria. To question a common practice under the Czechoslovakian communist regime, Havel uses the example of a greengrocer displaying the slogan "Workers of the World, Unite!" in his shop window. Havel postulates that the grocer displays the slogan not because he believes that the workers should unite, but rather because "these things must be done if one is to get along in life. It is one of the thousands of details that guarantee him a relatively tranquil life 'in harmony with society', as they say."[8] The slogan functions as a "sign," according to Havel, signifying the grocer's

FIGURE 9   Taxi cab with "cult" paraphernalia.

obedience and his desire to be left in peace, but not his actual belief in communist principles.

In Havel's "post-totalitarian" Eastern Europe, enforcement relied on what he calls "the principle of social *auto-totality*," meaning that people enforce each other's obedience without believing in what they do.[9] The same principle is at work in the example of Syria, with many of my interview subjects acknowledging the cult's potency by drawing on their experiences of its self-enforcing dimensions. A former Baʿth party official recounted a conversation in which he had praised Lenin, and one of his friends had responded, "Why aren't you praising Hafiz al-Asad?" The former Baʿthist, in the context of a general conversation about communism, felt compelled to laud Asad's virtues and to justify his praise of Lenin.[10]

Similarly, shopkeepers are rarely explicitly required to post official iconography in their windows, but many of them do so. Some store owners have to violate import laws in order to survive economically, so they hang a poster of Asad as a talisman to ward off harm, or in less magical terms, in the hopes that an outward sign of loyalty will discourage regime agents from disturbing business. Taxi drivers are avid users of cult paraphernalia, a practice that is understood by officials and dissidents alike as an effort to dissuade traffic police from giving drivers tickets (fig. 9). No one actually demands that iconography be displayed on private property, and failing to do so rarely results in actual punishment, but as one university professor argued, "People post the signs not because they love him, but because the system is self-enforcing and people are accustomed to it. People have internalized the control."[11] Indeed, even the circulation of stories such as M's might serve this purpose of self-enforcement, communicating the costs of transgression and the threats of punishment while justifying citizens' complicity by virtue of the safety it secures.[12]

For Havel, such practices mean that people are thereby made "agents of the system's general automatism and servants of its self-determined goals, so they may participate in the common responsibility for it, so they may be pulled into and ensnared by it, like Faust with Mephistopheles."[13] This "principle of social *auto-totality*" means more than bearing responsibility by being entangled in the system: it means that human beings "may create through their involvement a general norm and, thus, bring pressure to bear on their fellow citizens."[14] Moreover, people can:

> learn to be comfortable with their involvement, to identify with it as though it were something natural and inevitable and, ultimately, so they may—with no external urging—come to treat any non-involvement as an abnormality, as arrogance, as an attack on themselves, as a form of dropping out of society.[15]

This "auto-totality" is a "self-directed system." Havel claims that "what we understand by the system is not, therefore, a social order imposed by one group upon another, but rather something which permeates the entire society."[16]

As in Syria, in Havel's Czechoslovakia people are not required to believe the "mystifications" the regime puts forth, and they do not. They are required to act *as if* they did, and by so acting, to live "within the lie." They thus "confirm the system, fulfill the system, make the system, *are* the system."[17] Complicity matters for Havel because it means that human beings together sustain a system of rule that degrades them. People are degraded, in Havel's view, not because of the content of the norms, but because, while no one believes in them, everyone obeys and enforces them. Complicity is doubly degrading when people deny to themselves that they are behaving in complicitous ways. Ideology is insidious because it allows people to hide their reasons for obedience from themselves. Havel's critique of what degrades and what uplifts is problematic beyond the moralism that underlies his views. His analysis is sometimes tendentious, and minimizes the importance of the state's coercive mechanisms, perhaps because of the particular characteristics of "post-totalitarian" Czechoslovakia.[18] Nor does his claim that people treat noninvolvement as "arrogance" seem to fit the Syrian case. But his exposure of a system that is "self-directed," in which people together enforce mutual compliance with norms in which they do not in fact believe, offers at least a partial and provocative description of the way in which enforcement and complicity operate in Syria. While the threat of state punishment is always present, people also regulate themselves and each other to uphold the "norms" the regime prescribes. Enforcement under such circumstances means not that one group dominates another, but rather that "everyone in his or her own way is both a victim and a supporter of the system."[19] Surely there are different degrees of victimization and support, a point Havel acknowledges without analyzing adequately. Nevertheless, Havel's insight that everyone participates in the maintenance of the system, that "victims" also uphold the system through their participation, suggests that political systems can be reliant on, defined by, and functionally inseparable from people's habitual obedience to them. Under authoritarian conditions, political participation may not make people feel fulfilled, but it does make them feel safe.[20]

Iraqi expatriate Kanan Makiya, in his book *Republic of Fear*, about the regime of Saddam Husayn, offers one of the only Middle East–oriented accounts of the functions of obedience and complicity. The levels of compliance or obedience with which Makiya is concerned are also more dramatic than Havel's, and might seem for both reasons to be more applicable to the Syrian case. Of particular note is Makiya's brief discussion of show trial confessions, which share with the "dreams" of M's story the property of being enforced confabulations: both are made personal through each individual's own narration, which nonetheless operates according to regime-defined formulas. The Syrian regime's requirement that soldiers recount their dreams in M's story, like show trial confessions, is an explicit demand *not* to confess, but rather to produce an allegory that coheres with the regime's idealized and untroubled presentation of itself. Although Makiya's analysis is seriously flawed, its problems and insights help clarify the importance of public rituals for producing political power.

Makiya argues that complicity serves in particular to free the regime from accountability for its actions. He describes the spectacle of public confessions surrounding the 1979 purges in Iraq as follows:

> The first to "confess" was RCC [Revolutionary Command Council] member Muhyi ʿAbd al-Husain Rashid whose whole family was held hostage. The confession was filmed and then, as one version of the story has it, shown to an all-party audience of several hundred leaders from the entire country. A grief-stricken Saddam addressed the meeting with tears running down his cheeks. He filled in the gaps in Rashid's testimony and dramatically fingered his former colleagues. Guards dragged people out of the proceeding and then Saddam called upon the country's top ministers and party leaders to themselves form the actual firing squads.[21]

This account highlights the creation of an atmosphere of complicity, in which Rashid, Hussein, the top ministers, and party leaders all participate in "resolving" what appears to be an overwhelming national tragedy. Makiya concludes by arguing:

> Neither Stalin nor Hitler would have thought up a detail like that. What Eichmann-like refuge in "orders from above" could these men dig up in the future if they were ever to marshal the courage to try and depose the Leader? Can anyone devise a more brilliant tactical move to implicate potential foes?[22]

The story of the 1979 purges is extraordinary, but Makiya's analysis remains unpersuasive. He wants to show that Saddam Husayn represents a power even more insidious than Hitler's or Stalin's. However, the distinction he asserts between the obedience of Eichmann and that of Iraqi participants in the purges does not ultimately make sense. Does Makiya see "calling upon" as different from "ordering"? Nothing in his writing suggests what this difference might be. Surely the party leaders and ministers who formed the firing squads could claim that they were following "orders from above," that what they had done "was a crime only in retrospect,"[23] and that they were forced to comply lest they too be killed.

According to Hannah Arendt, whose book Makiya clearly has in mind when he invokes Eichmann, Eichmann's defense rested on the claim that he "had always been a law abiding citizen because Hitler's orders, which he had certainly executed to the best of his ability, had possessed 'the force of law' in the Third Reich."[24] The difference between Eichmann and Ba'thist party leaders, however, is that Eichmann was never required to kill anyone personally. Bureaucratic norms produced a peculiar kind of power that enabled individuals to disavow personal responsibility for their actions in a way that was particularly pernicious for politics, according to Arendt, an analogy that does not hold for this Iraqi example. Makiya, moreover, like many theorists of "totalitarian" politics, denies the fact of ambivalence or incoherence, the ways in which people are neither totally alienated nor totally inscribed in the relationships of domination the regime and its citizens produce.

Yet Makiya makes an important connection among victimization, participation, and complicity that is relevant to the soldiers' confabulations related by M. Although even participants can ultimately hold a regime accountable, complicity does make it harder for actors like the soldiers to represent themselves as having been mere victims of authoritarian caprice. As they recount their purported dreams of the night before, Syrian soldiers cannot help but be aware that they did *not* have these dreams, but are inventing them. The soldiers are made aware of the state's attempt to control their language for public display, but they are also made aware of their willingness to comply.

Richard Rorty, in his essay "Orwell on Cruelty," suggests that *knowledge* of oneself as someone who will obey has political and psychological consequences. He asks why it is important for O'Brien (the state torturer in Orwell's novel, *1984*) to make Winston (the tortured protagonist) "believe, briefly, that two and two equals five." Importantly, the statement is "not something O'Brien himself believes. Nor does Winston himself believe it once he is broken and released."[25] Rorty argues:

> The *only* point in making Winston believe that two and two equals five is to break him. Getting somebody to deny a belief for no reason is a first step toward making her incapable of having a self because she becomes incapable of weaving a coherent web of belief and desire. It makes her irrational, in a quite precise sense: She is unable to give a reason for her belief that fits together with her other beliefs. She becomes irrational not in the sense that she has lost contact with reality but in the sense that she can no longer rationalize—no longer justify herself to herself.[26]

Rorty borrows much of his analysis from Elaine Scarry's *The Body in Pain: The Making and Unmaking of the World*. Much of the time, according to Scarry, the aim of torture is not to get people to disclose information, but rather to use pain in such a way that even when the torture is over, the tortured person cannot reconstitute herself. According to Scarry, as the prisoner's "self," "voice," and "world" contract, the torturer's "self," "voice," and "world" expand. This dynamic allows the body's pain to be read as the regime's power.[27] The purpose of inflicting such agonizing pain on the body is to destroy the tortured person's sense of self and to remake his mind. Similarly, according to Rorty, O'Brien tortures Winston and thereby compels him to hold an irrational belief in order to destroy his belief system, without which he can no longer have a self he recognizes. O'Brien argues that the representative of the state has the power to "tear human minds to pieces and put them together again in new shapes of [his] own choosing."[28]

Despite the exaggerated formulation of the torturer as a representative of the state with limitless power, Rorty's and Scarry's analyses of torture can help us consider the acts of the individual Syrian soldiers in M's story who, unlike Orwell's Winston, were merely required to *say* they held irrational beliefs. Unlike O'Brien, the regime in M's story is unconcerned with whether anyone believes the irrational claims of the cult. The cult precludes belief. Nevertheless, the underlying points that both Rorty and Scarry make prove relevant to M's story: the Syrian soldiers are being coerced to say something manifestly spurious, which they otherwise would not say. By complying, each soldier demonstrates the regime's power to dominate him. The soldier comes to know about himself, and about the others, that each can be made to subordinate to state authority not only his body, but also his imagination; he knows that he is capable of inventing and declaring dreams that are unbelievable and not, in fact, his own.

Although the power involved in compelling such performances may seem to be of a lesser order than the power to alter beliefs, people are nevertheless required to enact a prescribed, politically congenial self for public presentation. Symbolic practices of power interfere with people's political "subjectivities," with their sense of themselves as political persons. As we shall see in chapter 4, Syrian popular culture, from editorial cartoons to televised political comedies, depicts the ways in which official rhetoric and orchestrated spectacles depoliticize people. Interviews with ordinary citizens attest to this depoliticization as well. Participation in a politics of dissimulation, according to numerous and diverse accounts, divests the citizen-subject of his or her "passionate excitement" (*wijdan*) and "dignity" (*karama*).[29]

The examples drawn from theoretical reflections on other cases, from interviews conducted in Syria, and from M's story demonstrate different levels of obedience: from the passive compliance of the green grocer with a poster in his shop window, to the Syrian soldiers and Iraqi leaders who are forced into lies, to torturers and party members wielding the weapons of state power. For Havel, the obedience of people who are not required to believe ideological "mystifications" but only to act as if they did reproduces a system that relies on, and is defined by, passive compliance. The division between ruler and ruled "runs *de facto* through each person, for everyone in his or her own way is both a victim and a supporter of the system."[30] For Makiya, whose example of Iraq demonstrates active participation rather than cynicism or apathy, the performance implicates participants in ways that make them aware of their complicity, and it is precisely this awareness that lends the experience of obedience its potency. For Rorty and Scarry, what is degrading and powerful in authoritarian state activities such as torture is not so much corporal punishment as such, but instead the way in which compelling people to do and say things against their will forces participants to surrender their sense of self, to become obedient, defeated, and sycophantic. In M's story, Syrian soldiers are made to know that they are capable of redirecting their imaginations, that the state's intervention means, in this case, its ability to define their obedience in this way. The Syrian regime, unlike "totalitarianism" as described by Orwell and others, need not reconstitute individual selves, but only "de-constitute" them, saturating them with experiences of state domination and producing "citizens" whose experience of political participation is largely theatrical.

A politics of "as if " registers the soldiers' complicity and the regime's power. But like all demonstrations of obedience, inducing complicity by enforcing public dissimulation also has its limitations. First, behavior that encourages awareness of one's complicity reminds each soldier that he and the regime are at odds, that a gap exists between performance and belief. Second, although this gap affirms the regime's power to induce complicity, complicity itself registers the regime's reliance on participants to uphold the system. Third, requiring citizens to act "as if " leaves the regime in the predicament of having to evaluate popular sentiment through the prism of enforced public dissimulation. Ritual dissimulation allows Syrians to keep their actual thoughts private.[31] Fourth, as M's example shows, professions of complicity sometimes become opportunities for subtle mockery or even outright rebellion.

M contradicts the obviously complicit mythology of his compatriots by choosing an alternative mythology that nevertheless situates his rebellion in the very rhetorical universe he seeks to reorder. He uses the regime's formulas and imagery to reveal the regime's corruption rather than glorify its power. For M, the nation is effectively fatherless; it is without precisely that strong masculine leadership Asad's cult claims he provides *par excellence.*

Some Syrian writers and artists, like the one who related M's story to me, are consciously repeating M's maneuver when they exploit the symbols of the regime to challenge the meanings and conditions authorizing Asad's rule. The following dialogue appears, for example, in Syrian author Usama Sa'id's poem "The Drunken Grave":

#1: I am his ambassador to illusion, his rusty sword, rusty from cutting the heads of illusions. I will leave him alone. I have nothing to do with him. Let him do what he likes.

#2: Oh, you make mistakes always. And in the wonders there are also wonders. You will die burning.

#1: Fire won't be able to burn me. I've been extinguished since the coming to power of my father.[32]

The vocabulary Saʿid uses, "since the coming to power of my father" (*wilayat abi*), derives from a slogan common during Asad's 1991 referendum. The poem was printed in *Alef*, a Syrian journal devoted to the experimental works of young Arab writers; the references Saʿid makes were not lost on Syrian censors, who removed the page on which this passage occurred before allowing distribution.

Saʿid's critique, like M's, uses the images and language of state power in order to undermine the system that sanctions their meaning. But there is an important difference between Saʿid's transgression and M's. M's defiant "dream" entangles him in the humiliation the state engineers, representing him as a voyeur with a prostitute for a mother. M resists in a way that turns the attack against himself. In that sense, M's attack testifies to the regime's power. Saʿid's poem distances the author from the "father" he challenges; it does not require that the author ridicule himself in order to criticize the regime. The distance Saʿid's *character* obtains, however, comes at the cost of his extinction, his death.

These examples provide us with legible instances of the ways in which "the line between ruler and ruled," as Havel puts it, "runs *de facto* through each person." Saʿid and M are engaged in skirmishes along that line, self-consciously bringing to our attention the ways in which the cult helps to make everyone both a victim and a supporter of the system.

CONCLUSION

Political practices that encourage dissimulation register participants' fluency in the rhetorical operations the regime puts forth. The regime's power resides in its ability to impose national fictions and to make people say and do what they otherwise would not. This obedience makes people complicit; it entangles them in self-enforcing relations of domination, thereby making it hard for participants to see themselves simply as victims of the state's caprices. Thus individuals' participation, and the attitude of impotence that attends compliance, uphold these mechanisms of control. A politics of "as if" carries important political consequences: it enforces obedience, induces complicity, identifies and ferrets out some disobedient citizens (such as M), and organizes the symbolic context within which struggles over the meaning of the nation, of selfhood, and of both political power and individual transgression take place.

The effects of Asad's cult, although powerful, are also ambiguous, indeterminate, and limited. Asad's cult demonstrates *only* that people can be brought to recite the slogans and to manipulate the mythological content orchestrated by leaders. Moreover, the vagueness and hyperbole of the rhetoric make Syria's symbolic universe unstable, which invites the kinds of subversive moments M publicly articulates in the story. M "works the weakness" of the cult by resignifying the symbolic order in ways that disrupt the regime's power to control fully citizens' language.[33] The cult, in particular, makes visible the paradoxically self-serving and self-defeating aspects inherent in the wielding of symbolic power.

M's act of subversion and its consequences register this paradox. A politics of "as if" both produces official power and imports into it a specific kind of fragility. M's punishment shows that the regime can blend coercive, material, and disciplinary-symbolic strategies to enforce its norms of external obedience. M is beaten and his ambitions as a university graduate seem to be dashed—but not before he has turned the power of the official rhetoric back on itself. The transgression itself turns out to be both radical and complex. Even as M displays his resistance to the cult's penchant for apotheosis, he does not relinquish a politics of "as if." Rather than taking up the language of direct discourse, M participates in the epistemic system of public dissimulation he seeks to disavow. He acts as if he too has had a dream. M might have said "I didn't dream" or "I didn't sleep." He could have recounted a neutral dream, or a dream he had actually had; he could have used the occasion for an openly defiant speech about the regime, or expressed his contempt by uttering any of a number of expletives. Any of these acts, though they might have been attended with greater or lesser concrete consequences, would have situated M more completely outside the epistemic system than his actual response did. But for that reason, any other choice would not have been as effective rhetorically: M's dream is insulting because it uses a politics of "as if" to dramatize the phoniness of the officers' request. By provoking the officers to punish him, M is making the officers implicitly admit that their question, like the soldiers' responses, is disingenuous.[34] M's punishment underscores the otherwise unacknowledged fact that the officers, too, are caught up in a politics of dissimulation.

M undermines the epistemic system of "as if" at the same time as he also destabilizes the conceptual system of language and symbols within which Asad's cult operates. And here again we have a paradox. The cult defines the discursive field through which M's resignification can occur. M appropriates the same familial metaphors conventionally invoked by the regime to express his resistance to official politics. In sharing in the conceptual system he seeks to undermine, M's subversion registers his entanglement in the world he insults. M remains the son in his narrative; and he obeys, if rebelliously.

Scholars of oppression and resistance have invoked such enmeshment to suggest that ruler and ruled are, in Tejumola Olaniyan's words "locked inextricably in the tyranny of language."[35] But it is unclear how worrisome such a tyranny should be, for how could resistance make sense outside of a shared conceptual system, such as the one supplied by Asad's cult? Without reference to an officially glorified object, how could M's speech function as an insult? In other words, M's "dream" is insulting not only because it exposes the regime's politics of pretense, but because it uses the very symbols supposed to glorify the regime in order to profane it. M's act shows us how transgression is conceptually and structurally dependent on the system that it opposes. But he also demonstrates that no one, not even a powerful authoritarian regime, owns a conceptual system. Perhaps most importantly, the story of M exemplifies the disposition of language to undermine its own authorizing logic.

M's is not the only instance of radical subversion registering what Douglas Haynes and Gyan Prakash have termed the "entanglement" of dominance and resistance.[36] The next chapter explores the ways in which Syrians are constantly waging skirmishes along the dividing line the cult establishes between ruler and ruled. The chapter analyzes the underground and tolerated jokes, cartoons, films, and television comedies that demonstrate self-conscious, quotidian contests over both the meaning and the disciplinary effects of official rhetoric. It asks: to what extent and in what ways do these signs of transgression amount to political resistance?

FOUR

Signs of Transgression

Syrian resistance is made up primarily of mundane transgressions that do not aim to overthrow the existing order. Some scholars have argued against designating these largely discursive triumphs as "political," because they cannot affect the overall situation of the regime's dominance. But ignoring these transgressive practices, as James C. Scott points out, may mean neglecting the lived circumstances in which collective action is generated and sustained; quotidian struggles can and do grow into large-scale and conscious challenges to the political order.[1] When they do not, they remain nonetheless the very stuff of ordinary political experience. Struggles imbued with explicitly political content are ever-present in the interstices of Syrian daily life.[2] The popularity of political satires and cartoons and the prevalence of jokes unfavorable to Asad tell us that although Syrians may not challenge power directly, neither do they uncritically accept the regime's version of reality. Comedies, cartoons, and films are among the forms taken by everyday political contests in Syria, no doubt in part because direct political engagement is generally discouraged by the fear of punishment or material deprivation.[3]

The implicit and explicit norms of the official rhetoric operate to demarcate boundaries between the acceptable and the unacceptable. Publicized Syrian comedies and cartoons are approved by the censors in accordance with guidelines specified by the Syrian Ministry of Information. According to a Deputy Minister of Information, these rules assure the maintenance of "national morals" by requiring journalists and writers to strike a balance between   *87* "responsibility" and "freedom of expression."[4] Syrian writers and actors generally understand that behind the rhetoric of the law lie prohibitions and limits not to be transgressed. Comedians cannot poke fun at religion or make references to sex. Criticisms directed at the regime must be directed only at state institutions, without naming names. Any reference to 'Alawis, or to any minority, is taboo.[5] Under no circumstances can the president's name, or that of any other high official, be mentioned in jest.[6] Tolerated political parodies tend both to operate within these specified guidelines and to probe the boundaries between publicly tolerated expression and the privately lived experiences of political power.

This chapter begins with a discussion of licensed political comedies and ends with a treatment of the jokes that are told in what might be termed "private enclaves of publicity." In the privacy of Syrian homes, among people who trust each other, criticism of the regime can and does thrive, often in the form of stories such as M's, and also as inside information, sheer speculation, rumors, and jokes. The popularity of these diverse practices demonstrates that in ordinary life Syrians are aware of the disciplinary effects of the cult and also seek to undermine them.[7] But paradoxically, rather than simply subverting the Syrian regime's power, it is precisely citizens' awareness of themselves as reluctant "conscripts" upon which a politics of "as if" depends.[8]

TOLERATED PARODIES OF POLITICS: CREATING AN AESOPIAN PUBLIC WORLD

In Arabic, the word *tanfis* means "letting out air" and is used by many Syrians to describe the perception that politically critical television serials and films operate as "safety valves," allowing people to vent frustrations and displace or relieve tensions that otherwise might find expression in political action. This claim has been echoed by scholars asserting that tolerated or authorized critical practices function to preserve a repressive regime's dominance rather than undermining it.[9] Others, by contrast, inspired by Mikhail Bakhtin's analysis of "carnival," celebrate the chaos-promoting effects and political potential of licensed rituals.[10]

There are problems in any conceptualization that poses a dichotomous alternative on this matter: that is, either the practice functions exclusively as a safety valve or it works as resistance. There is no *necessary* relation between carnivals, or any other forms of licensed political parody, and resistance; they may operate to reassert dominant patterns of behavior by providing moments of release and exception; they may offer enduring and politically incendiary criticisms of official hierarchy; and they may combine both effects to various degrees.[11]

Abstract juxtapositions of the "safety valve" formulation versus the idea of "resistance" obscure the ambiguity of these practices, which, however, are no less political for being ambiguous. Political scientists in particular tend to base their analyses of politics on the official or formal relations between ruler and ruled, either ignoring sites of cultural production altogether or situating them within this conventional juxtaposition. The cult is either good or bad policy. Licensed parodies of political power either uphold the regime (safety valves, good policy from the regime's perspective) or they inadvertently result in collective upheaval (bad policy). My observation of permitted comedies in Syria suggests, contrary to the dichotomous functionalist safety valve debate, that political parodies, feature films, and jokes are where Syrian political vitality resides and where critique and oppositional consciousness thrive. Artistic transgressions are the site of *politics*, of the dynamic interplay between the regime's exercise of power and people's experiences of and reactions to it. The line of friction between ruler and ruled—both in public among people differentially situated in the hierarchy and, as Havel teaches, internally to each person—is articulated and renegotiated in these practices. By unsettling the idealized representations of domination, artists produce memorable rhetorical performances, creating a transgressive counterculture that plays with the parameters of national membership.

Accounts assuming that any licensed act of subversion serves only the interests of a dominant elite are problematic, furthermore, because the intentions of policy makers do not necessarily correspond to the effects of any particular ritual or political parody.[12] A number of historians studying carnival, for example, show that the ritual may be designed to reaffirm the *status quo,* yet prompt collective action against it.[13] In the case of Syria, authorized political parodies generally involve a passive audience (television serials viewed in the home or plays viewed in a theater—the latter potentially more dangerous than the former because the theater is a public site where people gather as strangers). The point is not that such parodies threaten to generate collective action in the moment, but that they enable people to recognize the shared circumstances of unbelief. Seeing others obey in daily life makes each person feel isolated in his/her unbelief and thus helpless. Hearing the laughter of fellow spectators in a theater, sharing the experience of watching a television program satirizing official discourse, or discussing the program among friends afterwards, counteracts the atomizing conditions of the cult. A number of comedies explicitly identify charade-like practices and fraudulent slogans. This doubled representation of unbelief (the unbelieving character on stage or on screen and the unbelieving audience that laughs) dramatizes people's connection, rather than their isolation, and their connection is specifically in unbelief.

The problems with safety valve theories and, by extension, with conceptualizations of politics that ignore the everyday, lived experiences of opposition and critique, warrant the exploration of other explanations for the maintenance of these approved activities in public. Here I want to propose four alternative accounts of why transgressive practices might be allowed to persist under authoritarian conditions such as those in Syria.

First, these practices are not just sites of licensed critique; they are also hard won and defended by citizens in their contests for control over systems of signification.[14] For example, the Syrian state relaxed its control over film and theater productions in the late 1980s and early 1990s. This "thaw," to borrow the term applied at various times to Soviet cultural policy, was a response to the elimination of organized opposition, but also to the persistent attempts of individual, educated artists, playwrights, film directors, poets, cartoonists, and novelists to produce work offering an alternative to the regime's self-proclaimed ideals of omnipotence and indispensability. Increasing exchanges between Syrian and Western artists have also emboldened some to play more actively with official limits.[15] The regime's recent overtures to the private sector, enshrined in the passage of Investment Law #10 in 1991, have encouraged private sector entrepreneurs, some of whom are connected to regime officials, to develop television programs for commercial entertainment. Previously, Syrian television, which began broadcasting in 1960, had been a public sector enterprise devoted primarily to the propagation of official political ideals.[16] The proliferation of prohibited satellite dishes on the rooftops of most houses in Damascus is also a generalized manifestation of recent changes, signifying a victory for Syrian citizens seeking a measure of control over their access to sources of news and entertainment. Although these dishes are not permitted, the regime is choosing not to make people remove them. It may be that state ideologues imagine that the benefits of having citizens while away their leisure hours in front of their televisions outweigh whatever advantages of control might accrue from enforcing the ban.

Second, permitted critiques signal to both the regime and to citizens the shifting levels of commitment, obedience, and disobedience, which are otherwise driven underground. Permitted critiques may even help to identify and ferret out disobedient Syrians. For an authoritarian regime that relies primarily on public dissimulation, the existence of alternative yet carefully circumscribed visions of political life operates as a mechanism of surveillance—a barometer for reading (even tempting expressions of) contempt and frustration among ordinary citizens.[17]

Third, as Scott points out in his reading of Barrington Moore's *Injustice: The Social Bases of Obedience and Revolt,* oppositional consciousness and critique fall along a "gradient." The least rebellious expression of opposition is to "criticize some part of the dominant stratum" for having failed to live up to the standards by which they claim to rule. "The next most radical step is to accuse the entire elite" of violating "the principles of its rule." And the "most radical step" is to reject the "very principles by which the ruling group justifies its dominance."[18] Of course, these three "levels" barely begin to display the multiple ways in which people might actually oppose or experience themselves as resisting a regime. People might resist some policy or agency of the regime; opposition might be made manifest by supporting a permitted person or institution within the regime (e.g., the clergy, a cabinet minister who is a renegade on some issue, or an independent candidate for Parliament). People also tend to have different ways of expressing doubts, criticism, opposition and disaffection: from jokes to conspiracy to espionage or clandestine military preparations. For our purposes here, however, it is important to note that in Syria, permitted criticisms tend not to venture beyond the first level and do not challenge Asad's rule per se. Both the regime and people who criticize it have a finely calibrated sense of when transgressions go beyond the first level, and the regime stands ready to act upon such a breach, though it might not intervene in every instance.

Fourth and most important, if, as I have claimed, a politics of "as if" depends on a self-conscious submission to authority, which is to say, on the shared conditions of unbelief, then the recognition of that unbelief, within limits set forth by the regime and by each person's internal censors, actually reproduces the conditions of obedience under Asad. These conditions may not be optimal for either the regime or Syrians, but they are relatively stable and coherent and have the advantage of being easily recognized by all participants.

All of these accounts of the license for and restrictions on criticism help describe political life in Syria. They offer a four-pronged alternative to safety-valve arguments, suggesting the possible political motivations and observable effects of tolerating some criticism. They also hint at a rich, textured understanding of the struggles over power and meaning, or what Barbara Harlow, writing about colonization, calls a process of "challenge and riposte."[19] It is to the content of this process that we now turn.

Comedies

Tolerated comedies demonstrate the widely shared experience of unbelief in Syria and also probe the limits of the possible in various ways.[20] All of the comedic skits, plays, and films to be discussed in this section were immensely popular, have been shown (and sometimes rerun) on Syrian television, and are available for repeated viewing on video.[21] They highlight the discrepancies between official discourse and the political life experienced by most Syrians. The official rhetoric speaks of Arab unity, exalts ordinary citizens, and champions the wisdom and bravery of the regime's leaders; these comedies document the strife and divisions both within Arab countries and between them, demonstrate how demoralized the people are made by the regime's practices, reveal the corruption and brutality of the regime's leaders, and mock the arbitrariness and inefficiencies of state institutions.

In the play *Day'at Tishrin* (The October village, 1974), for instance, Syria's best known comedic actor and director, Durayd Lahham, and his long-time collaborator, the writer Muhammad al-Maghut, challenge certain official formulations of reality, parodying official power and allegorizing territorial loss.[22] In the play, thieves come and steal a vineyard, which is the dowry of a young bride. The wedding is postponed until the vineyard can be recovered. The *mukhtar* (village head) finally decides that the way to deal with the situation is to create feuds among the villagers so that they forget the lost vineyard. The *mukhtar* is finally toppled and another man assumes his position, then another, and another. Each time a new *mukhtar* comes to power, a patriotic speech ushers in the "authentic" leader, and villagers are warned against political plots.

The torture chamber, a familiar setting in Syrian comedies, appears in *Day'at Tishrin* as well; it both represents and inverts the relationship between official interrogator and citizen-victim. The torture chamber is a particularly harrowing location of state intrusion, but it enables al-Maghut and Lahham to "turn the world upside down," subverting conventional hierarchies both by interrogating the regime's practices and by doing so in a particularly unsettling context. In the atmosphere of coups and counter-coups, one of the villagers, Nayif, is arrested for complaining about the shortage of foodstuffs. (The village ran out of milk because the nationalized cow had ten bureaucrats appointed to attend to its milking.) In prison, Nayif is tortured and told that his complaints are unjustified. The village, in fact, has plenty of food, according to the interrogator: it is all in the house of the *mukhtar!* Ghawwar, the clown-like figure played by Durayd Lahham in most of his comedies, is also taken to the torture chamber, not because he has complained but because he has said nothing. The dialogue that transpires between Ghawwar and his interrogator exposes al-Maghut and Lahham's conception of the regime's anxiety and of the self-perpetuating practices that sustain it:

> THE INTERROGATOR: Here is the danger. Here is plotting more serious than Nayif's. Nayif spoke and we know what is in his mind. But you said nothing and we don't know what you are up to.
> GHAWWAR: You mean we aren't safe when we speak, and we aren't safe when we shut up?
> THE INTERROGATOR: What are you?
> GHAWWAR: I am nothing. I am a citizen. Nothing at all. (Ghawwar is then asked to sign a confession).
> GHAWWAR: Sign for what?
> THE INTERROGATOR: The things which you would have liked to say.

Ghawwar's status as a citizen renders him simultaneously a "nothing" and a threat to the regime. The practices of public dissimulation and silence mean not that people are uncritical, but rather that there are many things people would like to say and cannot. And of course, there are things the regime would like to know and cannot as well.

The play is sharply critical, but never explicitly of Asad or his regime. In fact, as in much of Lahham's subsequent work, *Day'at Tishrin* recovers Asad's cult from the critical wreckage, in this instance, by contriving an ending that celebrates the heroism of the final *mukhtar*. As the final *mukhtar* is chastised and reminded of his high ideals, he reforms and dedicates himself to the task of liberating the vineyard, which he succeeds in doing to the accompaniment of patriotic music. The play then can be read as an allegory for Asad's rise to power and the subsequent "victory" in the October War of 1973. The final leader rescues the village from the coups and failures of the 1950s and 1960s and recovers the lost territory.

The themes of political corruption, exploitation, and powerlessness challenge the discursive claims of the official rhetoric, but the intervention of a strong leader capable of correcting past ills and reclaiming lost territory coincides with the rhetorical declarations of Asad's cult. *Day at Tishrin*, then, can operate within the context of officially sanctioned political criticism in part because it can be read to situate Asad in the glorified, parody-free world of patriotism and recovery.[23] By contriving a positive ending to the story, the play distinguishes between good and bad leaders, thereby holding officials responsible for solving problems while, at the same time, accepting the institutional office of the *mukhtar*. The fact that the institution is authoritarian does not mean all *mukhtars* are bad; rather, there are good and bad *mukhtars,* and the good ones (like Asad) operate consistently to produce what the villagers want and need.

Not all of Lahham and al-Maghut's work simultaneously criticizes the regime's practices while rehabilitating Asad. The widely viewed, perhaps best-loved televised play, *Kasak Ya Watan* (Cheers! O homeland, 1979), lacks the hope and optimism that conclude *Day at Tishrin*. In a series of sketches, Ghawwar represents the common man, a good nationalist who cares about his "homeland" but suffers a series of indignities by virtue of his status as a "citizen." He lacks connections and seems helpless in the face of the powerful bureaucracy, corrupt officials, and the practices that sustain them. Ghawwar's ordinariness means that his infant daughter, Ahlam (literally, "dreams") does not get medical treatment and dies unnecessarily. The basic antibiotics are unavailable, at least to people without connections. When the doctor on duty finally arrives late at the hospital, Ghawwar, who has been waiting for hours to see him, must continue to wait while the doctor sees an official (the Arabic word, *mas'ul,* literally means responsible one) who is treated for impotence. When Ghawwar's turn finally comes, his daughter has died, poisoned by unpasteurized milk and "killed," as Ghawwar puts it, by the unjust and systemic practices that normalize the privileges of officials who are paradoxically both powerful and impotent. With his daughter's death, the dreams she symbolized also die. And the message is clear: the corrupt practices of the present destroy the wellsprings of the future.

The torture chamber again becomes the site for inverting relationships between ruler and ruled, but in this play the interrogators know everything, so that the point of the interrogation is not information-gathering but the assertion of power. Al-Maghut and Lahham both expose the fantasy of the regime's power and also invert it by charging the regime with excessive brutality and ineptitude. Ghawwar is taken to security headquarters, presumably because he has been inquiring into the death of his daughter and demanding to know who is responsible. The interrogator claims, "We know everything about you." And Ghawwar counters, "If you know everything about me, then why ask?" Ghawwar's impudence ultimately prompts an interrogator to order the use of electric shock. As the electric current reaches Ghawwar, his body trembles and he begins to laugh: "The electricity has reached me before it reaches our village!" Here a joke works both to announce in public what everyone knows—that the regime fails to live up to its promises and responsibilities—and to suggest that the regime is obligated to do so. The joke suggests that the regime, despite its excesses, can nevertheless be judged coherently by the obligations it announces.

Material shortages are explicitly related to rhetorical excess in two of the skits within *Kasak Ya Watan:* In one skit, Lahham and al-Maghut parody mainstream Syrian television and radio complaint programs, which are heavily orchestrated, providing only a simulacrum of democratic openness or even of consumerism. In the parody, a woman calls to complain about her electricity bill. The official who is responsible for solving consumers' electricity problems wears an enormous light bulb on his head. He responds to all of her complaints with tired patriotic slogans, which he speaks in the elevated Arabic of news broadcasts. In another scene Ghawwar returns home with takeout food for dinner. The meal consists of folded newspapers, suggesting that the papers may be more useful as food than as news; or, given the common practice in Syria of wrapping takeout food in newspapers, that the nourishment the pages are supposed to contain is absent. In both readings, Ghawwar's folded newspapers signal the emptiness of rhetoric. Ghawwar and his wife fight during the course of the meal, and Ghawwar raises his hand to hit her. He stops himself in time, and says: "they [the interrogators] hit me and I hit you. You hit the children, and the children hit other children. It's a vicious circle."

But despite Ghawwar's moment of restraint, there seems, as he fears, to be no way out of the exploitative patterns of behavior that perpetuate violence and misery. Ghawwar takes to drinking. During one of his drinking bouts he is visited by his dead father, a "martyr" who has died for the homeland. The ensuing conversation between father and son expresses al-Maghut and Lahham's patriotism, which consists of an appreciation for the land, for an authentic Arab heritage, and for a moral economy based on some form of distributive justice. But it is unclear who is at fault for the absence of this justice, and why the hopes that originally animated understandings of Arab and Syrian national liberation have not been realized. The sons have not been able to carry on the noble traditions of their fathers, the text suggests. But who or what is the reason for this failure?

The powerful seem to be most at fault, for they are the ones who victimize common people like Ghawwar. Those who are in charge respond to problems with tired slogans, exercise their power to gain special privileges, and use their offices for private gains. They mete out punishment arbitrarily and divert needed resources away from development projects toward the coercive practices that help maintain their power. But the text also suggests that the not-so-powerful people contribute to the system by being habituated to it; they empower the powerful through their complacency and despair.

Somehow citizens have become atomized and relations among them deeply unsatisfactory.[24] The powerful are responsible and ordinary citizens are victims, but the powerful are made powerful by a system that both supporters and victims uphold. And victimization is passed down the hierarchy of power: the interrogator hits the husband who hits the wife, who hits the children. The real victims are the children, who both signify the future and are genuinely powerless to alter their circumstances.

If there is any hope left in *Kasak Ya Watan*, it resides in somehow recovering the aspirations and standards that animated the nation's martyred fathers. This hope is rearticulated in Lahham and al-Maghut's last political film, *al-Taqrir* (1986), in which the solution to the country's problems resides explicitly in the person of the unnamed president. In *al-Taqrir*, Lahham plays a bureaucrat, 'Azma

Bik, who has discovered a vast scheme of corruption within his bureaucracy. He resigns in protest, fully expecting to be recalled. But when his resignation is accepted, ʿAzma Bik decides to document all of the corrupt practices that characterize daily life. The spectator sees luxury cars procured through extralegal means. ʿAzma Bik's daughter is followed and harassed by young men of the regime's nouveau riche class who, in one scene, while driving a red sports car, hit and kill a young schoolboy. The occupants of the car look like elite members of the *mukhabarat,* the secret police (reckless driving is especially common among secret police agents, who are not accountable to traffic laws and who have been known to drive on sidewalks). When the driver is later apprehended, his trial displays just another instance of regime corruption. The judge pronounces sentence, but when the telephone rings, a brief conversation prompts him to reduce it. ʿAzma Bik's taxi driver is a professor who cannot afford basic necessities on his university salary. At the airport, professionals prepare to emigrate to the West. At the site where the corruption scheme ʿAzma Bik is investigating was devised, a night club offers prostitutes from Sri Lanka, the Philippines, and other Third World countries, which prompts ʿAzma Bik to ask: "What, the Bandung Conference is *here?*"[25]

In a series of fantasy scenes, ʿAzma Bik prepares to deliver his report to the unspecified president, who is not in his office but at an important soccer game in which the team "East" plays the team "West." On the way to the stadium, ʿAzma Bik imagines himself first as a young revolutionary dressed in military fatigues leading a group of upstanding citizens to the nightclub. They overturn the table where the corrupt bureaucrats are seated drinking. In another fantasy, ʿAzma Bik and his group enter a torture chamber where a man hangs from a scaffold, having previously been whipped by his interrogator. The taxi-driving professor throws a gigantic pencil at the abdomen of the torturer, who doubles over defeated. The final scenario depicts ʿAzma Bik dressed as a knight on horseback, leading his group toward Palestine, as patriotic music plays in the background.

These increasingly grandiose fantasies both invoke familiar patriotic themes and also de-stabilize Asad's cult by positing an alternative hero in ʿAzma Bik himself. ʿAzma Bik becomes the conquering hero and the carrier of truth. The subversive implications of 'Azma Bik's fantasies are, however, at least partially obviated by events following 'Azma Bik's arrival at the stadium. The gesture of absolving the president from responsibility for corruption seems manifestly incomplete: first, 'Azma Bik never makes it to the president's box. He and the report are trampled on the field by the players, caught between East and West. Any fantasies of rivalry or substitution die along with 'Azma Bik, whose body remains sprawled on the field in his white suit long after the spectators have left. Second, 'Azma Bik's death ensures that the president remains both the solution to corruption and untainted by it: the president remains ignorant of any wrongdoing. But of course, the real president is not ignorant of Syria's problems, and Asad, were he to watch the film, would see its subversive message. The reassertion of the cult, therefore, seems manifestly hollow; by holding the "responsibles" responsible, Lahham can be read as implying that Asad is responsible too.

Al-Taqrir suggests two visions of community: one in which a strong leader can correct the relationships among people and change their patterns of behavior, and another suggesting the people themselves create, sustain, and can change the system in which they live. The latter vision is expressed most powerfully in the following scene: 'Azma Bik is in prison. His secretary, Rima, asks the policeman to release him. The policeman is depicted sympathetically and recognizes the charges to be unjust, but nonetheless claims he is powerless to help 'Azma Bik: "What's the use. You know you cannot change things." Rima replies: "No, I cannot and you cannot, but the words 'we can'. . . ." She does not finish the sentence out loud, and the policeman responds, "I wish." But the context makes it clear that while individuals separately cannot change the system, collectively people could be powerful. This message is reiterated, albeit ambivalently, in 'Azma Bik's fantasies of revolutionary heroism. Everyone helps to overturn the table at which the corrupt bureaucrats are seated. And it is the Professor, not 'Azma Bik himself, who spears the torturer with the pencil.

These potentially subversive moments are permitted by the censors. They are embedded in a context where the overall resolution of the problem remains the president. Lahham's films and plays, moreover, parody conditions that the regime itself would not defend (e.g., the regime does not claim that shortages are good). Moreover, the film and other such political satires are never specifically set in Syria. But the settings, the dialect, and the problems addressed are, in fact, characteristic of Syria, which is why Syrians find the scenarios so funny.

Yasir al-'Azma's work, like Durayd Lahham's, marks the boundaries of officially tolerated criticism, but also operates to renegotiate those limits. His highly popular television series, *Maraya* (Mirror), as the title suggests, reflects aspects of the political and social life of most Syrians.[26] Al-'Azma relates stories derived from people's lived experiences as he observes them.[27] *Maraya* criticizes the performance of state institutions and also challenges current relationships between men and women. Unlike Durayd Lahham, al-'Azma champions the virtues of the private sector and cautions women who work to make sure their homes remain their first priority. If Lahham's nationalism reflects a nostalgia for the lost hopes of the 1960s and 1970s, al-'Azma's works reflect the conservative, religiously inclined critiques of the 1980s.[28] Both men decry the habits of the nouveaux riches, but al-'Azma ultimately sees corruption as originating in the "weak morals" of the family.[29] Thus, whereas Lahham seems to situate political recovery sometimes in the innocence of children, sometimes in the collective actions of citizens, and sometimes in a strong national patriarch, al-'Azma suggests that it is the family patriarch who must be rehabilitated.

Al-'Azma's conservative critique and his emphasis on family values, however, is coupled with a strikingly astute depiction of political practices. Two of *Maraya*'s most pointed political skits are *Yawmiyyat Muwatin* (Days of a citizen, 1986) and *al-Khayyat Abu Sa'id Yuhanni' al-Umma al-'Arabiyya* (The tailor Abu Sa'id congratulates the Arab nation, 1988). In *Yawmiyyat Muwatin*, al-'Azma's character, Sa'id, is shopping in the market when a radio talk host asks to interview him. The character is extremely reluctant and complains about his tedious, hardship-ridden life. When the radio announcer informs him that he is on the air, Sa'id is incredulous and fearful. The initial exchange thereby sets up a division between speech appropriate in public and people's private, internal thoughts. This split is given explicit expression at the end of the interview when the announcer asks Sa'id what song he would like to hear, and Sa'id responds: "I am afraid to say what is in my heart," the title of a real song. Sa'id's (and of course, by extension, al-'Azma's) answer contains an ambiguity that could be used, if he were pressured, to disavow any intention to criticize. His remark is open to at least two interpretations. On the one hand, it can be read as a frank acknowledgment of his fear to say what he feels. On the other hand, Sa'id has also left open an avenue for his retreat: in naming a song, Sa'id has also complied with official instructions.

Al-'Azma's dialogue parodies existing television shows, in which interviews between official radio announcers and ordinary citizens simulate democracy by representing the regime as open and responsive. In *Yawmiyyat Muwatin,* al-'Azma makes explicit the links among enforced performative practices, political discourse, and coercive interrogation. In 1986 there were shortages of basic goods in the market place, and people were periodically allowed to complain about mundane discomforts. Al-'Azma thus uses grocery items as a symbol for all the sensitive issues that he cannot explicitly discuss. On the air, Sa'id exaggerates the abundance, even narrates what are obviously untrue accounts of excess and good fortune. Sa'id recites his grocery list, and the announcer asks whether he has found the listed items in the market. Sa'id says:

> Yes, of course, of course I found them. I went to the guy who sells propane gas [stoves in Syria require gas tanks]. I found my tank in a huge pile, piled to the ceiling . . . and there wasn't one customer. . . . And when he saw me carrying my jar on my back huffing and puffing and sweating, he relieved me of a potential hernia . . . and he brought the gas to our house.

Sa'id's anecdote draws attention to the actual situation by narrating its opposite: instead of plentiful supplies, gas and other basic necessities can be difficult to find. Customer lines are often extremely long, and store owners are rarely courteous or helpful. Such questioning and the responses of exaggerated plenitude continue, as each item on the grocery list is accounted for.

The interview simulates a government interrogation. The announcer tries to poke holes in Sa'id's account, by inquiring why, if such items are plentiful, Sa'id seems nervous and has to wipe the sweat from his face with a towel, rather than with (valued but often scarce) paper tissue. Sa'id's shopping experience in general operates as a homology for the official representation of politics: the exaggerative language and the counterposing of a problematic past to a trouble-free present orient would-be commentators in public and also effectively split public presentations from privately held beliefs. Sa'id explains:

> At home, the attic is filled with packages of paper tissues. 190 packages, 200 packages, I can no longer remember. And moreover, my wife, my wife, when she mops the floor of the house she doesn't mop it with a floor rag. No. She mops it with paper tissues. Why? Because they say it is cleaner and cheaper and plentiful like dough (*kishk*).[30] [Clears his throat.] It is not like in the beginning. In the beginning, we used to search for one box of tissues. For one tissue and we didn't find any. But now. This is it. The street vendors are selling tissues. Of course. They are yelling, we have tissues! Yo, we have tissues, people![31]

Sa'id's juxtaposition of past to present parallels the official presentations of history. In the past, there were problems, but the present is glorious and unassailable. Of course, this juxtaposition is ironic, meant not to celebrate the present but to criticize it. But the criticism always has a benign interpretation that allows the speaker to avoid trouble.

Al-'Azma's skit couples his exposure of material shortages with an irreverence for the language in which such problems are publicly discussed or ignored. The announcer ends by making explicit the connection between public dissimulation and the strategies of the regime when he asks the penultimate question: "Are you interested in politics?" (*Btehtamm bi-ssiyaseh?*) Now the announcer has Sa'id in a bind. If Sa'id says that he is not interested in politics, he may be considered unpatriotic or disloyal to the regime. If he answers that he is interested, however, he may be regarded as an insurgent. But Sa'id figures a way out of this bind. He answers in the affirmative, but reinterprets the word *as-siyaseh* in a different sense than the announcer intended. Besides "politics," the word also means "clever."[32] Sa'id says: "I mean, the owner of my house wants me to be clever or else he will throw me out. My wife wants me to be clever or else she will divorce me." The announcer has learned something from his questioning, although not what Sa'id thinks or feels. He (like the visiting officer in M's story) has learned that Sa'id (like the soldiers) can answer questions without either incriminating himself or disrupting the official world view. Sa'id's day as a citizen is not just about finding grocery items in times of shortage, but also about rising to the demand to act out a politics of "as if" in ways that avoid trouble and are spontaneously constructed.

Al-'Azma's skit highlights the ways in which the regime enforces obedience and induces complicity. People are habituated to provide publicly acceptable responses but not necessarily through outright lies. They use their imaginations to invent modes of evasion; they find ways of both speaking truth and yet reiterating the regime's idealized presentation of itself. From the regime's perspective, enforced dissimulation signals that citizens are willing to reproduce and are capable of reiterating an officially sanctioned vision of daily life. Although public dissimulation allows people's thoughts to remain private, practices that enforce such dissimulation also provide information about resistant behavior, from minor expressions of annoyance to deviant and limit-cases like M. In al-'Azma's skit the announcer's questions operate as a signaling device, registering who is willing to obey and who is not.

The shared practice of public dissimulation isolates people from one another by making it difficult for them to speak frankly in public and thus to trust each other or form new public relationships — to organize. We do not know that the announcer is an agent of the government, although his interrogating and demanding behavior suggests that he is. But the announcer's declaration that the interview is public immediately changes the interchange between announcer and citizen and isolates the two men from one another. The announcer's words further remind Sa'id (and the viewer) of the link between the existence of public fictions and the requirement that citizens sustain them: in one breath the announcer reminds Sa'id that the conversation must be "frank and open" and that "important people are listening." The skit thus both evades actual censorship and draws the viewer's attention to it. The external censors of the regime are coupled with the internal censors within each citizen, enabling him or her to navigate the politics of "as if."

Yet al-'Azma's comedy, by drawing attention to the shared circumstances that isolate people from one another, also helps to counteract those circumstances by providing an occasion for shared laughter and recognition. The viewer who watches the skit experiences his or her true thoughts being expressed in public, on television. The comic effect relies on the fact that viewers know the truth (there are shortages in the market) and therefore that Sa'id is not only lying, but engaging in one of the most basic of comic forms: the complete and exaggerated reversal of the true situation.

Al-'Azma's insightful critique of practices of dissimulation finds expression in another skit, *al-Khayyat Abu Sa'id Yuhanni' al-Umma al-'Arabiyya*. In this skit, al-'Azma pokes fun at the plethora of state holidays and at the requirements associated with them. The skit suggests that there are so many celebrations that it is difficult to care about or keep track of them. State holidays, as the skit reveals, are less about honoring a particular constituency or historical occurrence than about providing opportunities to collect revenue and to discipline subordinates. State holidays remind citizens of the state's power to enforce compliance, but they also serve to identify slackers who do not habitually sustain the regime's fictions.

In the first scene, a man enters Abu Sa'id's shop, asks Abu Sa'id to congratulate him, and inquires why the shop is not decorated. Abu Sa'id does not take his questions seriously until the visitor identifies himself as a "watchguard [secret police agent] of the capital's municipality" (*muraqib min amanat al-'asima*). Abu Sa'id does not know that the day commemorates "Arab knowledge," but he assures the security agent that he will decorate the store immediately. The agent, however, insists that Abu Sa'id come with him to jail and pay the requisite fine. Abu Sa'id tries unsuccessfully to avoid both the fine and the trip to jail by contriving an explanation that both justifies his negligence and enables him to criticize the state's education system: when he was in school, his teachers hit him, and he has had an ambivalent relationship toward knowledge ever since.

The scenario repeats itself in the next scene, in which Abu Saʿid has failed to decorate his shop in honor of Peasant's Day. Abu Saʿid again tries to explain his negligence to the watchguard (this time a representative of the township). There are few peasants left on the land. Most products are imported. To whom are they paying homage, anyway? Again, Abu Saʿid's explanation enables him both to offer a justification and to criticize Syrian policy. And again, he fails to dissuade the watchguard from taking him to jail.

In the penultimate scene, another agent enters the shop, and the following exchange takes place:

THE WATCHGUARD: Why haven't you decorated your shop?

ABU SAʿID: Today also. You see, brother, if today is Mother's Day, my mother's dead and she wasn't pretty. I rejoice in her death, as if I were malicious, God forbid.

THE WATCHGUARD: No. Today is not Mother's Day. Relax.

ABU SAʿID: Not Mother's Day. If it's the Day of Asian-African Co-operation, I already asked. They said we aren't involved, it's an official holiday not a popular one.

THE WATCHGUARD: No, not the Day of Cooperation.

ABU SAʿID: Not the Day of Cooperation. Ah, Wait a bit. I've become a lot more cultured in your absence. Wait a minute. Where is the notebook? Here it is. Is today Day of the Grape?

THE WATCHGUARD: No.

ABU SAʿID: Day of Hemp?

THE WATCHGUARD: No.

ABU SAʿID: Day of Cotton?

THE WATCHGUARD: No.

ABU SAʿID: Because we celebrate a lot of things that we don't have any connection to. Is it Manchurian Independence Day?

THE WATCHGUARD: No.

ABU SAʿID: The Discovery of Zenobia's Desert?

THE WATCHGUARD: No.

ABU SAʿID: The Subduing of the Summit of the Himalayas?

THE WATCHGUARD: No.

ABU SAʿID: The Continuation of the Television Program, the
Mirror?
THE WATCHGUARD: No.

At this point, Abu Saʿid's guesses begin gradually to move from the
ludicrous to issues of obvious political and economic relevance. By
compelling the watchguard to acknowledge that the holiday is not
celebrating, indeed *cannot* celebrate economic policy or official political practices, Abu Saʿid inverts the relationship between citizen
and state and begins to interrogate the interrogator. It is Saʿid who
asks pointed questions, and the watchguard who provides unsatisfactory answers.

ABU SAʿID: Discounting the price of fuel?
THE WATCHGUARD: No.
ABU SAʿID: Subsidizing sugar for citizens?
THE WATCHGUARD: No.
ABU SAʿID: Ending bribery and routine?
THE WATCHGUARD: No.
ABU SAʿID: Equality between citizens and important people?
THE WATCHGUARD: No.

It turns out that the holiday honors the Arab tree, and Abu Saʿid
is again compelled to go with the watchguard to jail. But by now
the trip has become a "habit" (*darab*).[33]

Habituation, however, has real consequences for one's relationship to oneself and for relationships among citizens. The next time
a stranger enters the shop, Abu Saʿid assumes he is another watchguard, and is prepared. Not only does he know what the official
holiday is, but he also has a statement for his visitor: "The tailor
Abu Saʿid congratulates the Arab nation in all of its national (*wataniyya wa qawmiyya*), social, political, and artistic occasions, and
he does so in order to relieve himself of responsibility. . . . The sig-
nature of Abu Saʿid. Me, I mean."

As Abu Saʿid reads the text he has written and signed in the
third person he suggests that his compliance has both a benefit
and a price: it relieves him of responsibility, but it thereby distances
him from himself. "Me, I mean" returns Abu Saʿid to the self he
recognizes, thereby putting a stop to the distancing mechanisms

his formal statement both exemplifies and produces. Moreover, the visitor, who knows nothing about the holiday, turns out to be an ordinary customer rather than a police agent. But Abu Sa'id has learned to suspect everyone. And what has become normal is not the entrance of ordinary customers, but what Pierre Bourdieu calls a society's "naturalization of its own arbitrariness," which in this case depends on the pomp and pageantry of endless state holidays.[34]

The comedic effect of these parodies relies on a widely shared experience of unbelief. The recognition of this common condition amounts to the creation of an Aesopian public world, where alternative conceptualizations of politics can be communicated. The skirmishes waged between official censor and artist are reproduced within each viewer as well. In the moment when the film or skit speaks with emphasis and is understood, the victory is that of both viewer and artist, who have somehow managed to speak to each other across the boundaries of censorial prohibitions and restraints.

Cartoons

Permitted theatrical and cinematic parodies offer one window into a political reality that is both structured by and critical of the official order. Cartoons provide another. On the back pages of the official newspaper, *Tishrin*, 'Ali Farzat's cartoons posit an alternative to the seamless web of the official narrative. He too must operate within the parameters of the permissible. But he too probes the limits and tests the sensibilities of Syria's censors. As shown in figures 10 through 28 at the end of this chapter, Farzat's cartoons demonstrate his trenchant political acuity; his reputation as Syria's foremost cartoonist suggests that his understanding is shared by many Syrians. When 'Ali Farzat was dismissed from *al-Thawra*, circulation reportedly dropped by 35 percent until he was reinstated one month later.[35]

Farzat's cartoons reiterate many of the themes presented in the slapstick comedies of Lahham and al-'Azma, but they do so in the uniquely succinct pictorial medium of the wordless cartoon. The popularity of these cartoons and the fact that one picture can convey to literate and illiterate audiences a widely understood critique of official political life suggests the power of Farzat's work: the moment the meaning of a Farzat cartoon dawns inside one's own head, the censor has been circumvented, and one's own sense of unbelief affirmed. The skirmish between Farzat and his publisher recurs inside the reader as well.[36] To the extent that Farzat's cartoons communicate unbelief in the regime's rhetoric, they represent a victory in the contest against enforced falsehood.

Farzat's cartoons offer concrete, detailed criticisms of the distance between rulers and ruled, of political oppression, corruption, inequality, exploitation, and conformity. My ordering of these cartoons produces its own political narrative, one which is, I believe, consonant with Farzat's own understanding of politics, and which coincides with the other critical discourses in this chapter.[37] Figures 10 through 14 are unified by their representation of power by a spatial metaphor (climbing up from the bottom). In figures 15 through 18, by contrast, all of the characters occupy the same spatial plane, and hierarchical power is signified by the discrepancy between the trappings of privileged officialdom, on the one hand, and the anxieties of ordinary citizenship, on the other. Figures 19 through 24 suggest that ordinary citizens together help to sustain the system that oppresses them, whether it be military authoritarian rule or Western capitalism. Although implicitly critical of the regime, all of these metaphorical and suggestive images fall within the bounds of permitted parody. Figures 25 through 28, however, violate the norms of permissible satire; they have never been published, and are unlikely ever to be published in Syria.

Figure 10 dramatizes the relationship between representation and rhetoric. The cartoon shows a man dressed in a civilian suit with buttons evocative of military decoration (signifying the civilian-military elite) at the top of a summit. He is tossing down a representation of a ladder to the ordinary man at the bottom. Ladders measure the distance between ruler and ruled. They also enable people to climb to the top from the bottom. But a *representation* of a ladder, of course, cannot be used for climbing. According to Farzat's cartoon, stratified relations rely not only on inequality, but on the *pretense* of its eradication. The cartoon suggests that the powerful person is obliged to do something, and therefore acts *as if* he were assisting the ordinary citizen without actually enabling him to ascend.

While this cartoon leaves unclear whether the powerful person is unable or unwilling to help his subordinates, figure 11 suggests that those who have real ladders deliberately prevent others from attaining official power (*sulta*, which Farzat typically signifies by a large, ornate chair). To arrive at a position of official power, however, is not necessarily to become powerful, as figure 12 illustrates: the man who has reached the chair is then sucked into its cushions. Official power swallows up those who attain it, and thereby also facilitates their resubordination (they are captive, sucked down into a place upon which another will sit). Figure 13 further complicates the depiction of the powerful by suggesting that they, like ordinary citizens, are incapacitated. An ethos of equality prompts the regime to extend a pretense of help to ordinary citizens. And ordinary citizens comply, thereby helping to enact the fiction by pretending that neither ruler nor ruled is crippled. A depiction of the regime as crippled does not, however, change the overriding facts of exploitation and inequality, as figure 14 suggests: ordinary citizens do the work and powerful people reap the benefits.

Figure 15 illustrates the polite face of exploitation. Maintaining the charade not only fails to ease the consequences of exploitation, it also occasions them: the healthy powerful visitor offers the ill patient flowers, while at the same time cutting off his oxygen supply, perhaps unintentionally, but with disabling effect. In figure 16, the consequences of not enacting the charade are explicit: the interviewer's microphone has its own noose. Like al-ʿAzma's skit, *Days of a Citizen*, the cartoon suggests that to speak frankly in public is to court punishment. Performative occasions require people to dissimulate in public while their actual thoughts remain unknown.

This is not true in figure 17, where a customs officer inspects the head—rather than the luggage—of a citizen who has apparently returned from abroad. The inspection of one's psychological interior or belief system leaves no room for maneuver, no way to avoid the intrusiveness and information-gathering capacities of the state. The cartoon is utterly explicit and seemingly damning, yet it was approved for publication. Perhaps its portrayal was far enough from the actual capacities of Syria's state surveillance to be permitted as an exaggerative jest.

Figure 18 was initially rejected by the censors. There is a certain arbitrariness to the implementation of censorship laws, and the judgments of individual censors vary according to personal predilections and historical events. Farzat thinks this one, which revisits the theme of state intrusion, was allowed by 1996. However, the prohibition of this cartoon in the late 1980s suggests that it might have been banned because it describes more accurately than figure 17 the actual lived experiences of ordinary Syrians. The state does not have the capacity to read minds, but it does consistently monitor conversations held in public. Farzat's caption in figure 18, which reads "From the Third World," specifies the generic character of his criticism, but censors were apparently not reassured.

The coercive and surveillance mechanisms of the state help create a society of people who conform. Figure 19 represents conformity by showing everyone wearing boxes on their heads. The man who has not conformed and who therefore can see is being taken away by a boxheaded person in uniform. Although figure 19 evokes the conformity of military rule, figure 20 evokes the conformity of Western consumerism by representing men's heads as computer barcodes. People's conformity upholds the system, which turns people into boxheads who cannot see (a system of military rule) or into commodities (Western consumerism).

Inequality, pretense, fear, and conformity characterize political life, but people are not mere victims of the system, they also behave in ways that sustain it. Figure 21 shows a man peering out from behind four prison bars, perceiving himself to be trapped. But the rest of the prison's bars have been cut, so that the man could escape were he to see his situation differently. Similarly, figure 22 shows a man trying to reach fruit from the tree. But he has ridiculously placed the ladders horizontally rather than vertically, thereby preventing his own satisfaction. The images in figures 21 and 22, then, indict not only the men in power and the system of dominance they represent, but also the *mentalité* of ordinary citizens. Everyone is responsible, not least the thinker, whose brain produces excrement (fig. 23). Even animals are puzzled and astonished that humans do not do a better job (fig. 24).

The last four cartoons (figs. 25–28) represent some of Farzat's boldest and most pointed criticisms of political power in Syria. None of them directly caricatures Asad; to do so would prompt certain punishment. No Syrian paper has ever printed even a favorable cartoon of Asad.[38] Crucially, the distinction between "official power" and Asad, which usually serves to distance Asad from the corruption and exploitation that critics document, breaks down in these latter cartoons. Figure 25 shows ordinary soldiers marching in single file up the stairs of a battle tank, into which they disappear to be expelled at the other end as blood, or perhaps as oil. No external enemy exists. Rather, an auto-regulating tank converts soldiers into blood or oil. The official claims of sacrifice, steadfastness, and struggle are a sham: victims are created by the very system these soldiers supposedly defend. The generals who are in charge are like filthy sewer rats (fig. 26). Their corruption is so complete that the urine of the innocent (signified by the naked boy holding a flower) drives them out of the sewer. A close-up of such a general shows us that he is a modern puppet, a robot who is turned off and on at the flick of a switch (fig. 27).

But who controls the switch? The figure of the robotic general manipulated by an external power allows two interpretations: either Asad is the general, which suggests that he too is manipulated by an external, not fully embodied power, or the cartoon depicts a general who is being turned on and off by Asad himself—the supreme manipulator of power, so powerful that he can never be represented publicly in jest. In this second interpretation, the hand is in fact a sign that signifies its own prohibition: it points to what it *cannot* show. What *is* visible is the state's pomp and pageantry, which Farzat likens to an extended roll of toilet paper (fig. 28). The spectacles are endless (indicated by the ways in which the two frames are drawn) and belong in the toilet.

In the last four cartoons, Farzat blends the pomp and pageantry of Asad's official power with the scatological. Farzat could never caricature Asad explicitly, but these cartoons insult both the form and the content of Asad's cult. The cartoons challenge the declarations of heroism, purity, populism, and pageantry that the cult claims for itself. They mark the boundary between what can and cannot be said in public. They demonstrate, perhaps more pronouncedly than those that were permitted, the gap between public adulation and private skepticism. And yet, because Farzat tried to submit these cartoons for publication, they too stop short of overtly undermining Asad. In Syria, professional critics of the regime explain that they must always "zigzag" around the object of their critique; in these last four cartoons, Farzat's zigzag produced an edge too jagged for public presentation.[39]

Film

Whereas cartoons and slapstick comedies enjoy a mass audience, Syrian films tend to appeal to the bohemian intellectual community;[40] it may be that the limited audience for feature films is what permits them to be produced at all, despite the censorship.[41] Many films critical of the regime have been produced by the National Film Organization, but not all have gained Syrian distribution rights. Censors approve production on the basis of a script that usually omits incendiary language or cinematic directions that might later be included in the actual film, but could be construed as blatantly critical. When a film is completed, the National Film Organization hosts an opening night to which dignitaries and some of the intellectual community are invited. Only after the premiere do government censors decide on the fate of its distribution. Some films emerge from the censors' offices to be shown to a general audience. Those that gain acceptance tend to be ones that have won recognition in Europe, are not particularly critical of the regime, or situate their criticisms in scenarios predating the Ba'thist era.

The National Film Organization was originally established in 1969 by the Ba'thist Regime of Salah Jadid to produce state propaganda films, but under Asad the Film Organization has not served that function.[42] Instead, artists have tended to struggle with the regime for control over cinematic signification, i.e., over representing the intersections between politics and everyday life. In 1974, four years after coming to power, Asad dismissed the Organization's director, Hamid Mar'i, and appointed a replacement who banned the production of documentary films. The regime, however, continued to permit critical films in fictional form, and has actually sponsored their production. As a result, the production and discussion of films have grown to become a center of intellectual life and discourse, especially when compared to other outposts of the intelligentsia such as the university. In the 1970s, film clubs (*nawadi al-sinama*), which exist in every Syrian city, became gathering places for Syria's intellectual elite and centers of secular oppositional activity.

The activities of the film clubs were sharply curtailed in the spring of 1980 as part of the regime's extensive efforts to eliminate opposition to its rule. Some of Syria's foremost film makers went into exile at this time. Yet despite increasing state intervention, a new group of internationally recognized, politically critical film makers emerged in the 1980s, under the auspices of the National Film Organization.[43] Some of the films they produced do not have an overtly political content. Others, although produced by the National Film Organization, have not been shown to general audiences because of their biting political commentary.

Nujum al-Nahar (Stars of the day) (1988) is perhaps the most politically critical film ever to have been made in Syria. Usama Muhammad, the film's director, initially sent the film abroad, where it won first prize at the Festival of Valencia and the International Festival of Rabat. The film was well-received at Cannes and gained commercial distribution in France, Spain, Germany, and Switzerland. In May 1989, Muhammad screened the film in Damascus at a special preview for an audience that included government officials and military officers. The censors decided neither to ban the film nor to approve it for distribution. Instead, the film remains in a curiously liminal position, neither available for general distribution, nor officially condemned.

Muhammad's film is an insightful and revelatory critique of the Syrian regime. Although taking the relatively safe form of a fictional narrative, the film's plot is a thinly disguised metaphor for political power and for Asad's cult. Muhammad, an 'Alawi, depicts the moral crisis of a rural 'Alawi family, some of whose members have moved to the city and have become involved in urban life and corrupt officialdom. As characters, they represent the regime's vulgarity and brutality. The main male protagonist, Khalil (played by real-life film director ʿAbd al-Latif ʿAbd al-Hamid), looks uncannily like Asad. Khalil is the controlling, manipulative, stingy brother and the *de facto* patriarch of the family. On his wall is a map of Lattakia, the region where most of Syria's ʿAlawi population originates. The dialect the family members speak is distinctively ʿAlawi and the language they invoke explicitly connects patriarchal family life to martial rule and political violence. A tire also hangs on the wall of Khalil's home, symbolizing *dulab*, a method of torture practiced in Syria. Khalil works as a telephone operator and listens in on people's calls. His sunglasses, and those of his brothers and male relatives, further signify their involvement in the security forces. Khalil's twin sons, dressed identically, repeat the same formulaic slogan in unison at key points in the movie:

> Papa bought me a rifle. Me and my brother are small children. We learned how to join the Army of Liberation. In the Army of Liberation we learned how to protect our homeland. Down, down with Israel. Long live the Arab nation.

In the context of the film, the slogan operates to parody the emptiness and tedium of official discourse, just as the character of Khalil, the brutal buffoon who looks like Asad, serves to mock the actual president and profane his cult. The attack on Asad's cult is made particularly explicit when Kasir, Khalil's deaf brother, arrives in Damascus. The capital city is papered with enormous pictures of a famous singer, who is also Kasir and Khalil's cousin. The style of the pictures and their strategic location on facades of public buildings make clear the reference to Asad's cult. Since Syrian directors film on location, the mechanics of taking down pictures of Asad and replacing them with images of, in this case, an actual Syrian singer, were exceptionally daring. Muhammad claims that he filmed those shots during a state holiday, and that members of his film crew charged with the task of taking down Asad's posters and replacing them with others knew the risk they were taking and were sympathetic to Muhammad's project.[44] These same crew members worked for the secret police, according to Muhammad, but in his estimation, they had come to admire Muhammad's project and to respect his critical sensibilities.

The film's title is a pun that invokes both the Arabic expression "I'll have you seeing stars at noon"—a threat of violence similar to American cartoon depictions of characters "seeing stars" when they get knocked out—and also Syria's contemporary political celebrities, or "stars of the day." The film suggests that there is no place to stand in contemporary Syria. The countryside, although filmed to show off its breathtaking beauty, is boring and unlivable or overrun with petty familial disputes and with the attitudes that Muhammad characterizes as "backwardness." The capital city is corrupt and the site of regime domination. The Arab nation may have informed collective fantasies of political belonging in the past, but what remains are vapid slogans. A sense of displacement, of being trapped and deadened, is dramatized by Kasir's experiences upon his arrival in Damascus. He becomes immediately stuck in the middle of a terrible, cacophonous traffic jam. In search of his cousin, the famous singer whose image is everywhere but whose person he cannot locate, Kasir visits two symbolically freighted sites in the city: a store in which birds in cages are for sale, and a tombstone engraver's workshop.

The film also suggests that there is no one with whom to identify positively. The sympathetic characters in the film are helpless victims: Sana', Khalil's sister, successfully refuses to wed her cousin whom she does not know and to whom she is not attracted, but when she falls in love with a humble Arabic teacher, Khalil forces her to marry a regime-identified thug, a relative who rapes her when she tries to run away from him. The grandfather is kind and wise, but bedridden and ineffectual. Kasir, Khalil's most endearing brother, is deaf because he was beaten by his father as a boy. Although his deafness distances him from his violent brothers, he too internalizes the family's norms, and, in one effort to conform to the brutality of his male relatives, delivers a merciless beating to Sana''s lover.

It is, in short, an extraordinary film that uses the symbols and language of the regime in order to subvert the regime's system of signification. It transgresses all of the boundaries of the acceptable, and unlike those cultural critics who indicate what they cannot represent, *Nujum al-Nahar* represents what it must not show. There is little distance between Asad and official corruption or arbitrary power in Muhammad's film: *Nujum al-Nahar* is an explicit attack on Asad's public glory.[45] It is also a defense of art, of the possibility of a politically engaged, aesthetically sophisticated visual experience that self-consciously struggles against internalized censors only to confront actual external ones.

The film, although never shown commercially in Syria, has had wide underground circulation among intellectuals and some general exposure at Syrian cultural festivals. Other films have been officially distributed, however, that are punctuated with moments of profound political criticism and can also be said to occupy, in less encompassing form, the border between the officially tolerated and the taboo.[46] I will elaborate on two.

Nabil Malih's *al-Kumbars* (The extras, 1993) lacks the breathtaking aesthetics of some other Syrian films, but politically it is remarkably daring. That the film was distributed commercially, Malih claims, was a matter of luck. An official from the Cairo film festival asked a key Syrian official why the film was not being commercially shown, thereby embarrassing the regime into releasing it.[47] The film is certainly shockingly explicit in its condemnation of political life, and the six *al-Kindi* theaters in Syria (the government theaters where art films are shown) were packed with viewers during its four-month run. The film has also been shown at international film festivals and at human rights events. *Al-Kumbars* focuses on a surreptitious meeting between Salim, a poor young actor, and his girlfriend, Nada. Salim arranges to borrow a friend's apartment to meet Nada in private, assuming, in Malih's words, that "by closing the door, they may obtain security, and liberate the ego."[48] But they are mistaken: "the outer world, with its many powerful pressures" intrudes, and they discover "their shameful impotency," leaving the apartment "as strangers."[49] In particular, the lovers encounter their own fears of intimacy, internalized taboos of sexual propriety and political pretense, and the actual intrusion of a secret police officer who claims to be concerned with the activities of a blind musician living upstairs above the apartment. The film's realism combines with surrealistic daydream sequences revealing

Salim's fantasies of a heroic response to the security police, while his actual behavior remains fearful and compliant. Malih explicitly links political and sexual impotence; Salim's role as a theatrical "extra" underscores Malih's vision of citizens as "extras" who perform in a theatrical drama in which they have little control of their political and personal lives, in which desire (political and sexual) remains mere yearning without fulfillment.

The following dialogue, in which Salim explains to Nada how, as an extra, he can play seven roles during one performance, demonstrates the ways in which Malih connects the theatricality of politics to citizens' degradation and depoliticization:

> SALIM: I play the role of a soldier in the first act, then I change my make-up and clothes to become a beggar in the second act, then a thief or a guard . . .
>
> NADA: And you die in all of the roles? That's unbelievable.
>
> SALIM: Oh God, you're a real theater expert! Dear . . . I die upon request. For instance, when I'm a soldier, I die for my homeland. When I'm a beggar, I die of hunger. When I'm a citizen, I die of depression. When I'm a thief, bigger thieves come and kill me. When I'm a demonstrator, I mean a revolutionary, they beat me up, make a file on me, and deprive me of ever being employed. I've discovered that the best professions are those of belly dancers and informers. It is said that they are always needed.

When Nada asks whether he is happy with roles such as that of a brutal prison guard, Salim responds: "It is not up to me; that was the way the director explained the role. It is none of my business." But the two fantasize rewriting the script, filling its scenes with the laughter and dance of which their own lives have been deprived. Their imaginings are interrupted by the actual knock at the door of the security police, and the pleasure they have discovered in their intimate fantasies is foreclosed. The film thus offers no solutions to, or redemption for, the problems it diagnoses. All that remains is the pain, "humiliation" (a word invoked repeatedly in the film), and sense of despair accompanying explicit portrayals of impotence.

In *Waqa'i' al-'Am al-Muqbil* (Chronicles of the coming year, 1986), director and writer Samir Zikra visits some of the same themes we have already encountered in other critical depictions of Syrian political experience. Produced by Syria's National Film Organization, *Chronicles* was banned from distribution in 1986 but shown three years later in a public theater. Munir Wahba, the protagonist, has aspirations to form and conduct a national orchestra. The film documents the everyday frustrations of dealing with the bureaucracy's philistine, corrupt officials. Statements such as, "The director is here. Play now and tune up later," capture Zikra's representation of official vulgarity. The film also highlights the patently spurious quality of Syrian discourse. In one scene at the "Ninth World Conference for the Deaf held in Palestine," an official lauds the "outstanding support the deaf, dumb, and blind of Syria have enjoyed." He announces, "The World Organization for the Deaf honored his Excellency, President of the Organization of Association for the Support of the Deaf, Dumb, and Blind in Syria by bestowing the highest medal upon an Arab official in the field of deaf and dumb education and by awarding . . . a medal of honor." As the official continues his speech, one character informs another that a car has run over one of the deaf students. The spurious content of the speech is revealed not only by its juxtaposition to one deaf person's actual death, but also by the mention of Palestine, which signifies both the false promises of the regime and the lost hopes of many Syrians.[50]

Most important, the film offers a critique of political power that invokes the imagery of personal omnipotence familiar to the cult in order, once again, to subvert it. A scene depicting a dreadful dream of the protagonist, Munir, exemplifies the renegotiations of Syria's symbolic universe in ways designed to undermine rather than uphold official power.[51] Munir dreams:

> The Sultan and his associates are in a large, luxurious room, which is filled with the smoke of water pipes. They are laughing obscenely. In front of them a man who has been seated on a stump, his hands tied, kneels down. "Take him," orders one of the rulers. Two men take the captured man away. His groans of pain are audible, but his torture is not shown. Instead, we see the Sultan and his men laughing raucously. The camera approaches the laughter and zooms in on the laughing men. One man is eating a large hunk of meat with his

fingers. Another's laugh exposes the absence of teeth at the side of his mouth.

"Bring him," the Sultan orders. "Bring him," echo the others. The servants enter with the man. His body, naked from the waist up, is marked with deep lacerations. He is positioned on the stump, his back once again to the camera. The laughter continues unabated.

"You were telling a joke about us. Tell us a joke," the Sultan orders, as he rips off a large drumstick from the carcass on a platter and tosses it to one of his friends. "Make us laugh even if it's about us." All are laughing. The Sultan tosses the drumstick to another who catches the leg and orders the tortured victim to speak. The beaten man raises his eyes and looks at the Sultan who returns the gaze and commands: "A joke."

The tortured joker responds: "Listen to this. I just remembered it." The joker begins to tell his joke, but the sound is cut off and the audience is unable to hear. The Sultan and his men, however, do hear the joke, and they are outraged. As the joker finishes his joke, the sound returns. The rulers are silent, and it is the laughter of the joker which fills the room. The Sultan draws his sword, exclaiming: "You bastard. You are laughing at the Ottoman Sultan, Commander of Land and Sea, Sultan of all Times." He approaches the victim, who is still laughing. The sword cuts off the joker's head, which rolls onto the floor. But even decapitation fails to silence the laughter: it is the joker, smile intact, who enjoys the last laugh.

This scene uses so many conventional subterfuges that it draws attention to the very need to use them to disguise criticism: Zikra's critique of authoritarian, arbitrary power is bracketed in the context of a dream; the men are not contemporary leaders, but Ottoman pashas; and the dangerous joke remains unheard. The spectators' imaginations, not the film itself, construct the joke's subversive content. This scene represents censorship in ways that both protect the audience from being implicated (by not letting them hear the joke) and also paradoxically implicate the audience by inciting them to imagine its content. The scene thus evokes the imagined or real watchguard positioned next to each viewer, and also seduces viewers to draw on their own jokes and circumvent their internalized censors, without which the scene could hardly make sense.

The scene operates as a metaphor for Asad's cult. Like M's story,

Munir's thoughts are presented in the world of dreams, where he cannot control (and therefore cannot be held fully accountable for?) his subversive thoughts. And yet even in the most private, inaccessible part of himself, his unconscious, the content of the joke remains censored and unknown. What we do know is that the joke is dangerous and titillating because its subject matter is the sultan himself, whose self-proclaimed omnipotence has somehow been threatened by the joker. In fact, we do not need to know *the* joke; any of a number of jokes profaning Asad will serve for this struggle over symbolic meaning. The room is not big enough for both "heads," the head of state and the mind of a subversive joker, and as the latter head rolls, it is nevertheless the joker's laughter that resounds in the room. The sultan is capable of killing the joker, but not of stifling his laughter. People can never be fully silenced and controlled, the film suggests. And articulations that undermine the symbolic power of the leader also undermine his effectiveness. The joker has refused to operate within the politics of "as if." Even his death cannot alter the fact of his transgressive power.

Jokes

Zikra's film makes explicit the connection between the unconscious processes common to dreaming and joke-telling. But whereas dreams are generally private and jokes public, Zikra reverses this relationship, making the dream public to his audience, while the joke remains private and inaccessible. Zikra is also suggesting the power of jokes by creating a scene in which the dreamer's expression of uncensored desire nevertheless censors its own most transgressive content. But in noncinematic life, in the privacy of Syrian homes, jokes do abound, the most politically charged and risky of them being about Asad and his cult.

In *Jokes and Their Relation to the Unconscious*, Sigmund Freud argues that jokes are pleasurable because they provide a release, representing an internal resistance overcome. The "secret of the joke's pleasure," in his view, derives from its "economy in psychical expenditure," which is a product of the joke's compression and consolidation of language, of the relationship between the joke and its context, and of the suppressed purposes (exposing the object of the joke, expressing hostility) communicated in the joke's telling.[52]

Scholars who draw on Freud in their treatment of jokes tend to focus on the inhibited hostile or aggressive wishes that the telling of a joke allows the teller to overcome. Certainly the expression of inhibited or repressed hostility is characteristic of many, if not all, Syrian political jokes. For example: **A man named Hafiz al-Khara' goes to the court because he wants to change his name. (Khara' means "shit.") The judge asks, "what name would you prefer to Hafiz?"** (1988; 1992)[53] This joke, and others like it, transgress the rules of hierarchy, discursively redressing the balance between ruler and ruled by making the officially exalted (Asad) base, while excrement becomes comparatively desirable.[54]

Discussing the necessarily public nature of jokes, Freud goes on to suggest political implications of joke-telling far beyond the leveling of elementary insults. A joke must be told to someone else. For it to be funny, the speaker and the listener must, in Freud's terminology, be in "sufficient psychical accord." And this requirement of "psychical conformity" means that jokes depend for their effectiveness on conditions shared between the teller and the audience of a joke.[55] In Syria, political jokes tend overwhelmingly to depend on the shared condition of unbelief; they are experienced as pleasurable in part because they communicate the sharing of this unbelief: **Asad needs an organ transplant. The officials know that many people will want to donate, so they hold a contest. They decide to drop a piece of crinkled paper into the crowd and whoever catches it wins. They drop the paper, and people blow it away chanting "With spirit, with blood, we sacrifice for you, O Hafiz"** (1988; 1992). The word *ruh* in Arabic means both "spirit" and "breath of life," punning on the meaning of the slogan. The joke suggests that people may look like they are enthusiastic about Asad, but they are actually using slogans of sacrifice in order to avoid sacrifice.

The existence of so many Syrian jokes specifically about the cult of Asad is evidence of the broad consensus in Syria that the cult is not credible. The jokes operate effectively as resistance to the cult to the extent that they allow tellers and listeners to overcome the isolation and atomization official performative practices induce. Both joker and audience experience the fact of having surmounted their own internalized censors, of violating taboos, and courting the danger of expressing unbelief even in the qualified "public" of one's trusted friends in a private home. Syrian political jokes, like the story of M, recapitulate the cult in reverse form, drawing on the official symbolism of political adulation in order to subvert it. They mark the point where the public shades into the private, countering the obedience dictated by the Syrian politics of "as if" with the disobedience of registering, if only for a light-hearted moment, the truth of near universal popular dissimulation. In doing so, they also evoke the themes we have so far identified as the primary ambiguities of the cult's power: isolation and atomization versus community and solidarity; hyperbole and dissimulation versus the common-sense apprehension of brute conditions; adulation versus discontent and hostility. The sheer abundance of jokes poking fun at Asad and his cult demonstrate yet again the fluency of Syrians in the official rhetoric; they manifest the widespread popular awareness of Syrian politics as a politics of "as if."[56]

One common and recurrent joke form uses fictive meetings among *heads of state* to undermine official claims of Asad's infallibility.[57] These jokes can be read to express the cynical point that all regimes are really alike, but they also suggest that under another regime things might be a bit better than they are under Asad. **Reagan, Gorbachev, and Asad get together. Reagan says, "I make 200,000 dollars per year." Gorbachev says, "I make 100 rubles per year." Asad says, "I make 10,000 Syrian lira per year." "How do you live on that salary?" the other two ask. "Oh, my children send me something every month"** (1988). The joke refers to Asad's self-proclaimed role as patriarch, his reliance on the self-sacrifice of young people, and the prevalent corruption that allows some Syrians (in this case, implicating Asad) to make considerably more than their regular income.

The following heads-of-state joke internalizes the claims of Arab inferiority and "backwardness" prevalent in colonial and Orientalist literature. But the joke also counters an official Syrian discourse that highlights "progress," links it to Asad's Corrective Movement, and aestheticizes Syrian development projects in public spectacles. **Bush, Mitterrand, and Asad all die. Bush asks God: "When will my people be developed?" God replies: "After**

50 years." Bush begins to cry. Mitterrand asks God, "When will my people be developed?" God answers: "After 100 years." Mitterrand begins to cry. Asad asks: "When will the Arabs be developed?" God starts to cry (1992).[58]

Another joke invokes the three-heads-of-state formula to underscore the distinction between loyalty and coercive compliance: Bush, Gorbachev, and Asad are in a race. Bush's bodyguard carries him until they reach a river. The river has crocodiles in it, and the bodyguard refuses to cross it: "I have children, family responsibilities. . . ." They return. Gorbachev's bodyguard carries him to the river, and he too refuses to cross it: "I have children, family responsibilities. . . ." They also return. Asad's bodyguard carries Asad to the river and dives in, dodging the crocodiles. The other bodyguards are amazed and ask: "How could you do it?" Asad's bodyguard replies: "I have children, family responsibilities. . . ." (1989). Actions, the joke suggests, may appear to be motivated by loyalty, but they are really inspired by fear.

Finally, the heads-of-state formula works to highlight the relationship between meaning and context, thereby distinguishing affective allegiance, which Syrians perceive to be common in Western democracies, from its Syrian simulacrum. Reagan, Mitterrand, and Asad meet. Reagan brags, "My subjects are so loyal that one regiment is willing to die for me." The other two leaders are incredulous. So Reagan summons the soldiers and sure enough, on being ordered to, the men begin to commit suicide. Horrified, Reagan orders them to stop. Mitterrand boasts, "My subjects are so loyal that two regiments are willing to die for me." Reagan and Asad are doubtful. So Mitterrand commands his soldiers to start committing suicide, and the troops begin to do so. Aghast, Mitterrand begs them to stop. Hafiz boasts, "My men are so loyal that three regiments are willing to die for me." Seeing the other two leaders doubtful, Asad orders his troops to start killing themselves. They do. Horrified, he begs them to stop. They keep committing suicide. Finally, there's only one man left. "Stop," Asad orders. "Why are you about to kill yourself?" he asks. The last soldier replies: "you think I want to stay around with you?" (1988) The greatest "sacrifice" is not death, but life with Hafiz al-Asad.[59]

Border jokes represent another popular genre. They always involve conversations between a Syrian and an Israeli soldier, and they run directly counter to the martial, Manichaean rhetoric of the official narrative: An Israeli and a Syrian are standing at the border. The Israeli says to the Syrian, "In Israel we've got running water, we've got electricity, and we've got working telephones." The Syrian, puzzled about how to reply, says, "Well in Syria, we've got Asad." [The word *asad* in Arabic means lion; the joke will pun on the dual meaning.] The Israeli is perplexed. He scratches his head and goes away. The next day the scenario is repeated. On the third day the Israeli comes back and says, "Now we have an 'asad' too." The Syrian, thinking that the Israelis have managed to get a hold of another Asad, responds, "Now you won't have running water, electricity, or working telephones either" (1985).

The following border joke registers perceptions of Israel's military superiority. It also provides a playful account of Syrians' ability to adapt, to make life work for them despite disadvantages. That the joke suggests extra-legal means to procure what one wants is a telling insight into the way Syrians view their world and their own ingenuity within it. A Syrian army officer wants a vacation from the army. He goes to the commanding officer. The commanding officer says, "Bring me an Israeli tank and you can have twenty days." The soldier complies and gets twenty days off. The soldier returns and, after a while, wants another vacation. So the commanding officer reiterates the same condition. Again the soldier complies. The commanding officer is astounded and asks, "How do you do it?" The soldier replies, "It's easy: I have an agreement with this Israeli guy—I give him two Syrian tanks, and he gives me one Israeli one!" (1989)

Orchestrated democracy is another theme that finds expression in Syrian jokes. The following example alludes to the orchestrated referendums by which the regime routinely simulates democracy. The frequently seen slogan "Yes to Asad" refers to these plebiscites, although the slogan is rather open-ended and can also suggest general obedience and support. A man had to go to the bathroom. So he entered the public restrooms at the Suq al-Hamadiyya [Damascus's large market]. He knocked on the door. The man inside said "Yes." He knocked on the door a second time. The man inside said "Yes." The man outside said, "Where do you think we are, at the polls?" (1989) This joke exposes the farcical nature of elections; voters can only vote "yes" and they can vote as many times as they want.

The charade-like character of presidential referendums and the dependence on coercion for enforcement find expression in this joke: **After the polls closed, men came to tell Asad that he had won by 99.2 percent of the vote. He said: I want the names of the other .8 percent (1992).**

During the elections, posters of Asad were plastered on walls throughout Syria. The serial repetition of Asad's image captures the particular ways in which the cult's paradoxicality becomes evident during an election "campaign." The orchestration of "democratic" elections and the rhetorical claims of Asad's multiplicitous occupations (he is the premier pharmacist, doctor, lawyer) draw attention to the possibility of multiple candidates and also to the political circumstances that foreclose the option. Asad is simultaneously the only and every presidential candidate. **A man goes to the eye doctor during the elections and says: "Doctor, something is wrong with my vision, all of the candidates look alike" (1992).**

The referendum of 1991 prompted not only the resuscitation of jokes familiar from other referendums, but also the creation of identifiably new jokes specific to the electoral discourse of 1991. During the 1991 election, Asad, who had previously been called Abu Sulayman as a term of endearment, became Abu Basil (father of Basil), which, as suggested in chapter 2, connoted the regime's dynastic ambitions. Also during the 1991 referendum, Asad released a number of political prisoners. **Three men are released. The guard says to the first prisoner: "Praise Abu Basil." So the first prisoner praises him: "God bless you, Abu Basil, our leader, symbol of steadfastness, etc." The guard says to the second man, "Praise Abu Basil," so he does: "God bless you, our leader, guardian of right and honor, etc." The guard commands the third prisoner to praise Abu Basil. And the third man replies: "O.K., but whatever happened to that other guy, Abu Sulayman?"** The joke draws attention to everyone's fluency in the regime's performative practices by underscoring this man's lack of such fluency, while also highlighting the interchangeability and generality of leaders as such.

Jokes that refer to Asad's sacred investiture may be gathered under the rubric of *charisma jokes*. In the following example of this form, rhetorical claims of regime longevity and dynastic ambition are counterposed to the ideological principles of Baʿthist socialism. Three people, a Saudi, a Libyan, and a Syrian, die and are resurrected. The Saudi hails "the Saudi Arab Republic." The kingdom has become a republic. The Libyan hails the "Libyan Arab Socialist Republic." The Libyans have become socialist. The Syrian hails, "The Syrian Arab Socialist Republic under the leadership of Hafiz al-Asad the 16th" (1989). Hafiz al-Asad's immortality, secured through his paternity, is fundamentally at odds with the party's former revolutionary precepts.

This joke mocks Asad's Christ-like rhetorical status: Asad dies. Officials begin searching for a grave, but do not find one. They search the whole world in vain. They finally go to Jerusalem and ask for a grave. They meet a priest in the Church of the Holy Sepulchre (where Christ is buried). The officials say to the priest: "We want this grave." The priest replies: "There isn't any room, but if you pay 5 million dollars, I'll see what I can do." The officials reply: "Oh, that's expensive, we only need it for three days" (1992).[60]

The metonymical relation between Asad and the twelfth century Kurdish hero Salah al-Din, established in the official narrative, is the subject of this joke, which also pokes fun at the uneducated officials in charge of education: A history teacher gives a lecture and asks his students: "Who killed Salah al-Din?" The students become frightened and begin crying. "We didn't do it, teacher. We swear." The teacher is surprised and sends for the principal. The principal comes and asks, "What is the matter?" The teacher says, "I asked them who killed Salah al-Din and no one answered." The students begin to cry again. The principal asks: "Do you suspect any one of them?" (1992)

Jokes *about fear* also abound. This one emphasizes the point that Syrians are compliant, in part, because they are afraid: A drunk man sees a picture of Asad and calls him a dog. A young boy standing at the bus stop with his father overhears the drunk. As they mount the bus the boy sees another picture of Asad and says to his father, "Look at that dog." The father looks around and says: "Has anybody lost his son?" (1992) The drunk's alcohol intake enables him to circumvent his internal censors, and the boy's innocence and impressionability mean that he too fails to uphold the unspoken rules of the cult. Fear distances fathers from sons and routinely reinforces understandings of appropriate public speech and conduct specified by Asad's cult.

This fear not only distances people from one another, but also alienates ordinary citizens from themselves: A red BMW hits a taxi. The taxi driver is angry and curses. He leaves his taxi and goes to yell at the driver of the BMW and to seek recompense. The BMW's windows are smoked, concealing the identity of the occupants. The window opens a crack, and a young woman slips a card with her phone number into the furious, cursing taxi driver's hand. He calls the number and a man answers. The taxi driver begins to yell: "I work hard for my money, you son of a bitch." The man replies, "Do you know with whom you are speaking?" "No," the driver replies. "This is Hafiz al-Asad," the man says. The driver says, "Do you know with whom you are speaking?" Asad says "No." The driver says: "Thank God," and hangs up (1992).

Jokes *about 'Alawis* are another category that, as the following example illustrates, may violate a number of discursive taboos simultaneously. This joke speaks explicitly of the 'Alawi nature of the regime, identifies 'Alawis with vulgarity and stupidity, and juxtaposes the religion of the mosque to the arbitrary excess of Asad's cult: An officer wants to pray. He asks his guards: "Is there an 'Alawi mosque here?" The guards go and search and come back without finding one. They tell him that there is only a Sunni mosque in the area. The officer says, "It's O.K. Let's enter it and pray." They enter to pray. He sees an Imam delivering a speech, and shouts at him, "Stop that blathering." He orders one of his guards to complete the speech. The guard ascends and begins the speech. When he finishes, he asks the officer, "How was my speech, was it good?" The officer replies, "You are a donkey. You said Muhammad is the cousin of Asad and we believed you. You said God is his uncle and we believed you. But how can we believe that the Ka'ba [a shrine in Mecca dating from pre-Islamic times and holy to Muslims] is among the achievements of the Corrective Movement?" (1992) The joke's comical significance resides in its attention to the transparently bogus "achievements" of the Corrective Movement, and to the arbitrariness of officials who define the limits of discursive excess.

The regime's 'Alawi character finds expression in this joke as well: **the telephone is ringing in Asad's palace: qrn, qrn** (1989; 1992). The 'Alawi dialect retains the vocative "q," which in most Syrian dialects becomes a glottal stop. This joke suggests that the regime is so entirely made up of 'Alawis that even the phones ring in 'Alawi dialect.

The following joke about 'Alawis inverts the standard jokes about people from Homs, who are conventionally depicted in jokes as particularly bumbling and stupid (not dissimilar to Sa'idi jokes in Egypt or Polish jokes in the United States): **An 'Alawi is selling a rabbit. A Homsi passes by and asks him: how much is your donkey? The 'Alawi says, "You Homsis are really stupid. Can't you see that's a rabbit?" The Homsi replies, "I was talking to the rabbit!"** (1996)

Finally, *everyday problems* are thematized, usually by drawing attention to the disparity between official representations and people's frustrations. The paradoxicality of Asad's cult finds expression in this joke, for on the one hand, official rhetoric claims Asad to be omnipotent and omniscient, but on the other hand, Asad is not supposed to be responsible for any of Syria's problems. **A man goes to market and notices that there is no olive oil available. He asks his companion, "Where's the olive oil? I thought Syria was full of olive oil." The secret police overhear him. They say, "You've insulted the President." They take him away and kill him. The second man goes to market and notices that there is no sugar in the market. He asks his companion, "Hey, what happened to the sugar? I thought Syria was full of sugar." The secret police overhear him and say, "You've insulted the President." They take him away and kill him. A third man, having witnessed the fate of the other two, says to his companion: "I hear Anisa (the**

President's wife) is pregnant . . . but the President does not have anything to do with it" (1989). In this joke, the insult depends on misunderstanding the guidelines put forth by the cult in ways that challenge Asad's manliness; Asad can control the activities of the marketplace, but not the sexual practices of his wife.

Life with Asad, rhetorical claims notwithstanding, is intolerable: Asad is passing by the American consulate. He notices a long line outside the door.[61] He asks his bodyguards, "Why is there such a long line outside the American consulate?" The bodyguards only shrug their shoulders. Asad goes into the consulate and demands to see the consul. He asks the consul, "What are all these people doing waiting in line outside the consulate?" The consul replies, "They all want visas to go to America." Asad thinks for a moment, and then says, "Give me a visa too; I want to go to America." So the consul obliges and gives him the visa. He steps outside only to find that no one is waiting in line. The place is empty. "What happened?" Asad asks his bodyguard. The guard replies, "When they found out you were going, they decided to stay" (1985; 1988; 1991). Like all of the Asad jokes, these jokes about everyday life indicate a shared and rueful understanding of the gap between official rhetoric and lived experience in Syria.

Syrian political jokes represent the point at which the regime's symbolic management breaks down, where the generation of meanings definitively exceeds the control of both state administrative and symbolic powers. Jokes parody the requirements of public praise by supplying consolidated narratives that demystify Asad and strip him of his sanctity. They offer a differentiated image of Syrian political power, depicting a political reality that can be found neither in the official discourse nor in conventional political and economic studies.

CONCLUSIONS

People who offer alternative visions of politics can be said to "resist" to the extent that they challenge the official meanings and idealized version a regime claims as its own. This resistance works not only by renegotiating, subverting, or appropriating rhetorical meanings, however, but also by undermining the disciplinary effects associated with the discourse and its attendant practices. In the case of Syria, resistance resides in the rhetorical practices, both permitted and forbidden, that recognize the shared conditions of unbelief the cult produces.

If the cult isolates and atomizes Syrian citizenry by forcing people to evaluate each other through the prism of obligatory dissimulation, then the comedies, cartoons, films, and forbidden jokes work to undo this mechanism of social control. These unofficial, sometimes "hidden" practices point emphatically to the gap between compliance and belief. They help to establish an Aesopian public sphere, an alternative space in which official rhetoric and imagery are invoked only to be criticized, undermined, transgressed, or subverted. The permitted and forbidden comedies, cartoons, films, and jokes do not eliminate complicity, but they suggest that Syrians are aware of the ways in which their participation upholds and confirms the system. This Aesopian public world is an alternative system that Syrians also create and sustain. This system relies on a language that communicates a far-reaching shared recognition of unbelief, which counteracts the atomizing effects of the politics of "as if" conducted in public.

Most forms of resistance generally operate within a conceptual system shared by the regime. The fact that jokes, cartoons, films, and slapstick comedies function within the same conceptual system—that there is no "exteriority," to borrow from Foucault— suggests the power of the regime and the limitations of resistance.[62] But a common conceptual system is also what makes the resistance comprehensible and intelligible. To accept the vocabulary of the cult is also to be able to use it to undermine rather than to glorify.

Moreover, it is not clear who or what owns any conceptual system. The regime appropriates cultural meanings and may reinvent them, but it does not own them. Just as the regime clutters public space with its symbolic displays of power and magnificence, the jokes, films, and slapstick comedies that poke fun at the regime are ways in which people create and commemorate more or less alternative conceptions of politics. These contests over the signification and effects of political discourse are important, in part, because they are the form everyday transgressions assume in Syria. The discourse contains and structures both the guidelines for obedience and the material for subversion.

Because organized opposition is not tolerated, language and the courage it takes to speak with others establish the foundations of what might ultimately eventuate in organized opposition. But a joke, a movie line, or a cartoon is politically relevant not only insofar as it may have consequences for or help define the parameters of future political upheavals; in the moment when a joke is told, when laughter resounds in the room, people are also cancelling the isolation and atomization manufactured by a politics of "as if." People are affirming with each other that they are unwilling conscripts, that the cult is both unbelievable and powerful.

And yet, paradoxically, it is precisely this shared acknowledgment of involuntary obedience that also makes the cult so powerful. Or to put it differently, Asad's cult is powerful, in part, because it is unbelievable. These acts of transgression might counteract the atomization and isolation a politics of "as if" produces, but they also shore up another of the cult's mechanisms of discipline, namely, the ways in which the cult relies on an external obedience produced through each citizen's unbelief. If Asad's cult disciplines citizens by occasioning continual demonstrations of external obedience, and if external obedience relies on a self-conscious submission to authority, then recognizing the shared conditions of unbelief reproduces this self-consciousness without which a politics of "as if" could hardly be sustained.

Careful analyses of transgressive practices require a corresponding identification of the strategies and logic of a particular regime's domination.[63] In the case of Syria, identifying the ways in which Asad's cult operates to discipline citizens by enforcing obedience, inducing complicity, and isolating participants enables us to assess the ways in which transgressions can undermine some aspects of the regime's power while reinforcing others. Conversely, interpreting transgressions can help us to gain a nuanced understanding of the ways in which power works. Systems of domination are never total, and everyday forms of resistance suggest the partial, less-than-optimal ways in which power is exemplified and produced in Syria. This chapter has been an attempt both to acknowledge the ways in which people cope in courageous and humorous ways, and also to show that the cult is nonetheless a markedly effective, low-cost mechanism of social control. Everyday practices of transgression not only alert us to the discrepancies between public performances of deference and privately held sentiments of unbelief, they also teach us about the complex structure of Syria's official symbolism and about the power that even acts of resistance can generate for the regime.

FIGURES 10–28   From the archives of the cartoonist ʿAli Farzat. All the cartoons were drawn in the late 1980s and early 1990s. Figures 10–24 were permitted by the censors, but figures 25–28 were disallowed.

FIGURE 10

FIGURE 11

FIGURE 12

FIGURE 13

FIGURE 14

FIGURE 15

FIGURE 16

Figure 17

Figure 18

FIGURE 19

FIGURE 20

FIGURE 21

FIGURE 22

Figure 23

Figure 24

Figure 25

Figure 26

FIGURE 27

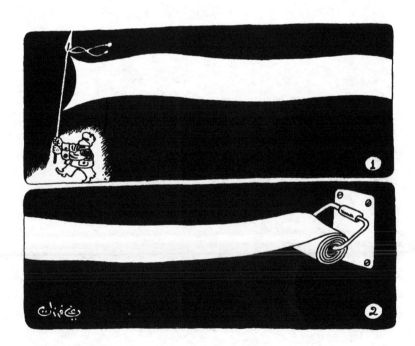

FIGURE 28

Five

Complicating Compliance

If you knew your Excellence from what burden you have delivered me. You have liberated me from the ingratiating honor of being the head of 5 million inhabitants all of whom consider themselves politicians emeritus. Half claim for themselves the vocation of leader. One-fourth believe themselves to be prophets; ten percent at the least take themselves to be gods. You will have the guardianship of people who adore God, fire, and the devil.[1]

These were the reported words of Syrian President al-Quwatli in 1958 when he turned governance of Syria over to Egyptian President Gamal 'Abd al-Nasir.[2] Read now against the backdrop of Asad's era, Quwatli's statement has the ring of nostalgia. By all accounts, Syria had a politicized population from the period of the French Mandate through to the creation of the United Arab Republic in 1958. Syrians experienced a period of vigorous parliamentary activity in the early to mid-1940s, followed by a series of coups and counter-coups (three occurring in 1949 alone). The nascent institutions of the Syrian state were not always able to contain conflicts within democratic confines, but the atmosphere of turmoil in the 1940s, continuing into the 1950s, reflected a capacity in Syrian society for translating diverse political orientations into publicly meaningful points of view and active organizations. None of these organizations could obtain an electoral majority, and many employed extra-parliamentary means to achieve their goals.

The depoliticization that arguably began when Syria unified with Egypt in 1958 became increasingly obvious after their separation, especially under the Ba'th Party monopoly established in   *143*

1963. Even so, early Ba'thist rule was not well consolidated and currents of opposition continued actively. It would not be until the 1970s under Asad that popular depoliticization became an increasingly observable phenomenon in public life. Asad's regime has used a variety of means to discourage political opposition: it has allocated resources and passed out rewards to those who play by the rules and it has deployed its security forces against those who do not. Like most if not all newly formed nation-states, Syria has tried to negotiate ethnic and political difference in the difficult circumstances of simultaneous state- and nation-building, to keep the peace, and to channel potentially regime-destructive energies along regime-constructive lines. Important parts of this negotiation take place symbolically, as the regime attempts to manage meanings in ways that are consistent with and reproductive of civic order.

My analysis of Asad's cult has examined in detail some of the disciplinary mechanisms by which a nation-state in formation generates compliance but also invites transgressions. This concluding chapter seeks to answer two broadly comparative questions: What are the implications of this investigation for understandings of power and compliance more generally? What are its implications for studying political symbolism?

Current understandings of compliance generally stop short of considering the ways in which symbolic displays of power generate obedience for regimes. Drawing on Max Weber's conceptualizations of authority and the state, social scientists typically rely on one or another version of a representative taxonomy according to which there are: (1) legitimate or "voluntary *normative* compliance, usually due to consensus on values or outcome"; (2) "*utilitarian* compliance, compliance benefiting the individual or group"; and (3) "*coercive* compliance, based on compulsion by force, violence, and terror or the threat of them."[3] But Asad's cult manifestly fails to produce "legitimacy," and thus cannot fall under the rubric of "voluntary normative compliance." The cult does appropriate meaningful narratives and it inscribes Asad into existing systems of signification. But voluntary normative compliance requires that values and goals be shared, which is quite distinct from the unbelieving submission to authority called for by the fictions of the cult.

The maintenance of Asad's cult undoubtedly relies on utilitarian and coercive strategies to some degree, since the failure to perform may result in economic hardships or punishment, and performing well helps promote security and possibly enhances economic and political opportunities. Nevertheless, utilitarian compliance implies a bargain rather than obedience; and a bargaining system is two-sided, only working over the long run when the bargains are kept. Coercive compliance need not imply submission, but may, like utilitarian compliance, derive from a simple calculation of expediency, the terms of which may be reconsidered whenever conditions change. Moreover, formulations of both coercive and utilitarian compliance focus on material rewards and punishments, rather than on the role of ideology as a mechanism of control in the absence of belief or emotional commitment.

The evidence marshaled here for the status of rhetoric and symbols as disciplinary devices calls for the articulation of a subsystem of coercive compliance hitherto unspecified in the literature—what might be termed "disciplinary-symbolic" power. Discipline denotes control gained by enforcing obedience or order. Disciplinary-symbolic practices, then, would refer to the ways in which power is generated through its representation, and also to the insinuation of formulaic rhetoric and self-serving state symbolism into the daily lives of citizens, habituating people to perform the gestures and pronounce the slogans constitutive of their obedience. The cult of Hafiz al-Asad does not simply depend for its efficacy on other mechanisms of enforcement; rather, *the cult is itself such a mechanism.*

DISCIPLINARY-SYMBOLIC POWER
AS A FORM OF CONTROL

It is easy to understand how orchestrated spectacles and gala events provide *occasions* for enforcing compliance: as we have seen, attendance at state spectacles is sometimes compulsory and other forms of participation in the cult are matters of both police and self control. People are even careful about how or whether they speak of the president in the most informal public settings, such as during a bus ride, in a store, at the park, or in a café. Unscripted comments are generally assumed to be insulting rather than glorifying of Syria's leader, implying that Asad's power resides not only in orchestrated displays of obedience, but also in the silence about domestic politics that characterizes everyday life.

The ways in which representations of power and obedience themselves operate to *produce* power and obedience, however, require further explanation. Within the category of coercive compliance, regimes rely not only on the fact of, but also or mainly on the anticipation of actual punishment. The focus of coercive compliance is not the actual meting out of punishments to those who disobey, but the dissemination of credible *threats* of punishment. Although threats, to be credible, must at least occasionally be carried out, in general they suffice to ensure the compliance of most citizens. In coercive compliance, people obey because they *fear* being punished.

Sustaining the threat of punishment requires what Lacanian historian Louis Marin terms "the placing in reserve of force in signs," suggesting that there is an important connection between the representation of political power and its creation.[4] To the extent that power in its crudest sense means the capacity to apply force, Marin argues, political cults and their attendant spectacles operate as a punitive force that is not exerted, but is nevertheless manifested through the representation of its potential. In the case of Syria, through the fantastic, magnified, multiplicative effects of Asad's image alongside those of obedient citizens, physical violence is deferred or converted into coercive potential.

The images of citizens delivering panegyrics to Asad's rule, collectively forming his face, signing oaths in blood, or simply displaying a picture of him in their shop windows communicate to Syrians throughout the country the impression of Asad's power independent of his readiness to use it. As James C. Scott notes, "effective display may, by conveying the impression of actual power and the will to use it, economize on the actual use of violence."[5] To this extent, Asad's cult is an effective mechanism of power because while economizing on the actual use of force, it also works to generate obedience. Asad is powerful because people treat him as powerful; spectacles are enactments of people treating him as powerful, thereby helping to make him so. In other words, political systems are upheld not only by shared visions, material gains, and punishments, but also by unstable, shifting enactments of power and powerlessness, which are no less real for being symbolic. Spectacles not only provide an occasion to enforce obedience, but also represent this enforcement, thereby serving to create a *mentalité* of popular powerlessness that helps produce the regime's power anew. And the greater the absurdity of the required performance, the more clearly it demonstrates that the regime can make most people obey most of the time.

Asad's cult and its attendant spectacles are also central to the construction of what T. Fujitani, writing about the Japanese monarchy, calls "a kind of ocular domination," in which citizens behave as if they are being watched because they might be.[6] Asad's image as the transcendent leader, his gaze monitoring the actions of Syrian citizens, by signifying the anonymous, panoptic security forces—in the words of one Syrian, Asad's "eyes and ears"[7]—allows the police to be "present" even when one knows that they are not. Although certainly not the only apparatus through which Syrians have come to discipline themselves, the image of the ubiquitous, all-seeing Asad and the proliferation of occasions for citizens to demonstrate their obedience to him have facilitated the construction of a nation-state composed of people who have internalized their own surveillance, imagining themselves as objects of the regime's observation.

The effect of the regime's power is manifest in the active compliance of mobilized citizens, but also in citizens' passive compliance, in the cynical apathy of those who obey because they have become habituated to the cult or in order to be left in peace. The reproduction of empty narratives and gestures, the endless festivities, the sheer length of official occasions, tire out the bodies and minds of those who produce and consume them. Inspiration is difficult to sustain over time even in revolutionary regimes, and it is all the more so in the Syrian context, which is not only nonrevolutionary, but also, in part thanks to the cult, in a certain sense postpolitical. The tedium of official pomp and pageantry, paradoxically, is part and parcel of the cult's strength. Official language and symbols operate to kill politics prophylactically before it emerges, to depoliticize people by orchestrating public performances in which people's compliance ensures their safety but, more importantly, forecloses the individual and group engagement customarily associated with ideas of political fulfillment.

Depoliticization, however, is never total in any regime. First, there are always those who remain politicized and opposed to the regime in varying degrees. In authoritarian circumstances it is difficult to create an organized group that significantly threatens the existing order, but uprisings do occur. Even when they are defeated, they prove that people who are not apathetic and cynical continue to exist among those who are.[8] Moreover, the performative practices authoritarian regimes require enable people to conceal their internal thoughts from public scrutiny, which means that people may not only dissimulate greater loyalty than they feel, but may also act more cynical and apathetic than they are.

Second, despite the depoliticizing effects of tired slogans and tedious festivals, "intellectual life under dictatorship," to borrow the title of Andrei Plesu's essay on the subject, not only exists, but may even thrive, especially in the privacy of one's home. Plesu's teacher, Constantin Noica, makes the point without qualification: "For intellectual life bad conditions are good and good conditions are bad."[9] The truth may be more complex than this simple claim, but Noica is far from alone in maintaining that the conditions of authoritarian rule—the proscriptions and limitations with which citizens contend every day—may enhance and intensify intellectual engagement and political thinking rather than only produce cynicism and apathy. Reading forbidden texts in whatever setting surely seems a more significant and exciting activity than reading texts that are permitted. As Plesu writes:

> The existence of censorship led to the elaboration of ingenious subtexts, allusions, and camouflage techniques practiced with great virtuosity and assimilated promptly by the mass of readers. . . . Intellectual life under dictatorships has a dramatic, fiery aspect, capable of mobilizing the whole being of its protagonists, their ultimate resources.[10]

Such "camouflage techniques" seem to be practiced under all authoritarian regimes. And although regimes may be vigilant in prohibiting certain books or films, there are always "cracks" or "loop-holes" in the system. Robert Darnton, writing about the former East Germany, reports on the way that forbidden books were:

> circulated through networks of trusted friends. A friend would appear with a volume and give you a time limit, often two days, to read it. You would shut yourself up in a safe place and pore over the text, day and night. The effect was overwhelming. . . . Dissident authors of the current generation . . . got away with heresies by putting them in foreign settings, just as Montesquieu and Voltaire had done. And everyone learned to read between the lines.[11]

Similarly in Syria, forbidden short stories, novels (such as Salman Rushdie's *The Satanic Verses*), and films circulate among groups of friends, as do human rights reports, prohibited political journals, and even individual pages that have literally been excised from permitted texts by the censors. This insistence on creation and circulation, on devising ways of communicating politically incendiary ideas, suggests that, along with cynicism and apathy, authoritarian power also produces conditions conducive to critical *engagement*. As the Czechoslovakian director Milos Forman, in comparing artistic life under communism with life under market society, explained: "When you're not allowed to talk you know what you want to say. . . . Censorship identifies what's worth talking about. But when you're free, you have to decide what's important. And that's more difficult."[12] Forman is not advocating state censorship, but he is suggesting that authoritarian regimes structure the terms of transgression in ways that orient would-be dissidents. People who interpret transgressive materials must, as Darnton writes, learn to "read between the lines," overcoming their own internal censors to decipher what is funny or damning (or both) in the coded messages. There is a kind of "unspoken conspiracy" between artist and audience, a connection forged through the shared experiences of unbelief.[13]

The production of apathy and cynicism, in other words, like other mechanisms of social control, while powerful, is never absolute. To the extent that the production of cynicism is a tool of the regime for control, then it needs a cult people can*not* believe. But this does not mean that all of the evidence of satire and transgression in Syria necessarily serves the state's interests or that "unspoken conspiracies" and the titillation of reading forbidden texts can substitute for substantive discussions of political issues in public. What it does imply is that intellectuals, in particular, find ways of coping with fear and of communicating alternative ideas to receptive audiences who can imagine remaking their world even if they do not act politically.

Like other forms of social control, requirements and prohibitions in the realm of the disciplinary-symbolic invite skirmishes with a regime over the meanings of lived experiences by both producers and consumers of symbolic messages. The line of demarcation between ruler and ruled runs: (1) psychologically through each individual; (2) externally or "behaviorally" in each struggle; and (3) contextually: the person who is "ruler" in one skirmish may be "ruled" in the next. If one takes seriously Havel's insight that people sometimes enforce on each other what none believes, presumably even Asad is sometimes compliant to someone.[14]

Bearing in mind the complex and shifting lines of demarcation between ruler and ruled, it becomes possible to imagine disciplinary-symbolic power as a continuum along which, in any regime, the enactments of everyday political contests can be charted. On one end of the continuum is the credible threat of reprisal, implying the stimulation of fears of bodily punishment, economic disadvantage, political "excommunication," or social disapproval. On this end, it is the individual's perhaps temporary overcoming of her or his fear that produces words and deeds critical of an existing order. The skirmish is located not only between ruler and ruled but, like Havel's line, within each individual. One recognizes the skirmish in uprisings that overwhelm a regime's ability or "willingness" to respond coercively. The "velvet revolutions" in 1989 in Eastern Europe are recent examples. At the other end of the continuum lies the fatiguing, depoliticizing, cynicism-producing effects of the discourse. The struggle here resides in the ways that people every day devise strategies to counteract the deadening effects of tired rhetoric, to breathe, in the words of Gabriel Liiceanu, "stolen oxygen."[15]

The friction between ruler and ruled on all points of the continuum may be visible in collective action or in individual symbolic triumphs around the globe. The latter are notable rhetorical performances, testimony to what Lauren Berlant calls the "unrealized potential for subaltern political activity . . . when a person stages a dramatic coup in a public sphere in which she does not have privilege." Berlant continues,

> Flashing up and startling the public, she puts the dominant story into suspended animation; as though recording an estranging voice-over to a film we have all already seen, she renarrates the dominant history as one that the abjected people have once lived sotto voce, but no more; and she challenges her audience to identify with the enormity of the suffering she has narrated and the courage she has had to produce, calling on people to change the institutional practices of citizenship to which they currently consent.[16]

Although sustained collective rebellion may be rare in both stable authoritarian regimes and in hegemonic liberal democratic ones, individual triumphs that call on shared conditions of suffering or unbelief are visible everywhere: the injustices and arbitrariness of state officialdom invite transgression in the most blatantly coercive regimes and in the most placid-seeming liberal democracies.[17] Some examples might be: Usama Muhammad, the Syrian filmmaker discussed in chapter 4, whose explicit violation of official taboos creates a transgressive counternarrative to the regime's official claims of harmonious unity. Or in the American context, Marlon T. Riggs, a gay black American poet and filmmaker whose film, *Tongues Untied,* not only celebrates but is itself the occasion of voices being raised in a chorus of otherwise unheard, nonetheless commonplace experiences of homophobia and racism, on the one hand, and of erotic pleasures and political pride, on the other.[18] It is as if, in such acts of symbolic overcoming, dominant practices are turned inside out, revealing, if only momentarily, a form of counter-power drawn from the fluid potential of human self-assertion.

Individual transgressive practices, although important, are not necessarily transformative of institutionalized political life or capable of prompting collective action. Rational choice theories, in construing shifts from quiescence to overt political action in terms of "tips" or "cascades," may help to explain why.[19] If a person thinks that everyone will participate in a state-sponsored spectacle, for example, then she is likely to regard refusal as an act that will be punished. If she believes, however, that many others will also refuse to obey, then caution no longer dictates remaining compliant. As more people assess that others will refuse to comply, political life can "tip" from compliance to protest. To the extent that people decide whether to obey or to rebel on the basis of what they think others will do, Asad's cult—from public spectacles to posting signs in shop windows—reinforces the expectation that most everyone will obey most of the time. The cult displays obedience, thereby helping to ensure it. The persistence of transgressive practices and the alternative possibilities such practices summon may help to reinvigorate institutional politics eventually. From the perspective of a "tipping" model, however, such acts would have to go beyond demonstrating the shared conditions of unbelief, to convince participants that others are willing to protest actively. The transgressive practices discussed in this book do not yet do so.

AMBIGUITIES OF DOMINATION

Symbolic power is inherently fragile and less determinate, but also more economical and more encompassing than forms of power involving overt violence and coercion. Exertions of symbolic power in authoritarian regimes tend not only to invite transgression but also to define what thoughts and practices are deemed transgressive. In Syria, the existence of contestations about the cult testifies to the power of the rhetoric's absurd statements. And yet if the cult of Asad is a holding in reserve of police violence, then the shared sensibility of unbelief, along with parodic television skits, films, and jokes may also be a holding in reserve of a potential counter-violence.

This recognition of ambiguity is not to be confused with what some social scientists might call the "unfalsifiability" of my underlying argument. This account could be falsified by demonstrating the existence of a regime in which tired slogans and empty gestures foster allegiance and actually generate people's emotional commitments to the regime. Moreover, this work does not imply that the cult is the only way to produce power for a regime. The absence of a cult (in Asad's aftermath, for example) would probably mean that other disciplinary controls would be needed to sustain obedience. A post-Asad regime might increase its use of brute force, or it might introduce liberal market mechanisms as another way to regulate citizens.[20] Or it might fall from power. Under Asad, the cult has so far been an effective means by which mundane practices reproduce the regime's dominance by normalizing external compliance in ways that are often prosaic, banal, and powerful.

The ambiguities generated by a politics of "as if," in particular, may have to do with the ways in which public dissimulation depends, in part, on self-enforcement. The cult's logic is clear, its effects interpretable, and yet it is unlikely that anyone specifically designed a policy calling for transparently phony rituals of obeisance. For this reason, the significance of official discourses is to be found, in Foucault's terms, in "the conditions of their manifest appearance," the "transformation which they have effected," and "the field where they coexist, reside, and disappear," rather than in "silently intended meanings," or in the explicit intentions of leaders who formulate these discourses.[21] In other words, if we look at cults as strategies without a strategist that produce citizens' compliance and resistance, rather than as a series of policy initiatives, it becomes possible to grasp the political importance of the cult without relying on unanswerable questions of intention. The cult has consequences whether or not anyone intended them, or it.

This "Foucaultian" claim of strategies without a strategist might seem out of place when applied to an authoritarian political environment. Indeed, Asad's rule is often characterized as "personalistic," suggesting anything but the sorts of self-enforcing mechanisms to which this book has largely been devoted. And yet even in authoritarian regimes, where control is relatively hierarchical and concentrated in the form of one sovereign, be it a single political party or a leader, power is nevertheless multiplied and diffused through people's everyday habits of conformity and the meanings they attach to them. There is no all-powerful person who manipulates the world at will and brings about political changes all by himself. Rather, there are perceptions and practices, internalized by citizens and made manifest in a historically contingent process of regime survival. The effectiveness of authoritarian power in Syria resides not only in the technologies available to monitor and punish some citizens while rewarding others, but also in the ways in which coercive power is made disciplinary, often through patently spurious discursive practices that require the cooperation and participation of the regime's citizenry.

The habituation to obedience—the combination of cynical lack of belief and compliant behavior—may be characteristic of authoritarian regimes, but it is not confined to those settings. Havel invites us to consider the former authoritarian politics of Eastern Europe as simply "an inflated caricature of modern life in general," another form of consumer and industrial society, which stands "as a kind of warning to the West, revealing [the latter's] own latent tendencies." Havel claims that in the West the "effortless spread of social auto-totality" is connected to the reluctance of consumption-oriented people "to sacrifice some material certainties for the sake of their own spiritual and moral integrity."[22] Havel treats such "integrity" as if it were natural to humans rather than learned. But his observation that all regimes rely on self-enforcing mechanisms suggests that the experiences of obedience and complicity identified in authoritarian circumstances have analogues in Western consumer-capitalist countries. In the latter, Havel suggests, people opt for complacency and material certainty over the possibility of satisfaction gained by leading an engaged political life. Žižek, too, identifies the combination of cynicism and compliant behavior not only in the East European "split" between public dissimulation and private belief, but also in what he discerns as the Western Enlightenment's paradoxical celebration of public freedoms and private submissions to authority. Kant, according to Žižek, was "not simply restating the common motto of conformism, 'in private, think whatever you want, but in public, obey the authorities!,' but rather [articulating] its opposite: in public, 'as a scholar before the reading public,' use your reason freely, yet in private (at your post, in your family, i.e., as a cog in the social machine) obey authority!"[23] Žižek's reading of Kant may be disputable, as is his conflation of private authority with the "social" dynamics of bureaucratic rule, but his main point is helpful. In both authoritarian and "post-ideological" Western liberal contexts, Žižek notes, "even if we do not take things seriously, even if we keep an ironical distance, *we are still doing them.*"[24] And "doing them," that is to say, behaving obediently, is what counts politically.

Certainly there are significant differences between authoritarian regimes and liberal "democratic" ones. Cynicism and parody do not operate everywhere with the same effects and the same relevance to politics. In liberal democratic regimes, there are institutional-ized checks and balances on the power of rulers, and competition for election is somewhat open, even if, at least in the American context, dominated by money. As a rule, moreover, most personal freedoms in a liberal context enjoy legal protection, while in au-thoritarian regimes they do not. Liberal regimes have a measure of hegemonic security that most authoritarian ones lack. People seem to embrace the principles of democratic citizenship even if many do not have access to or are cynical about their fulfillment. In this sense, the relatively nonhegemonic, transparently phony character of Syria's discursive universe may make the polity more vulner-able to conflict and more unstable than a regime that can win the "hearts and minds" of its citizens. The fact that liberal forms of power are not as dependent on the acumen or whim of individual leaders as authoritarian forms also makes liberal regimes seem par-ticularly durable, natural, and for many, desirable. In this sense, Syria remains open to radical contestation, especially in the after-math of Asad's rule, in a way that seems remote from the American example.

The point is not to collapse experiences of Western liberal de-mocracies into those of authoritarian rule or vice-versa, but to un-settle the attitudes of some who see in the fall of communism the triumph of democratic citizenship, or who might interpret this study to be solely about authoritarian "otherness." By tracking the politics of rhetoric and symbols in a particularly dramatic, but am-biguous, case, I want to invite others to rethink the ways in which political spectacles (from made-for-television national party con-ventions in the United States to cults of personality in postcolonial countries) help to foreclose possibilities for political thought and action, making it hard either to imagine or enact a truly democratic politics.

CONCLUSIONS

An emphasis on everyday political realities and on the symbolic mechanisms of control that inform political life has implications for the ways in which both compliance with regime requirements and political symbolism are understood. The questions posed by Max Weber, "When and why do men obey? Upon what inner justifications and upon what external means does this domination rest?" have remained central to the study of politics.[25] The answer mostly has taken the form either of accounts of political "authority" or "legitimacy" based on Weber's ideal typology (traditional, charismatic, and legal-rational) or of compliance mechanisms such as those discussed above (normative, instrumental, and coercive). People obey because they believe in the values, norms, and standards within which a particular regime operates, because it is in their material interest to do so, or because they fear the coercive consequences of *not* obeying. All of these are no doubt good explanations of why people obey, but they remain incomplete. They fail to account for the ways in which language and symbols mediate, structure, define, and continually reassert political power and obedience.

Beyond the barrel of the gun and the confines of the torture chamber, political cults work to generate compliance by producing, through symbolic displays, the potential for coercive power while also economizing on its actual use. A leader's control over intelligence networks and coup-deterring elite militias may be critically important to the maintenance of his/her power, but coercive control itself relies as much on the threat as on the fact of being used. The threat is sustained not only by occasionally deploying police and army units to eliminate organized opposition, but also through signifying practices such as those constitutive of Asad's cult. The Syrian case suggests that these practices help to ensure people's habitual obedience, specifying the terms of citizens' conformity in displays of public dissimulation and rhetorical excess.

Asad's cult is part of the way in which the Syrian regime tries to manage contests over signification. In exercising its capacity to appropriate meanings and to insist on the momentary stability of signs, the regime advertises its power. By representing this power the regime creates it anew, continually upholding the circumstances that produce citizens' compliance. As illustrated by an insightful Syrian joke, Asad is powerful because citizens make him so: **The reporter goes to the Pharaoh and asks him, "why did you become a sun god?" The Pharaoh replies, "because no one stopped me."** By imposing its fictions, the regime may not be able to create an extraordinary leader, in Weber's sense of the charismatic individual believed to be endowed with supernatural powers, but it does make Asad extra-ordinary in the sense that people are publicly obedient to *him*. [26] The fact that people watch others behave sycophantically and submissively toward Asad consistently re-produces this extra-ordinariness.

All polities have some way of generating the shared orientation that is constitutive of political membership. In the postcolonial context, where regimes are often forced to build an effective state and enforce their dominance *while* cultivating a sense of national identification, political cults, in particular, may serve to redefine the terms of national membership by both occasioning the enforcement of compliance and also generating the shared experience of that compliance. In such cases, membership rests, in part, on the generalized orientation toward public conduct and speech a cult provides. Cults may also contribute to nation-state building by helping to territorialize official politics. It is generally within the boundaries of the nation-state that people from the Syrian capital and its hinterlands, for example, are exposed to countless photographs of Asad and are expected to chant the slogans and listen to the panegyrics lauding the president's accomplishments. National membership is expressed through people's facility with the vocabulary and the regime's ability to reproduce the symbolism of Asad's rule. The nation-state, in this sense, extends as far as the cult does.

Asad's cult and the features it seems to share with post-Stalinist East European political cults and ideology suggest a potentially general understanding of language and symbols as political strategies that clutter public space, producing acts of narration that are depoliticizing.[27] This study invites further research on the ways in which political cults and ideological formulations might have similar disciplinary effects in any non-revolutionary or post-national-liberation regime. In places that have (or had) political cults, such as Zaire, Haiti, Rumania, Iran (under the Shah), or the Philippines, to name a few, the rhetoric and iconography may also work to enforce obedience and induce complicity, perhaps even less ambiguously than in Syria where aspects of regime rule (as opposed to cult practice) can produce belief in the regime's appropriateness.

Arab countries suggestive of fruitful comparative analysis include Jordan and Tunisia. Even a casual acquaintance with these cases reveals forms of symbolic rule and evidence of popular ambiguity that call for comparative investigation. In Jordan, King Husayn is descended from the Prophet Muhammad and his rule is officially represented as being invested with the sanctity that his genealogy implies. Regime iconography depicts the king as guardian of Muslim holy places as well as leader of the nation-state; ideologues have a repertoire of resonant symbols with which to produce idealized, hagiographic versions of his rule. In Jordan, unlike in Syria, there is no single political party that mobilizes participants for the enactment of ritualized spectacles. Some scholars of Jordan, moreover, identify Husayn as "charismatic," thereby accepting widespread representations of the king without examining the relationships among the disciplinary dimensions of symbolism, the concept of charisma, and the fact of regime durability. A cursory look at Tunisia suggests another variation on cult practice. The cult of President Bin 'Ali is a second-generation one, emerging from that of the founder-hero, Habib Bourguiba, whom Bin 'Ali deposed in 1987. The Tunisian cult is much less intense than Syria's; posters are generally pervasive only during holidays or in the region from whence the President came. There are also no statues to immortalize the President. The presence of liberal market mechanisms of control, combined with a strong security force, may make the cult less necessary or desirable in the Tunisian case. In summary, the content and intensity of personality cults, the relative recourse made to police repression, the local institutions of mobilization, the presence of markets, and the ability of the regime to provide goods and services differ in these cases in ways that beckon comparison.

Liberal democracies generally do not rely on the "personality cult" of a particular leader. The survival strategies of the liberal state are based heavily on "voluntary" compliance, at least compared to the coercive controls of authoritarian regimes. By focusing on the existence of compliance mechanisms, however, this study implies that an analysis of what I have termed disciplinary-symbolic power is relevant to liberal, market-oriented regimes as well. Signifying practices that generate habitual obedience might help to explain why the institutions we define as democratic in the American context do not seem to stimulate engaged, lively political involvement among citizens. Spurious advertising claims saturate American politics. Money, much more than popular conviction, dominates electoral campaigns. Debate by television sound bite threatens to relocate political discussion to the self-consciously bogus world of consumer consumption. A *mentalité* of powerlessness, widespread and unmistakable, is no less real for being self-fulfilling.

Of course any regime's power is always partial, fragile, and subject to change or to renegotiation. The example of Syria makes apparent the paradoxical effects of symbolic mechanisms of social control. On the one hand, the cult is risky, as it invites the very subversion it seeks to manage. On the other hand, the methods of resistance open to most Syrians, although frequently courageous and ingenious, are by themselves incapable of significantly altering "the order of things." These forms of transgression, however, are nonetheless important: recognizing shared conditions of unbelief, creating foundations for alternatives, sustaining visions of collectivity and humanity always have the potential for political possibility. The fact that changes do take place, but almost always with reference to the language and symbols of the past, suggests the power of symbolic mechanisms of control. That a regime cannot completely control the significance or meanings of its symbols suggests the inherently intangible and contestable dimensions of any symbolic project. In other words, it suggests the central political importance of symbolic mechanisms of social control. Such findings are not meant to suggest that no charismatic leaders exist, that all regimes operate without requiring belief, or that symbols fail to generate feelings of loyalty and love of the ruler in the ruled, as some students of fascism, for example, claim they do. Rather, this study argues that language and symbols are politically fundamental even in the absence of belief or loyalty.

Examining political practices of obedience and also looking at the ways in which people subvert them suggests, as Paul Veyne puts it, that "political life does not gravitate exclusively to the poles of spontaneity and constraint. It is more varied."[28] This variety consists of constant friction along the demarcation lines between rulers and ruled, and within each person. Symbolic displays of power offer us the opportunity to "watch" these skirmishes as they are represented in a regime's idealized presentation of itself and in people's experience of their political lives.

CHAPTER ONE

1. Volker Perthes, *The Political Economy of Syria under Asad* (London: I.B. Taurus, 1995), p. 161.

2. Middle East Watch, *Syria Unmasked: The Suppression of Human Rights by the Asad Regime* (New Haven: Yale University Press, 1991), p. 30.

3. Interview with Syrian cartoonist ʿAli Farzat, September 1992.

4. Author's interview, 1996.

5. Children are mobilized through the regime's youth organizations. The group, Vanguard of the Baʿth (Talaʾiʿ al-Baʿth), organizes students in elementary school; the Revolutionary Youth Organization (Shabibat al-Thawra) takes charge of junior and senior high school students. These organizations are quasi-mandatory. The university students' union is not compulsory, but is the organization representative of Syria's university students and largely operates as a mechanism to monitor peers. These groups also participate in organizing military training in schools and universities, as well as recruiting students for elite military and intelligence training.

6. Author's interview, 1992. There are a number of such examples. One wealthy Sunni entrepreneur showed me that in the reception room of his large offices, for example, he has a gigantic portrait of Asad, a gift from an ʿAlawi general. Hanging opposite this portrait is the slogan of his factory, *Laqad karramna bani Adam,* a Qurʾanic verse which means "we have honored the sons of Adam" (17:70). Chuckling, the factory owner explained that he meant the juxtaposition of Asad's portrait with the Qurʾanic saying to demonstrate the contrasts between Asad's rule and his own in the factory. He was self-consciously   *161*

distancing himself while still seemingly conforming to the dictates of Asad's cult.

7. For example, a government official in charge of patriotic programs for Syrian youth told me that he understood the concept of "love for the pan-Arab nation" (*umma*) to be "just a slogan." Author's interview, 1992.

8. Author's interview, 1996. In numerous conversations, the words to describe the regime even by those who value its continued rule were *munafiq* (hypocritical) and *kadhdhab/kadhib* (lying). For a description of the ways in which lies saturate daily life and implicate ordinary citizens, see Usama Muhammad, "Sadiq al-kadhdhab, sadiq al-munafiq," in *al-Hayat*, June 1996, p. 8.

9. See Raymond A. Hinnebusch, *Peasant and Bureaucracy in Ba'thist Syria: The Political Economy of Rural Development* (Boulder: Westview Press, 1989), p. 302.

10. See Karl Marx, *The Eighteenth Brumaire of Louis Bonaparte* (New York: International Publishers, 1963).

11. See, for instance, Patrick Seale, *Asad: The Struggle for the Middle East* (Berkeley and Los Angeles: University of California Press, 1988), p. 339; Robert Scott Mason, "Government and Politics," chap. 4 in *Syria: A Country Study* (Washington, D.C.: Department of the Army, 1988), p. 212. Volker Perthes's *The Political Economy of Syria under Asad* is probably the most informative book on Syria to date, and although it too pays little attention to the cult, Perthes indicates that the cult seems to demand only outward signs of obedience, and implies that further exploration of the phenomenon might be of critical importance.

12. For an overview of the recent literature on authoritarianism in the Middle East, see Jill Crystal's "Authoritarianism and Its Adversaries in the Arab World," *World Politics* 46, no. 2 (January 1994): 262–89. All of the works Crystal discusses are primarily concerned with the causes of authoritarianism, rather than the conditions of its reproduction by regimes, and Crystal herself focuses mainly on "materialist" concerns. Yet, while claiming that ideology works to promote "legitimacy," she does suggest, without elaboration, that ideological conformity can have the effect of depoliticizing people (280–81)— a point that will become important as this study proceeds. See also anthropologist Abdellah Hammoudi's recent book *Master and Disciple: The Cultural Foundations of Moroccan Authoritarianism* (Chicago: University of Chicago Press, 1997). Unlike the books Crystal reviews,

Hammoudi's is an attempt to investigate the ideological and "cultural" bases of authoritarianism in Morocco. Hammoudi concludes that the foundations of authoritarianism are located in Sufi practices: relationships of "absolute authority and absolute submission" between Sufi master and disciple inform major aspects of Moroccan personal and political life, and operate to "legitimate" authoritarianism and to "repress" alternative understandings. Hammoudi seems more interested in repression than in the ways citizen-subjects are actually constituted under authoritarian regimes.

13. This formulation is overly general. Nevertheless, the recognition among "materialists" that the symbols of power may operate in contradiction to actual policies (e.g. conjuring up images of Gamal 'Abd al-Nasir in Syria while pursuing policies antithetical to pan-Arabism) has prompted many to dismiss or ignore symbolism and official rhetoric altogether, rather than to explore the nature of the disjuncture.

14. See, for example, Raymond Hinnebusch, *Authoritarian Power and State Formation in Syria: Army, Party, and Peasant* (Boulder: Westview Press, 1990); Steven Heydemann, *Successful Authoritarianism: The Social and Structural Origins of Populist Authoritarian Rule in Syria, 1946–1963* (rev. Ph.D. diss., Univ. of Chicago, January 1992); Elizabeth Picard, "Arab Military Politics: From Revolutionary Plot to Authoritarian Regime," in *The Arab State,* ed. Giacomo Luciani (London: Routledge, 1990).

15. This summary of the political culture school necessarily simplifies a complex group of approaches. The "classic" study is Gabriel A. Almond and Sidney Verba, *The Civic Culture: Political Attitudes and Democracy in Five Nations* (Princeton: Princeton University Press, 1963). For one of the most recent influential books in this genre, see Robert D. Putnam, Robert Leonardi, and Raffaella Y. Nanetti, *Making Democracy Work: Civic Traditions in Modern Italy* (Princeton: Princeton University Press, 1993). Arguments that use culture as the strong independent variable often ignore other domestic and international factors that govern decisions, facilitate coalitions, and possibly determine outcomes. For a critique of political culture studies of the Middle East, see Edward W. Said, *Orientalism* (New York: Vintage Books Edition, 1978); see especially pp. 284–328. For a critical but sympathetic discussion, see Gabriel Ben-Dor, "Political Culture Approach to Middle East Politics," *International Journal of Middle East*

Studies 8 (1977): 43–63. For a compelling critique of cultural "essentialism," see also Ronald Inden, *Imagining India* (Cambridge, Mass.: Blackwell, 1990). And for a political science analysis of political culture that combines anthropological insights from Clifford Geertz and Abner Cohen with Gramsci's understanding of hegemony, see David D. Laitin, *Hegemony and Culture: Politics and Religious Change among the Yoruba* (Chicago: University of Chicago Press, 1986).

16. In general, scholars of political culture fall into three traps. First, their arguments tend to be circular. Behavior implies values that then appear determinative of behavior. Second, scholars tend to be vague and slippery about the values they claim to identify as causes. Third, political culture analysts often fail to extend their argument to a comparison with other cases. Characteristics attributed to one allegedly bounded "political culture" are not necessarily peculiar to that experience. The notion of "culture" as a bounded entity in which identifiable essences inhere to a particular group has recently been revived by some rational choice theorists. See, for example, contributors in the *American Political Science Association–Comparative Politics Newsletter,* "Notes from the Annual Meetings: Culture and Rational Choice" (summer 1997): 5–21; and Avner Greif, "Cultural Beliefs and the Organization of Society: A Historical and Theoretical Reflection on Collectivist and Individualist Societies," *Journal of Political Economy* 102, no. 5 (1994): 912–50.

17. Clearly *compliance* and *obedience* do not mean exactly the same thing, although I use the two terms interchangeably in this book. In ordinary usage, "compliance" has the sense of yielding to another's desires or wishes, of accommodating another. "Obedience" conveys the sense of submitting to the rule and authority of another, compliance with or performance of command or law. One complies with wishes or demands, but obeys orders, commands, or laws. Being compliant is a character-trait; being obedient need not be. Political scientists, however, often use the term "compliance" in relationship to legal and political situations, a custom I follow.

18. I am indebted to an anonymous reader for the journal *Comparative Studies in Society and History,* who first formulated my project in this way.

19. My findings correspond to those of other observers of Syrian politics. See, for example, Hisham Melhem, "Syria between Two Transitions," in *Middle East Report* 27, no. 2 (spring 1997): 4. Recent

works on the Syrian regime's regional interests and the peace process include Alasdair Drysdale and Raymond E. Hinnebusch, *Syria and the Middle East Peace Process* (New York: Council on Foreign Relations Press, 1991); and Raymond E. Hinnebusch, "Does Syria Want Peace?" *Journal of Palestine Studies* (autumn 1996): 42–57.

20. Achille Mbembe notes in his study of postcolonial rule: "Elites try to impose their views and not, simultaneously. They seek to establish the legitimacy of their power and privilege but, at the same time, they can do without legitimacy." Achille Mbembe, "Prosaics of Servitude and Authoritarian Civilities," *Public Culture* 5, no. 1 (fall 1992): 128. Mbembe's conceptualization suggests that legitimacy is something that a regime either has or doesn't have. I want to suggest that "legitimacy" is a complex, usually contradictory bundle of beliefs and emotional commitments, but that nevertheless the cult does not operate primarily to produce "legitimacy" nor is it likely that regime officials expect to "impose their views" by producing preposterous claims.

21. Samuel P. Huntington, *The Third Wave: Democratization in the Late Twentieth Century* (Norman: University of Oklahoma Press, 1991), p. 46.

22. John H. Schaar, *Legitimacy in the Modern State* (New Brunswick: Transaction Publishers, 1989), p. 20.

23. 'Alawis make up 11 percent of the total population but hold a disproportionate number of key political and military positions. For sophisticated discussions of the 'Alawi character of the regime, see Yahya Sadowski, "Ba'thist Ethics and the Spirit of State Capitalism," in *Ideology and Power in the Middle East,* ed. Peter J. Chelkowski and Robert J. Pranger (Durham: Duke University Press, 1988), pp. 160–84; and Perthes, *Political Economy.* See also Elizabeth Picard, "Clans militaires et pouvoir ba'thiste en Syrie," *Orient* (1979): 49–62; and Hanna Batatu, "Some Observations on the Social Roots of Syria's Ruling Military Group and the Cause for Its Dominance," *Middle East Journal* 35 (summer 1982): 331–44.

24. For a description of Islamicist opposition to the regime, see Hanna Batatu, "Syria's Muslim Brethren," in *Middle East Report* 12, no. 9 (November–December 1982): 12–20, 34, 36; Fred H. Lawson, "Social Bases for the Hamah Revolt," *Middle East Report* 12, no. 9 (November–December 1982): 24–28. See also my chapters 2 and 5. After the massacre of Muslim Brotherhood and Islamicist forces

at Hama in 1982, Islamicist oppositional activity has been rare. But many Sunni Muslims attend mosque prayer on Fridays, participate in Qur'anic reading groups, and wear modest clothing.

Although it is difficult to measure, it seems to me (and to a number of my interview subjects in Damascus in particular) that more women are veiling in 1997, for example, than did in 1985. Many people (both women who wear the head scarf (*muhajjabat*) and men and women who do not) interpret the practice of veiling as signifying subtle Sunni distance from, if not opposition to the regime. Of course, the fact that the regime tolerates Islamic dress also suggests confidence among leaders that the practice no longer implies actual political threats to Asad's rule as it did in the late 1970s and early 1980s. Veiling is also a way to indicate piety, chastity, and to enable women to be in public places where they otherwise might feel uncomfortable. Approximately 80 percent of Syria's population is Sunni, and it is unclear how many are religious and whether the adoption of religious practices will have any political ramifications, especially in the aftermath of Asad's rule.

25. See George L. Mosse, *The Nationalization of the Masses: Political Symbolism and Mass Movements in Germany from the Napoleonic Wars through the Third Reich* (New York: New American Library, 1975), p. 4.

26. For a discussion of the impact of land reform on the Syrian countryside, see Hinnebusch, *Peasant and Bureaucracy*, p. 302. See also Françoise Métral, "Land Tenure and Irrigation Projects in Syria: 1948–1982," in *Land Tenure and Social Transformation in the Middle East*, ed. Tarif al-Khalidi (Beirut, 1984), pp. 465–81; and id., "State and Peasants in Syria: A Local View of a Government Irrigation Project," in *Arab Society: Social Science Perspectives*, ed. Nicholas Hopkins and Saad Eddin Ibrahim (Cairo: AUC Press, 1985), pp. 336–56; and Volker Perthes, "Social Structure and Class Relations," chap. 3 in *The Political Economy of Syria under Asad*.

27. Seymour Martin Lipset, *Political Man* (Garden City, N.Y.: Doubleday, 1960), p. 77, cited in Schaar, *Legitimacy in the Modern State*, p. 20. Weber's own understandings of the term are extremely slippery and complex. Weber sometimes seems to conflate "claims to legitimacy" with "belief in legitimacy" and with the "ideal types" of legitimate authority he uses to classify different modes of rule. See Max Weber, *Economy and Society*, ed. Guenther Roth and Claus Wittich (Berkeley and Los Angeles: University of California Press, 1978), pp. 212–54.

28. The most prominent opponents to Asad's rule were the Muslim Brotherhood and its Islamicist allies, who were defeated in Hama in 1982. Although some violent attacks were made in the mid-1980s, these were isolated events and it is unclear who or what groups engineered them. According to one scholar who studies Syria's opposition, the Islamic Front (al-Jabha al-Islamiyya fi Suriya), a coalition of *'ulama'* (Islamic clergy) and Islamicist groups has "ceased to exist, and in the early 1990s there is no organized Islamist movement inside the country." See Hans Gunter Lobmeyer, *"Al-dimuqratiyya hiyya [sic] al-hall? The Syrian Opposition at the End of the Asad Era,"* in *Contemporary Syria: Liberalization between Cold War and Cold Peace,* ed. Eberhard Kienle (London: I.B. Taurus, 1994), pp. 85–86. Organized secular opposition to the regime has also been effectively destroyed, and the leftist groups that remain are extremely weak. Among the secular parties who still have some members are the Party of Communist Action (Hizb al-'Amal al-Shuyu'i), the CP-Politbureau, and the oppositional wing of the Arab Socialist Union (ASU).

29. Perthes, *Political Economy;* Hinnebusch, *Peasants and Bureaucracy;* Sadowski, "Ba'thist Ethics"; Elisabeth Longuenesse, "Bourgeoisie, petite bourgeoisie et couches moyennes en Syrie: Contribution à une analyse de la nature de classe de L'état," *Peuples Mediterraneens,* no. 4 (July–September 1978): 21–42; Longuenesse, "The Class Nature of the State in Syria," *Middle East Research and Information Project Reports,* no. 77 (May 1979): 9–10.

30. Psychoanalytic accounts of fascism suggest that this connection is rooted in libidinal desires for the primal father or the mother, depending on the interpretation. Sigmund Freud, *Group Psychology and the Analysis of the Ego,* trans. James Strachey (London: Hogarth Press, 1949); Theodor W. Adorno, "Freudian Theory and the Pattern of Fascist Propaganda," in *The Essential Frankfurt School Reader* (New York: Urizen Books, 1978), pp. 118–37; Klaus Theweleit, *Male Fantasies* (Minneapolis: University of Minnesota Press, 1987).

31. For a discussion of the ways in which the "Fuhrer myth" reflected Hitler's popularity and also seemed to fulfill people's "yearnings for security, progress, and national greatness," see Detlev J. K. Peukert, *Inside Nazi Germany: Conformity, Opposition, and Racism in Everyday Life,* trans. Richard Deveson (New Haven: Yale University Press, 1982), p. 75.

32. Hannah Arendt, *Totalitarianism,* part 3 of *The Origins of Totalitarianism* (New York: Harcourt, Brace, 1968); Robert Tucker, "The

Dictator and Totalitarianism," *World Politics* 27, pp. 555–83. See also studies of Maoism, such as Mayfair Yang's *Gifts, Favors, and Banquets: The Art of Social Relationships in China* (Ithaca: Cornell University Press, 1994), especially pp. 245–86.

33. Interestingly, Gramsci himself does not give us a clear or precise definition of "hegemony." As Jean and John Comaroff rightly note, the definition most often quoted in recent commentaries—"the 'spontaneous' consent given by the great masses of the population to the general direction imposed on social life by the dominant fundamental group" is a description of what Gramsci called "the subaltern functions of social hegemony and political government." See A. Gramsci's *Selections from the Prison Notebooks*, ed. Quintin Hoare and Geoffrey Nowell-Smith (London: Laurence and Wishart, 1971), p. 12. There are dozens of references to hegemony in the text, but no single dominant meaning. The point is not to determine Gramsci's intended definition, but to show the ways in which the term is commonly used in scholarly works.

David Laitin, for example, defines hegemony as "the political forging—whether through coercion or elite bargaining—and institutionalization of a pattern of group activity in a state and the concurrent idealization of that schema into a dominant symbolic framework that reigns as common sense." See Laitin, *Hegemony and Culture*, p. 19. See also John Gaventa, *Power and Powerlessness: Quiescence and Rebellion in an Appalachian Valley* (Urbana: University of Illinois Press, 1980), which is cited at length in James C. Scott's critique of hegemony; and James C. Scott, *Domination and the Arts of Resistance: Hidden Transcripts* (New Haven: Yale University Press, 1990). For a lucid treatment of the concept, see Jean Comaroff and John Comaroff, *Of Revelation and Revolution*, vol. 1, *Christianity, Colonialism, and Consciousness in South Africa* (Chicago: University of Chicago Press, 1991), especially chap. 1.

34. Stuart Hall, "The Toad in the Garden: Thatcherism among the Theorists," in *Marxism and the Interpretation of Culture*, ed. Cary Nelson and Lawrence Grossberg (Urbana: University of Illinois Press, 1988), p. 44. Hall's interpretation of this term is similar to Raymond Williams's characterization in *Marxism and Literature* (London: Oxford University Press, 1977), 108f.; see ibid., n. 14.

35. Comaroff and Comaroff, *Revelation and Revolution*, p. 23. See also Pierre Bourdieu, *Outline of a Theory of Practice*, trans. Richard Nice (Cambridge: Cambridge University Press, 1977), p. 94.

36. See Louis Althusser, "Ideology and Ideological State Apparatuses (Notes towards an Investigation)," in *Lenin and Philosophy and Other essays by Louis Althusser* (New York: Monthly Review Press, 1971), p. 168; and Stuart Hall, "Signification, Representation, Ideology: Althusser and the Post-Structuralist Debates," in *Critical Studies in Mass Communication* 2, no. 2 (June 1985): 100.

37. Althusser, "Ideology," p. 169.

38. Ibid.

39. Many works might fall under the rubric of "spectacles." Of those, some key works that do not get discussed in-depth in this study are the following: Guy Debord's *Society of the Spectacle* (Detroit: Black and Red, 1983), which was one of the first works to examine what he might have termed the "culture of spectacles." Debord focuses primarily on the contemporary Western experience and on the Stalinist Soviet Union. In Michael Rogin, *Ronald Reagan, the Movie, and Other Episodes in Political Demonology* (Berkeley and Los Angeles: University of California Press, 1987), and id., "'Make My Day!': Spectacle as Amnesia in Imperial Politics," in *The New Historicism Reader*, ed. H. Aram Veeser (New York and London: Routledge, 1994), pp. 229–54, Rogin examines the countersubversive tradition central to American politics. In essays relating politics to Hollywood movies, Rogin argues that films represent and shape political sensibilities, and political realities sometimes seem indiscernible from filmic fantasies. Murray Edelman, another political scientist, argues that "spectacles" and "art" influence public perceptions, opinions, and policy-making. See Murray Edelman, *From Art to Politics: How Artistic Creations Shape Political Conceptions* (Chicago: University of Chicago Press, 1995); id., *Constructing the Political Spectacle* (Chicago: University of Chicago Press, 1988). Michel Foucault's works have inspired a number of theorists to write on spectacle. Thomas Laqueur, for example, develops insights produced by Foucault and places them in the English context in his essay, "Crowds, Carnival and the State in English Executions, 1604–1868," in *The First Modern Society*, ed. A. L. Beier, David Cannadine, and James M. Rosenheim (Cambridge: Cambridge University Press, 1989), pp. 305–55.

40. See, for example, Clifford Geertz's *Negara: The Theater State in Nineteenth-Century Bali* (Princeton: Princeton University Press, 1980).

41. Ibid. See also Clifford Geertz, "Centers, Kings, and Charisma," in *Local Knowledge: Further Essays in Interpretive Anthropology* (New York: Basic Books, 1983), especially pp. 130 and 134.

42. See also Frances A. Yates, *Astraea: The Imperial Theme in the Sixteenth Century* (London: Ark Paperbacks, 1975), pp. 124–26. On the cult of Queen Elizabeth I, see also Roy Strong, *The Cult of Elizabeth: Elizabethan Portraiture and Pageantry* (Berkeley and Los Angeles: University of California Press, 1977).

43. Yates, *Astraea*, p. 101.

44. Ibid., p. 111.

45. Mona Ozouf, *Festivals and the French Revolution*, trans. Alan Sheridan (Cambridge: Harvard University Press, 1988), p. 83. See also pp. 41, 43, 44, 54, 79, 117.

46. James Von Geldern, *Bolshevik Festivals 1917–1921* (Berkeley and Los Angeles: University of California Press, 1993), p. 10.

47. For a discussion of "invented tradition" in the Israeli context, see Yael Zerubavel's *Recovered Roots: Collective Memory and the Making of Israeli National Tradition* (Chicago: University of Chicago Press, 1995); and id., "The Historic, The Legendary and the Incredible: Invented Tradition and Collective Memory in Israel," in *Commemorations: The Politics of National Identity* (Princeton: Princeton University Press, 1994), pp. 105–23.

48. See E. J. Hobsbawm and Terence Ranger, *The Invention of Tradition* (Cambridge: Cambridge University Press, 1983).

49. Scholars of revolutionary spectacles, in particular, show how festivals "recast space and time." Ozouf argues, for example, that revolutionary planners in France attempted to erase spatial and temporal reminders of the past by avoiding the processional routes favored by the Catholic Church and by the French monarchy. Revolutionaries constructed new calendars to express their fundamental break with the past. Ibid., chaps. 6 and 7. In Bolshevik Russia, in Robespierre's France, and in Queen Elizabeth's England, the state's secular holidays replaced the Church's religious ones, or religious ones were renamed to fill the void left by the intended destruction of an ecclesiastical past. The last Shah of Iran also attempted to create a new calendar, not, however, to symbolize a break from the past, but to reaffirm "traditions" that had been threatened by reforms.

50. In Elizabethan England and sixteenth-century France, according to Yates, symbols functioned to "buttress" the monarchy and to undermine the papacy. Yates, *Astraea*, pp. 9–10. In Morocco, "sacred performances" have consistently "renewed the power and legitimacy of the Moroccan monarchy," an institution that has existed for over twelve hundred years. See M. E. Combs-Schilling, *Sacred Performances:*

Islam, Sexuality, and Sacrifice (New York: Columbia University Press, 1989), p. 186. In Iraq, the state's attempts to "penetrate 'low culture' initially represented an attempt to enhance its legitimacy" relative to that of its rival, the Iraqi Communist party. See Eric Davis, "The Museum and the Politics of Social Control in Modern Iraq," in *Commemorations: The Politics of National Identity*, ed. John R. Gillis (Princeton: Princeton University Press, 1994), p. 99.

I do not mean to suggest that Davis argues that the revival of folklore served *only* to legitimate the regime. Davis does mention at the beginning of the article that "even the most repressive regimes, of which the Iraqi Ba'th is an exemplar, seek to develop ideologies that generate 'self-discipline' among the populace at large" (p. 90). But he does not develop this point. Or, according to another observer of Iraq, the Ba'thist regime of Saddam Husayn created spectacles and enacted charades, such as the January 1969 hangings or the 1979 purge trials, that symbolized "the general process of legitimation"—a legitimation based on fear and "designed to adduce 'proof' of the organic relationship between Ba'thism and its masses." See Kanan Makiya, *Republic of Fear*, p. 235. Bolshevik festivals were intended to "propagate legitimizing genealogies," and the Bolshevik party sought "to develop new identities that would legitimize its rule." Spectacles have the potential power to "sway minds," a function that appealed to both Robespierre and the Bolsheviks, according to James Von Geldern. Von Geldern, *Bolshevik Festivals*, pp. 12–13.

51. Mona Ozouf, by generally avoiding reliance on terms such as "legitimacy," rightly challenges an understanding of spectacle that conflates the effects of spectacle with the intentions of ideologues. Nevertheless, it remains unclear in Ozouf's treatment what spectacles *do* do. Her discussions of the results of spectacles can be ambiguous and confusing. For instance, she argues that the festivals failed to provide a compelling substitute for Catholicism, while also asserting that festivals were able to "sacralize" new values: "The transfer of sacrality onto political and social values was now accomplished, thus defining a new legitimacy." See Ozouf, *Festivals and the French Revolution*, p. 282. Ozouf's account is influenced by Emile Durkheim's work on religion and community.

52. Louis Marin's *Portrait of the King* emphasizes the mimetic dimensions of absolutist spectacles. Marin's concern with the ways in which power is defined and represented through the ruler's image as exemplar coincides with Geertz's formulations in *Negara*. But unlike

Geertz, Marin's work is structured by a Lacanian understanding of the *imaginaire.* Marin's formulations of the relationship between representation and power, although provocative, remain ambiguous and sometimes tendentiously asserted, as in his assumptions about how these texts were received and interpreted. Readers of the official royal historical narrative are presumed to be admiring, to take pleasure in, and be captivated by texts glorifying the King. At times, he suggests that readers are supposed to believe what the text represents, and to imagine themselves at the King's side. See Louis Marin, *Portrait of the King,* in Theory and History of Literature, vol. 57, trans. Martha M. Houle (Minneapolis: University of Minnesota Press, 1988).

53. For an explanation of the "interpretive" approach in anthropology, see Paul Rabinow and William M. Sullivan, eds. *Interpretive Social Science: A Second Look* (Berkeley and Los Angeles: University of California Press, 1987). See especially id., "The Interpretive Turn: A Second Look," pp. 1–30; Geertz's well-known essay "Deep Play: Notes on the Balinese Cockfight" is also reprinted here. But the more persuasive interpretive analysis by Geertz is presented in his case study, *Negara: The Theatre State in Nineteenth Century Bali.* For a discussion of Geertz's interpretive analytic, see Clifford Geertz, *The Interpretation of Cultures* (New York: Basic Books, 1980), and id., *Local Knowledge: Further Essays in Interpretive Anthropology.*

54. Geertz, *Negara,* p. 120.

55. These formulations of "state" and "nation" are not meant to be definitive, but are rather intended to get at the difference between state- and nation-building. Indeed, major problems in the scholarship are what is *meant* by "nation," "state," and "nationalism" and how applicable generalizations based on early modern European history are to late twentieth-century regimes like Syria. As Timothy Mitchell points out, the state is both a system of formal governmental institutions and a "common ideological and cultural construct" that "occurs not merely as a subjective belief, incorporated in the thinking and action of individuals [but] represented and reproduced in visible everyday forms." See Timothy Mitchell, "The Limits of the State: Beyond Statist Approaches and Their Critics," *American Political Science Review* 85, no. 1 (March 1991): 81.

56. Charles Tilly, "On the History of European State-Making," in *The Formation of National States in Western Europe* (Princeton: Princeton University Press, 1975), p. 6; Gianfranco Poggi, *The Development of the Modern State: A Sociological Introduction* (Stanford: Stanford

University Press, 1978); Perry Anderson, *Lineages of the Absolutist State* (London: Verso, 1979), especially chaps. 1, 2, 4, 5. For essays on states as "organizational structures" or as "potentially autonomous actors," see Peter B. Evans et al., eds., *Bringing the State Back In* (Cambridge: Cambridge University Press, 1985). For a discussion of state-formation as a structured, long-term process of development in which kings and aristocrats gradually became increasingly dependent on and constrained by subjects who were themselves increasingly disciplined or "civilized," see Norbert Elias, *Power and Civility*, vol. 2 of *The Civilizing Process* (New York: Random House, 1982).

57. Eric Hobsbawm, *Nations and Nationalism since 1780* (Cambridge: Cambridge University Press, 1990); id., *The Age of Empire, 1875–1914* (New York: Random House, 1987), chap. 6. For a discussion of the evolution of the nation-state, see Ernest Gellner, *Nations and Nationalism* (Oxford: Basil Blackwell, 1983). In a yet unpublished article, "The French Revolution and the Emergence of the Nation Form," William H. Sewell Jr. argues that the nation "as the principle of sovereignty" was established by the French revolutionaries during the summer and early fall of 1789. Although the nation had figured in French political discourse before the revolution, its meaning changed with the proclamation of the new National Assembly. As Sewell argues, "the King, who had previously been the sovereign, now became a *representative* of the nation—a particularly august representative to be sure, but nonetheless ultimately subordinate to the nation's will" (p. 5).

58. Liah Greenfeld, *Nationalism: Five Roads to Modernity* (Cambridge: Harvard University Press, 1992); "Transcending the Nation's Worth," *Daedalus* 122, no. 3 (summer 1993): 47–62. Greenfeld's understanding of the early modern origins of "modern" British nationalism is shared by an increasing number of British historians.

59. Eugen Weber, *Peasants into Frenchmen* (London: Chatto and Windus, 1979); and Susan Cotts Watkins, *From Provinces into Nations* (Princeton: Princeton University Press, 1991).

60. Hobsbawm, *Nations and Nationalism since 1780;* Gellner, *Nations and Nationalism.*

61. The nation, in this respect, is one form of what Benedict Anderson calls "imagined communities." Benedict Anderson, *Imagined Communities,* rev. ed. (1983; London: Verso, 1991).

62. Arab nationalism first arose in the nineteenth century as a reaction against the Ottoman Empire. For important and divergent

views, see George Antonius, *The Arab Awakening: The Story of the Arab National Movement* (London: H. Hamilton, 1938); Sylvia Haim, *Arab Nationalism: An Anthology* (Berkeley and Los Angeles: University of California Press, 1962); Albert Hourani, *Arabic Thought in the Liberal Age, 1798–1939* (London: Oxford University Press, 1962); C. Ernest Dawn, *From Ottomanism to Arabism: Essays on the Origins of Arab Nationalism* (Urbana: University of Illinois Press, 1973); Philip S. Khoury, *Urban Notables and Arab Nationalism* (Cambridge: Cambridge University Press, 1983); Rashid Khalidi et al., eds., *The Origins of Arab Nationalism* (New York: Columbia University Press, 1991).

63. Clifford Geertz, "The Integrative Revolution: Primordial Sentiments and Civil Politics in the New States," in *The Interpretation of Cultures* (New York: Basic Books, 1980), pp. 255–310; Nikolaos van Dam discusses the sectarian, regional, and tribal rivalries within the Syrian armed forces and in the Ba'th party in his book, *The Struggle for Power in Syria: Sectarianism, Regionalism, and Tribalism in Politics, 1961–1978* (New York: St. Martin's Press, 1979).

64. For a recent scholarly account of the state's failure to realize the national aspirations of Arabs, see Burhan Ghalioun, *Le malaise arabe: L'état contre la nation* (Paris: Éditions la Découverte, 1991).

65. For a description of the way in which the state has used patronage services in order to channel scarce resources, see Sadowski, "Ba'thist Ethics." For a description of state policy toward economic "development," see Hinnebusch, *Peasant and Bureaucracy.* For a discussion of the importance of the state in promoting economic development among "late-developing countries," see Alexander Gerschenkron, *Economic Backwardness in Historical Perspective* (Cambridge: Belknap Press of Harvard University Press, 1962), pp. 5–30, 353–64.

66. This is also the case for "systems-building" regimes. See Ken Jowitt, *New World Disorder: The Leninist Extinction* (Berkeley and Los Angeles: University of California Press, 1992), pp. 61–62; see also ibid., pp. 8–11 for a discussion of Stalin's cult; Ernst H. Kantorowicz, *The King's Two Bodies: A Study of Medieval Political Theology* (Princeton: Princeton University Press, 1957). Kantorowicz argues that in France the state became "a personification in its own right which was not only above its members, but also divorced from them" (p. 382).

67. Jowitt, *New World Disorder*, pp. 91–92, n. 9.

68. The "physiological fiction" of the King's Two Bodies was especially developed in Tudor England. For instance, the Elizabethan jurist Edmund Plowden wrote, "The king has in him two Bodies, a Body natural and a Body politic. His Body natural . . . is a Body mortal, subject to all infirmities that come by Nature or Accident. But his Body politic is a Body that cannot be seen or handled . . . and this Body is utterly void of Infancy, and old Age, and other natural Defects and Imbecilities." Kantorowicz, *The King's Two Bodies*, p. 7; Rogin, *Ronald Reagan, the Movie*, p. 81. In France under Louis XIV, leader and state were even less distinguishable than in England, as suggested by the King's famous claim, "l'état c'est moi." Kantorowicz argues that in France, the individual living king had features of a *persona idealis.* The Crown in late Medieval England was not a fictitious person such as the continental "state" became during the sixteenth century and especially under Louis XIV. Statements like "le roi ne meurt jamais" were current in France since the sixteenth century, p. 409. For an especially insightful discussion of the ways in which Louis XIV's regime disciplined the court aristocracy, see Norbert Elias, *The Court Society,* trans. Edmund Jephcott (New York: Random House, Pantheon Books: 1983).

69. In *Economy and Society*, Max Weber defines the charisma of office to mean "the belief in the specific state of grace of a social institution," p. 1140. For the "routinization of charisma," see pp. 246–51; for a discussion of "legal authority," see pp. 215–26.

70. Broadcast on 11 March 1980; cited from Moshe Maoz, *The Sphinx of Damascus* (New York: Weidenfeld and Nicolson, 1988), pp. 156–57.

71. It is interesting to note that Queen Elizabeth I assumed both the pastoral persona of a queen of shepherds and that of a humble milkmaid. Louis Adrian Montrose argues that Elizabeth created for herself a "rustic, 'mere English' version of pastoral," which suggests to me the beginnings of national consciousness in England. But for Montrose Elizabeth used such rhetoric to affirm that "she herself is *not* a milkmaid." See Montrose, "'Eliza, Queene of Shepheardes' and the Pastoral of Power," in *The New Historicism Reader,* ed. H. Aram Veeser (New York and London: Routledge, 1994), p. 90. None of the monarchical cults could ever have asserted the democratic, leveling claim: "X is no one but one of you."

72. Of course, Hobbes would have hated such mysticism.

73. I am indebted to an anonymous reader for the journal *Comparative Studies in Society and History* for the formulation of this insight.

74. For examples in Middle Eastern studies, see Timothy Mitchell's *Colonising Egypt* (Berkeley and Los Angeles: University of California Press, 1991), which draws on Foucault and Jacques Derrida to document and analyze the disciplinary effects produced by British colonial rule in Egypt. His is one of the most compelling uses of poststructuralist theory in the Middle Eastern context. See also Brinkley Messick, *The Calligraphic State: Textual Domination and History in Muslim Society* (Berkeley and Los Angeles: University of California Press, 1993), which analyzes the changing relationship between Islamic writings and "authority" in the "textual polity" of Yemen.

75. To name a few: Elaine Scarry, *The Body in Pain: The Making and Unmaking of the World* (New York: Oxford University Press, 1985); Thomas Laqueur, *Making Sex: Body and Gender from the Greeks to Freud* (Cambridge: Harvard University Press, 1990); id., "Orgasm, Generation, and the Politics of Reproductive Biology," *Representations*, no. 14 (spring 1986): 1–41. Other antecedents include Kantorowicz's pioneering and brilliant study of the Tudor "physiological" fiction that connected the mortal body of the king to the immortal body of the realm, *The King's Two Bodies*.

76. Michel Foucault, *Discipline and Punish: The Birth of the Prison*, trans. Alan Sheridan (New York: Random House, Vintage Books, 1979), p. 194.

77. Ibid., pp. 293–308.

78. See T. Fujitani, *Splendid Monarchy: Power and Pageantry in Modern Japan* (Berkeley and Los Angeles: University of California Press, 1996), p. 26.

79. For the ways in which public narratives frame understandings of citizenship in the American context, see Lauren Berlant's *The Queen of America Goes to Washington City: Essays on Sex and Citizenship* (Durham: Duke University Press, 1997). Berlant makes the important point that people are not consumed by their identity as citizens even during political campaigns or patriotic events. "Yet the rhetoric of citizenship does provide important definitional frames for the ways people see themselves as *public,* when they do" (p. 10). She also intentionally uses the language of advertising to describe the ways in which certain conceptions of national life deploy the "very strategies of linking happiness to desire that advertising uses" (p. 11).

80. Unofficial reports claim that at least two children died of sunstroke during drilling because insufficient water and protection were provided. People from different regions and different class backgrounds told me the story, but there was no way to verify it; the story may have been a widespread rumor, but it is plausible. According to interviews with a member of the Sports Federation who was responsible for organizing the opening ceremony, women participants who told their trainers that they might be menstruating during the ceremonies were given pills to inhibit menstruation.

81. See, for instance, Ian Buruma, "Playing for Keeps," *New York Review of Books,* 10 November 1988, pp. 44–50. For a description of "mass Games" in North Korea, see Urban C. Lehner, "Group Think, For North Koreans' Mass Games Are Sport—and Indoctrination," *Wall Street Journal,* 15 August 1989, p. 1; Kong Dan Oh, *Leadership Change in North Korean Politics: The Succession to Kim Il Sung* (Santa Monica: Rand Corporation, 1988), pp. 2, 24–26.

82. Archival research was conducted at the Asad Library in Damascus (Maktabat al-Asad), the Ministry of Foreign Affairs in Paris (Ministère des Affaires Étrangères) and the Ministry of Defense, Vincennes (Ministère de la Défense). In 1985, while studying Arabic, I lived with a Lebanese family in Abu Rummaneh, an affluent neighborhood of Damascus. In 1988–1989, under the auspices of an IIE-Fulbright grant, I lived in the women's dormitories at the University of Damascus, in the Palestinian refugee camps, and in a rented apartment in Salahiyya, a middle-class neighborhood near the center of town. In 1992, I rented an apartment on the border of the middle-class, conservative neighborhood of Muhajirin during a year-long stay supported by a Fulbright-Hays doctoral dissertation fellowship. And in 1996, funded by a grant from Wesleyan University, I returned for the summer and lived in the Institut Français d'Études Arabes de Damas. During the course of my research, I interviewed over one hundred people, including prominent government officials, leaders and rank-and-file members of the "popular" organizations, peasants, sports coaches, school teachers, principals, entrepreneurs, artists, poets, film directors, economists, historians, and political dissidents. The majority of these interviews were conducted in Arabic. Many of those interviewed must remain anonymous.

83. William H. Sewell Jr., "The Concept(s) of Culture," in *Beyond the Cultural Turn: History and Sociology in the Age of Paradigm Breakdown,* ed. Victoria Bonnell and Lynn Hunt (Berkeley and Los Ange-

les: University of California Press, forthcoming), discusses the slippery usages of the term "culture" in anthropology and sociology. As Sherry Ortner suggests, if we think of culture not as "a deeply sedimented essence attaching to or inhering in particular groups," but rather as the activity of "meaning-*making*," then we can examine the ways in which symbolic constructions are generated and received by "real historical actors," who are "always trying to make sense of their lives, always weaving fabrics of meaning, however fragile and fragmentary." Sherry B. Ortner, "Introduction," *Representations* 59 (summer 1997): 8–9.

84. See Sherry B. Ortner, *Making Gender: The Politics and Erotics of Culture* (Boston: Beacon Press, 1996), chap. 1. Like Ortner I do not think one has to choose between "total constructionism and total voluntarism, between the Foucauldian discursively constructed (and subjected) subject, or the free agent of Western fantasy" (p. 11).

85. See Comaroff and Comaroff, *Of Revelation and Revolution*, 1:17.

86. See H. Aram Veeser, *The New Historicism Reader* (New York: Routledge, 1994), p. 2. This understanding of the relationship of critical thought to power draws from the work of Michel Foucault. In *The History of Sexuality, Volume One*, Foucault asks: "Did the critical discourse that addresses itself to repression come to act as a roadblock to a power mechanism that had operated unchallenged up to that point, or is it not in fact part of the same historical network as the thing it denounces (and doubtless misrepresents) by calling it 'repression'? Was there really a historical rupture between the age of repression and the critical analysis of repression?" (p. 10).

87. For a provocative critique of Foucault's formulation of power, see Neil Brenner, "Foucault's New Functionalism," *Theory and Society* 23 (1994): 679–709.

88. Most of the writings that deal directly with authoritarianism were published prior to the 1980s. See, for example, Juan Linz, "Totalitarian and Authoritarian Regimes," in *Macropolitical Theory*, vol. 3 of *Handbook of Political Science*, ed. Fred Greenstein and Nelson Polsby (Reading, Mass.: Addison-Wesley, 1975); and Samuel P. Huntington and Clement Moore, eds. *Authoritarian Politics in Modern Society* (New York: Basic Books, 1970). There is also a considerable literature on bureaucratic-authoritarianism, which emphasizes the causal relationship between the "deepening" of import substitution strategies and the intervention of a bureaucratic-military elite to control potential labor

unrest. See, for instance, David Collier, ed., *The New Authoritarianism in Latin America* (Princeton: Princeton University Press, 1979). Earlier works on the related phenomenon of so-called "totalitarianism" include Hannah Arendt, *The Origins of Totalitarianism* (New York: Harcourt, Brace, 1968); and Carl Friedrich, *Totalitarianism* (Cambridge: Harvard University Press, 1954). The recent "transitions" literature is too lengthy to cite, but I have in mind books like Adam Przeworski's *Democracy and the Market: Political and Economic Reforms in Eastern Europe and Latin America* (Cambridge: Cambridge University Press, 1991).

89. This figure is the estimation of the Paris-based Committee for the Defense of Democratic Freedoms and Human Rights in Syria (CDF) cited in *Human Rights Watch World Report*, 1997, p. 300. There have been a series of Presidential amnesties in the 1990s. One of the most recent occurred in late November 1995: according to reports, 1,200 prisoners were released, most of whom were suspected to have connections to the Muslim Brotherhood. There are also allegedly fifteen different security and paramilitary forces that monitor one another and Syrian citizens. See Middle East Watch, *Syria Unmasked: The Suppression of Human Rights by the Asad Regime* (New Haven and London: Yale University Press, 1991), p. xiii. The military is another institution that provides the regime with an important political constituency and protects the regime from internal opposition. The heads of the security forces are among Asad's top advisers. And they, like the President, tend to be military officers from the minority 'Alawi sect. A third basis of Asad's rule is the Ba'th party, which holds an absolute majority in all of its organizations and is the only party permitted to operate among students and inside the armed forces. In 1990, Asad did expand the number of seats in Syria's Parliament (majlis al-sha'b) to allow independent candidates to run. Some independent campaigners, representing the local private sector, advocated economic reforms, but none criticized the government explicitly. See Volker Perthes, "Syria's Parliamentary Elections: Remodeling Asad's Political Base," *Middle East Report* 22, no. 1 (January–February 1992): 15–18.

90. James L. Gelvin identifies the origins of what he terms a "populist political sociability" in Syrian institutions, discourses, and public ceremonies responsive primarily to French and British intervention in the aftermath of World War I. See "The Social Origins of Popular

Nationalism in Syria: Evidence for a New Framework," *International Journal of Middle East Studies* 26 (1994): 645-61. For an extensive discussion of the origins of Syrian populism, see James L. Gelvin, *Popular Mobilization and the Foundations of Mass Politics in Syria, 1918-1920* (Ph.D. Dissertation, Harvard University, September 1992). In the Iranian context, Ervand Abrahamian argues provocatively that Khomeini's interpretation of state and society resembled Third World populism, especially its Latin American variant, rather than "conventional fundamentalism." See *Khomeinism: Essays on the Islamic Republic* (Berkeley and Los Angeles: University of California Press, 1993), especially chap. 2. For Abrahamian's definition of populism, see p. 17.

91. See for instance, Katerina Clark, *The Soviet Novel: History as Ritual* (Chicago: University of Chicago Press, 1981) and "Utopian Anthropology as a Context for Stalinist Literature," in *Stalinism*, ed. Robert Tucker (New York: W. W. Norton and Co., 1977), pp. 180-98. For a description of the iconography of early Bolshevik festivals, see Von Geldern, *Bolshevik Festivals 1917-1920*, and Victoria E. Bonnell, "The Representation of Women in Early Soviet Political Art," *Russian Review* (July 1991):267-88. According to both Von Geldern and Bonnell, many of the early Bolshevik images were inspired by the neoclassical symbols and allegories transmitted via the French Revolution. For descriptions of the French symbols, see Lynn Hunt, *Politics, Culture, and Class in the French Revolution* (Berkeley and Los Angeles: University of California Press, 1984). Also, Maurice Agulhon, *Marianne into Battle: Republican Imagery and Symbolism in France, 1789-1880* (Cambridge, England: Cambridge University Press, 1979); and Ozouf, cited earlier.

92. Katerina Clark calls political narrative based on the family "utopian kinship models," in "Utopian Anthropology as a Context for Stalinist Literature," p. 182.

93. Hinnebusch, "Political Recruitment and Socialization in Syria: The Case of the Revolutionary Youth Federation," *International Journal of Middle East Studies* 11 (1980): 143-74, cited in Sadowski, "Ba'thist Ethics," p. 161.

94. For a discussion of the centers and origins of charisma, see Clifford Geertz, "Centers, Kings, and Charisma," in *Local Knowledge: Further Essays in Interpretive Anthropology* (New York: Basic Books, 1983), pp. 121-46.

95. For details on the palace, see Daniel Le Gac, *La Syrie du Général Assad* (Éditions Complexe, 1991), p. 112.

96. Jowitt, *New World Disorder,* see pp. 1, 4–5, 9–12, 18, 21–23, 114–15, 125–26.

97. Interestingly, Asad's father is never invoked. See chapter 2, which analyzes the invocation of familial metaphors in detail.

98. See chapters 2 and 3.

99. Clark, "Utopian Anthropology," pp. 180–98.

100. Kanan Makiya (then writing under the pseudonym Samir al-Khalil) *The Monument: Art, Vulgarity and Responsibility in Iraq* (Berkeley and Los Angeles: University of California Press, 1991), pp. 3–4. An article on postage stamps in Iraq by Donald Malcolm Reid, while superficial, does pay attention to the symbolic in Iraq, which most scholarly work, with the exception of Makiya and Davis, does not. See "The Postage Stamp: A Window on Saddam Hussein's Iraq," *The Middle East Journal* 47, no. 1 (winter 1993): 77–89.

101. Despite the French mandate's own divide-and-rule policies, which enabled rural, middle class peasants from minority sects to gain a disproportionate amount of military and, later, political power in Syria, the commercial and business classes remained extremely influential under the mandate. In the radical period of Ba'thist rule the political and economic power of these groups was severely curtailed. Outside the formal institutions of power, however, current business classes have some influence in economic policy-making. Those businessmen from the pre-1963 bourgeoisie currently compete not only with emergent entrepreneurs in small industry, manufacture, commerce, and services who profited from economic liberalization in the late 1980s, but also with the upper echelons of the nouveaux riches who use their connections with state elites to gain lucrative holdings in real estate, construction, agrobusiness, tourism, and transportation. See Joseph Bahout, "The Syrian Business Community, Its Politics and Prospects," in *Contemporary Syria: Liberalization between Cold War and Cold Peace,* ed. Eberhard Kienle (London: I.B. Taurus, 1994), p. 74, cited in Fred H. Lawson, "Private Capital and the State in Contemporary Syria," *Middle East Report* 27, no. 2 (spring 1997): 11. And institutions such as the Chamber of Commerce in Damascus have some input in the regime's financial decisions. On the influence of Damascus's Chamber, see Steven Heydemann, "Taxation without Representation," in *Rules and Rights in the Middle East,* ed. Ellis Goldberg, Resat Kasaba and Joel Migdal (Seattle: University of Washington Press, 1993).

102. For a discussion of the groups that comprise this civil society, see Raymond Hinnebusch, "State and Civil Society in Syria," in *Middle*

East Journal 47, no. 2 (spring 1993): 243–57. For a remarkably detailed discussion of classes and status groups in Iraq see Hanna Batatu, *The Old Social Classes and the Revolutionary Movements of Iraq* (Princeton: Princeton University Press, 1978). And for a problematic contrast between Iraq and Syria's "fundamentally different political cultures," see Robert Springborg, "Baathism in Practice: Agriculture, Politics, and Political Culture in Syria and Iraq," *Middle Eastern Studies* 17, no. 2 (April 1981): 191.

103. For a description of Saddam Husayn's personification of Bedouin values and of "machismo" in Iraqi comic strips, see Allen Douglas and Fedwa Malti-Douglas, *Arab Comic Strips: Politics of an Emerging Mass Culture* (Bloomington: Indiana University Press, 1994), pp. 46–60. In comic strips, Saddam Husayn is portrayed as the lone hero, which contrasts markedly with Syrian official comics depicting Asad as the "father" of Syria. Asad's role as the metaphorical father is discussed in chapter 2.

104. See Kanan Makiya (Samir al-Khalil), *Republic of Fear: The Politics of Modern Iraq* (Berkeley and Los Angeles: University of California Press, 1989). This book offers an account of the way in which fear in Iraq establishes Saddam Husayn's authority. See also Makiya, *Cruelty and Silence: War, Tyranny, Uprising and the Arab World* (New York: W. W. Norton and Co., 1993). For critical Arab responses to his third book, see, for instance, Ahmad Dallal's review in *al-Hayat*, 23 May 1993; Edward Said, "The Intellectuals and the War," in *Middle East Research and Information Project Reports*, no. 171 (July–August 1991): 15–20; As'ad Abukhalil, "Arab Intellectuals on Trial," *Middle East Journal* 47, no. 4 (autumn 1993): 695–706. These authors do not dispute the characterization of the Iraqi regime as cruel and terrifying, but they do dispute some of the facts Makiya claims to present, and they challenge his portrayal of Arab intellectuals. For another account of terror in Iraq, see 'Isam al-Khafaji, "State Terror and the Degradation of Politics in Iraq," *Middle East Report* 22, no. 3 (May–June 1992): 15–21.

105. I am indebted to Yahya Sadowski for this analogy.

106. By using the word "non-totalizing" here I am not suggesting that there actually exists a totalitarian or totalizing regime; I'm merely implying that some regimes are more totalizing than others, e.g., that they have greater abilities and aspirations to regulate citizens than other regimes do. This position should become clear in chapter 2.

CHAPTER TWO

1. Achille Mbembe, "Domaines de la nuit et autorité onirique dans les maquis du Sud-Cameroun (1955–1958)," *Journal of African History* 31 (1991): 120.

2. My analysis here derives, in part, from extensive readings in the official newspaper, *al-Ba'th*, from 1969 (one year before Asad took power) to 1996. For a history of the newspaper and its positions on various political issues, see Turki Saqr, *Jaridat al-Ba'th fi sab'a wa thalathin 'aman* (Damascus: Dar al-Ba'th, 1983). All translations from the Arabic are my own.

3. See James C. Scott's discussion of the "public transcript" in *Domination and the Arts of Resistance: Hidden Transcripts* (New Haven: Yale University Press, 1990), pp. 45–69.

4. Author's interview, 1992.

5. Patrick Seale, *Asad: The Struggle for the Middle East* (Berkeley and Los Angeles: University of California Press, 1988), p. 339.

6. Telephone conversations with Yahya M. Sadowski and his personal notes on the "Cult of Personality in Syria."

7. Robert Scott Mason, "Government and Politics," in *Syria: A Country Study*, chap. 4 (Washington, D.C.: Department of the Army, 1988), p. 212.

8. This is an excerpt from Ba'thist party member Ahmad al-Khatib's speech on the occasion of the Ba'th's anniversary. *Al-Ba'th*, 8 April 1971, p. 1.

9. Indeed, Asad visited Cairo almost immediately after coming to power. Upon his return, he paid tribute to Nasir: "I felt touched during my visit to Cairo by the continuing good fortune of the departed President and the growth of his thoughts and his deeds." *Al-Ba'th*, 2 December 1970, p. 1.

10. Asad also visited North Korea in September 1974 and may have been inspired by the cult there. In *al-Ba'th*, images of the trip depict the North Koreans holding posters of Kim Il Sung and of Asad. See especially *al-Ba'th*, 6 October 1974, p. 5.

11. While the economic prosperity of the 1970s, due primarily to the Arab oil-producing countries' donations and the remittances of Syrian workers from abroad, created vast sums of wealth, the proliferation of development projects often disproportionately benefited those associated with the regime. Some of the money went to fund increas-

ingly ambitious state-initiated five-year plans. But kickbacks and commissions also created "instant millionaires" who pursued their private interests at the expense of the public good. Corruption, and the ineffectiveness of campaigns waged against it, angered many Syrians who resented the ostentatious displays of wealth by those businessmen, politicians, and military men associated with the regime. See Seale, *Asad,* chap. 19.

12. The "Muslim Brotherhood" challenged the regime's authority from 1977 to 1982. It was a term used in official accounts to describe the Muslim opposition to the regime—an opposition that actually included several distinct guerilla groups with different leaders from various parts of Syria.

13. *Al-Ba'th,* 24 February 1982, p. 3.

14. See, for example, Hamdan Makarim and Tawfiq Kuttab's book *Masirat al-wafa' wa al-'ata'* (publisher unknown, 1988). The introduction depicts Asad's acceptance of the "will of the people" and is full of imagery concerning contractual obligation. Asad's message to the people includes statements such as "And you pledged allegiance to me (*baya'tumuni*) and I pledged allegiance to you and you contracted with me (*'ahadtumuni*) and I contracted with you to sacrifice. . . ." In later chapters, the book provides an official view of what the exchange between Asad and citizens entails. The regime promises not only to protect but also to supply goods and services such as health care, education, and economic development projects conducive to prosperity.

15. This definition, including some of the precise wording, is taken from the *Encyclopedia of Islam* (Leiden: E.J. Brill, 1960), vol. 1, pt. 2, pp. 1113–14.

16. Some examples are Hani al-Khalil, *Hafiz al-Asad: al-idyulujiyya al-thawriyya wa al-fikr al-siyasi* (Damascus: Dar Tlas, 1986); *Hafiz al-Asad: al-dawla al-dimuqratiyya al-sha'biyya* (Damascus: Dar Tlas, 1987); Iskandar Luqa, *Hafiz al-Asad: qiyam fikriyya insaniyya* (Damascus: Dar Tlas, 1986); and Anwar Salim Sallum and George 'Ayn Malik, *Hafiz al-Asad: al-qiyada wa al-tarikh* (Damascus: Dar Ibn Hani, 1985).

17. Author's interview with publisher, 1996.

18. Author's interview, 1992.

19. Songwriters associated with the regime invented lyrics that praised Asad's leadership. Even Asad's body parts were the subject of adulation. High foreheads, which connote cleverness, were the theme of a song by 'Ali Hulayhil, a Syrian-Lebanese composer who was un-

known before the publication of his song, "Abu Basil" ("Father of Basil") from the tape *Aghani Wataniyya: Abu Basil Qa'idna*.

20. Author's interviews, 1992.

21. Ulrike Freitag, *Geschichtsschreibung in Syrie 1920–1990* (Hamburg, 1991: Deutsche Orient Institut). See especially pp. 46–83, 362–409, 423–27.

22. Syria and Egypt unified and became The United Arab Republic in 1958. Nasir's decision to unify was contingent on Syrian leaders' willingness to dismantle all Syrian political parties. The Ba'th Party, one of the key initiators of the union, was therefore, like other parties, dissolved. In the aftermath of the union's dissolution in 1961, leaders of the Ba'th Party were faced with the daunting task of recruiting fresh cadres at a time when the first experiment in union, for which the Party pushed, had failed. As a consequence, many Ba'thists recruited members of their families, relying less on ideological commitment and more on kin reliability, to fill the ranks.

23. Countless editorials and newspaper headlines beginning in October 1973 until 1976 invoke this vocabulary. See, for example, *al-Ba'th*, 16 November 1973, in which the October War "gave ideas practical reality" and "unified the hearts, feelings, and energies" of the people against "the enemies of fate," p. 1. See also ibid., 7 April 1974; ibid., 6 October 1974.

24. Hannah Arendt, "Truth and Politics," in *Between Past and Future* (New York: Viking Press, 1968), p. 231. The actual text reads: "The chances of factual truth surviving the onslaught of power are very slim indeed; it is always in danger of being maneuvered out of the world not only for a time but, potentially, forever."

25. Ibid., p. 258.

26. Hannah Arendt, *The Origins of Totalitarianism* (New York: Harcourt, Brace, 1968).

27. William A. Rugh makes this observation in his book, *The Arab Press: News Media and Political Process in the Arab World*, 2d ed. (Syracuse: Syracuse University Press, 1987), p. 35.

28. See Frederick M. Dolan, "Political Action and the Unconscious: Arendt and Lacan on Decentering the Subject," in *Political Theory* 23, no. 2 (May 1995): 330, 337.

29. Author's interview, 1996.

30. Ibid.

31. Ibid.

32. Two women parachutists were slain in their beds. Women

parachutists were particularly offensive to the Muslim Brotherhood, according to Seale. *Asad,* p. 332.

33. *Al-Ba'th,* 23 February 1982, p. 3.

34. Ibid.

35. *Al-Ba'th,* 24 February 1982, p. 3.

36. *Al-Ikhwan al-muslimun: nash'a mashbuha wa tarikh aswad* (Damascus: Maktab al-I'dad, 1985). These volumes are published by the Ba'th Training Bureau. No author is mentioned. The books provide a standard history, but also divulge details of the conflicts between 1976 and 1982 not publicized at the time of their occurrence.

37. Niccolò Machiavelli, *The Discourses,* in *The Prince and the Discourses* (New York: Random House, 1950), 3:1, 3:3. For a discussion of these passages, see Hanna Fenichel Pitkin, *Fortune Is a Woman* (Berkeley and Los Angeles: University of California Press, 1984), pp. 246–51.

38. John Adams, "A Dissertation on the Canon and Feudal Law," in *The Political Writings of John Adams,* ed. George A. Peek, Jr. (Indianapolis: Bobbs-Merrill Educational Publishing, 1954), p. 17.

39. Jeffrey Merrick, "Patriarchalism and Constitutionalism in Eighteenth-Century Parlementary Discourse," *Studies in Eighteenth Century Culture* 20 (1990): 319, 321, 323, cited in Lynn Hunt, *The Family Romance of the French Revolution* (Berkeley and Los Angeles: University of California Press, 1992), pp. 18–19.

40. *Al-Ba'th,* 6 October 1974, p. 6.

41. "Family Romances," in *Standard Edition of the Complete Psychological Works of Sigmund Freud,* trans. James Strachey (London: Hogarth Press, 1959), 9:238–39, cited in Hunt, *Family Romance,* p. xiii.

42. Hunt, *Family Romance,* and Michael Paul Rogin, *Fathers and Children: Andrew Jackson and the Subjugation of the American Indian* (New York: Alfred A. Knopf, 1975).

43. Hunt, *Family Romance,* p. xiii.

44. Rogin, *Fathers and Children,* chap. 1. As Michael Rogin has pointed out to me, Freud meant the boy's wish to substitute noble parents for his own. Hunt and Rogin reverse that wish in a way: Their understanding of the family romance begins not with escaping real parents, but with attacking noble ones—and replacing them, of course, not with actual parents (though Rogin argues that in the United States the substitute parents were often real ones because of the family-based order), but with new symbolic family relations. When Rogin actually uses the term "family romance," it refers (in the chapter with that title)

to Andrew Jackson's wish to escape his own parents and be the father of himself. *Fathers and Children* alludes both to this wish and to Jackson's fantasies of patriarchal authority over Native Americans.

45. See Pitkin, *Fortune Is a Woman,* p. 199.

46. Halim Barakat, "The Arab Family and the Challenge of Social Transformation," in *Women and the Family in the Middle East: New Voices of Change,* ed. Elizabeth Warnock Fernea (Austin: University of Texas Press, 1985), p. 28. This essay is reprinted in Barakat, *The Arab World: Society, Culture and State* (Berkeley and Los Angeles: University of California Press, 1993), chap. 6.

47. Suad Joseph, "Gender and Relationality among Arab Families in Lebanon," in *Feminist Studies* 19, no. 3 (fall 1993): 469. Hisham Sharabi's *Neopatriarchy: A Theory of Distorted Change in Arab Society* (New York: Oxford University Press, 1988) was an influential book from the point of view of political activism. As an analysis of family forms, however, the book assumes, wrongly, the specificity and uniformity of Arab families. It also posits "culture" as monolithic, fixed, and static; and it makes problematic claims about the relationship between family arrangements and political ones, sometimes suggesting that the state is a family *writ large* or that Arab family structures are responsible for both authoritarian political relations and for the ways in which people revolt when they do.

48. See Paul Ricoeur, "The Metaphorical Process as Cognition, Imagination, and Feeling," in *On Metaphor,* ed. Sheldon Sacks (Chicago: University of Chicago Press, 1979), p. 146.

49. Joseph, "Gender and Relationality," p. 472. Joseph's discussion focuses on Arab families in the urban working-class district of Camp Trad. But her findings are consistent with mine in Syria.

50. Ibid., p. 468.

51. Ibid.

52. Ibid.

53. Ibid.

54. As scholars of Syria agree, most Syrians had already come to expect the state to provide certain goods and services previously offered by families and by charitable organizations, or formerly not provided at all. To some extent, such expectations reflect the relationship between the weakened authority of leading families and the growing role of the state.

55. *Awraq min Tishrin* (Dar Talaʾiʿ al-Baʿth lil-Tibaʿa wa al-Nashr), n.d., p. 9.

56. Ibid., p. 28.

57. Ibid.

58. The 1956 Suez War was considered a victory for the Arabs and contributed greatly to creating an Arab nationalist hero in Gamal 'Abd al-Nasir.

59. The film *al-Layl* (1992), directed by Muhammad Malas, depicts the famous incident in which Syrian President al-Quwatli discovered that officers were providing their troops with bone fat rather than cooking oil. For a description of the "cooking fat scandal," see Patrick Seale, *The Struggle for Syria: A Study of Post-War Arab Politics* (New Haven: Yale University Press, 1965), pp. 41–44. For a discussion of Syrian troops' ill-preparedness, see pp. 33–34.

60. Seale, *Asad*, chap. 10, especially p. 144.

61. In the weekly newspaper published by the National Union of Syrian Students, for example, a typical article reads as follows: "The masses of students contract (*tu'ahid*) with the father, the leader Hafiz al-Asad in the pursuit of scientific knowledge and military preparation (*al-i'dad al-nidali*) in order to deepen their role in building a society of progress and socialism" (9 September 1988, p. 4).

62. A pamphlet about Asad and Syria's Republican Guard, for example, is entitled: "With the father, the dearly beloved (*al-mafdi*) leader Hafiz al-Asad on the road to victory and liberation." (Note: *al-mafdi* means "the object of self-sacrifice" and also is used following the name of a leader or the word "homeland"—*watan*—to mean "dearly beloved" or "dear"; both connotations seem applicable here). "The father, the leader Hafiz al-Asad made history in the victorious journey of the Ba'th, and the leader of the nation (*umma*) on the road to strong victory from our sacrificing (or giving, *i'ta'na*) of our combative identities in this epoch, and we have emerged as masters after slavery and with dignity after a long period of subjugation and humiliation" (p. 7). The pamphlet concludes with an address to the Republican Guard in which Asad refers to them throughout as sons.

63. In *Tishrin*, for example, after Ghada Sha'a' won a gold medal at the Olympics in Atlanta, a caption read, "The family of our hero Ghada Sha'a' congratulates the homeland (*watan*) and the leader of the homeland;" Asad is referred to as the "guardian (*ra'i*) of sports and of athletes and of heroism (*butula*)." Here the "family" (*usra*) refers to the Arab world.

64. See, for example, Asad's statements in the aftermath of Basil's

death in which he claims that people telephoned saying "All of us are Basil, all of us are your sons," cited in 'Izzat al-Sa'dani, *Basil fi 'uyun al-Misriyyin* (Basil in the eyes of the Egyptians) (Cairo: al-Ahram, 1995), p. 78. Asad goes on to say, "Every citizen in this country in my mind is a brother or a son like Basil. . . . We are one large family" (p. 79).

65. See, for instance, *al-Ba'th*, 16 November 1973, p. 7, and 3 October 1975, p. 1, in which the headline reads, "The October War is the war of manliness, honor, and liberation." Asad has mentioned the importance of *rujula* in at least thirty-four speeches, most often in association with the holiday, Army Day; television advertisements for the army also celebrate *rujula*. Masculinity is rarely invoked in contexts other than martial ones.

66. Hani Khalil, *Hafiz al-Asad: al-idyulujiyya al-thawriyya wa al-fikr al-siyasi*, dedication.

67. *Al-Ba'th*, 6 October 1989, p. 1.

68. Of course, constructions of the nation as feminine are widespread in the world (e.g., France and India, to name two oft-repeated examples). In Arabic there are at least two words meaning "nation." The word *umma* generally refers to the pan-Arab nation, without the artificial boundaries imposed during colonial rule. The word *watan* also means "nation," or sometimes "homeland"; it comes from the root "residence" and is more likely than *umma* to suggest a specified, bounded territory. Sometimes *watan* conveys an ambiguous, pan-Arab meaning, and sometimes *watan* seems to mean the nation-state. When the nation is explicitly personified as feminine, the word *umma* tends to be invoked.

69. Adonis, *Kitab al-tahawwulat wa al-hijra fi aqalim al-nahar wa al-layl* (Book of transformations and migrations in the regions of day and night) (Beirut: Dar al-Adab, 1988), p. 143.

70. Mary Layoun, "Telling Spaces: Palestinian Women and the Engendering of National Narratives," in *Nationalisms and Sexualities* (New York: Routledge, 1992), p. 417. Layoun discusses two novels by Sahar Khalifa: *al-Subbar* (The cactus) and *'Abbad al-shams* (The sunflower). See also al-Tayyib Salih's *Mawsim al-hijra ila al-shamal* (Season of migration to the north), a novel that uses the trope of landscape as woman and connects it to rape, without the explicit Palestinian context. My attention to the trope of nation or landscape as woman is not meant to suggest that these evocations exhaust the range of meanings that may be at play here.

71. Cited in Ghassan Salamé, ed., *The Foundations of the Arab State* (London, New York, Sydney: Croom Helm, 1987), p. 167. See also Zaki al-Arsuzi, *al-Muʾallafat al-kamila* (The complete works) (Damascus: Matabiʿ al-Idara al-Siyasiyya lil-Jaysh wa al-Quwwat al-Musallaha, 1973), 4:213; see also ibid., 2:341–52, 359–79; and Salim Barakat on Zaki al-Arsuzi, *al-Fikr al-qawmi wa ususuhu al-falsafiyya ʿinda Zaki al-Arsuzi* (Damascus: Matbaʿ Muʾassasat al-Wahda lil-Sihafa wa al-Tibaʿa wa al-Nashr, 1979), pp. 107–8, 234–36. For a description of Arsuzi as the "spiritual father" of the Baʿth, see Sami al-Jundi's book, *al-Baʿth* (Beirut: Dar al-Nahar, 1969), p. 19.

72. Salamé, *Foundations*, p. 167. But in this article, *rahmaniyya* is translated as "uterine" rather than as "womb-like." The word *al-Rahmaniyya* is a neologism. Taking philological license, al-Arsuzi interprets "al-Rahman," one of the appellations of God, as a compound of the words *rahim/rihm* (womb), *anam* (mankind) and *ana* (I). *Al-Rahmaniyya* (or Rahmanism) emerges out of this morphological fusion as a master-concept, a state of being that unites divinity with creation and mankind with the individual ego through the intermediate, encompassing vessels of womb and nation. I prefer to translate *rahmaniyya* as womb-like because this rendering is less clinical (just as throat would generally be more appropriate than trachea) and conveys the sense of an "experience" better than "uterine." (I am indebted to Engseng Ho for much of this formulation.)

73. This painting, according to the guard at the mausoleum, was painted approximately eight to ten years before Naʿisa's death; it was the property of Naʿisa's doctor. The artist was unknown to the guard and to other artists I questioned.

74. After Naʿisa's death in 1992, reproductions of the painting were displayed primarily by secret police agents (*al-mukhabarat*). Copies of the painting were taped to the windows of many white Peugeots, which were cars widely recognized to be favored by Syria's secret police at that time. Security guards at the Asad library also exhibited the picture. It is difficult to know exactly why these images were distributed primarily to agents of the secret police. Perhaps the pictures were meant to underscore the role of these agents as protectors of the nation, rather than as perpetrators of violence; perhaps, too, some agents identify with Asad in ways that inscribe them more intimately than ordinary Syrians in the regime's narrative of kinship. Indeed, certain elite members of these security organizations are Asad's blood kin or are connected to him through marriage.

75. Robert Scott Mason, "Government and Politics," in *Syria: A Country Study*, chap. 4 (Washington, D.C.: Department of the Army, 1988), p. 212.

76. Najah al-ʿAttar, "Ummuna allati rahalat" (Our mother who departed), *Tishrin*, 23 July 1992, pp. 1 and 11.

77. Ibid., p. 11.

78. Ibid., p. 1.

79. Ibid., p. 11.

80. Ibid. The example of a human mother who gives birth to a God-like son may remind Westerners of Mary giving birth to Christ. Indeed, the ʿAlawi religion, of which Asad is a member, considers Mary holy. Moreover, 8 percent of Syrians are Christians. There may therefore be a connection between this political imagery and the story of Christ's birth. A postal stamp also suggests the connection: a Mary-like figure releases Syrian cadres from her cloak. This imagery may also be derived from Bolshevik iconography, which still suggests that the referent is Mary.

81. Author's interviews, 1996.

82. *Basil fi ʿuyun al-Misriyyin* (Cairo: al-Ahram), p. 69. Chapter 15, devoted to Bashshar and entitled "Bashshar the Hope," reiterates this dynastic principle, pp. 261–85.

83. In Syria, the establishment in 1967 of a state-sponsored organization for women, the Federation of Women, coincided with other state policies that increasingly encouraged women to enter the work force. Policies of "state feminism" functioned to transform what Mervat Hatem calls the "reproductive and productive roles of women" by providing them with access to education and with incentives to work outside of the home. See Mervat F. Hatem, "Economic and Political Liberation in Egypt and the Demise of State Feminism," *International Journal of Middle East Studies* 24 (1992): 231–32. Scholars often construe policies of "state feminism" as "public patriarchy," meaning that women increasingly rely on the male-dominated state as they depend less on their patriarchal families. Importantly, though, policies of "state feminism," at least in Syria, also underscore the *importance* of the family and the state's commitment to preserving the possibilities for family life in an increasingly complex economic and political system. See, for example, the Syrian Labor Law, which allows for generous maternity leave, allots time for nursing mothers to breastfeed their babies, and provides for the establishment of daycare facilities in public sector workplaces.

84. The Fourth Conference of *Ittihad Shabibat al-Thawra,* reported in *al-Ba'th,* 16 April 1985. Asad made reference to Muhaydli a second time on 14 June 1985.

85. In 1991, in the wake of the Gulf War, Syrian ideologues began to emphasize Asad as the "man of peace" as well as the "knight of war." Images of Muhaydli no longer presented the appropriate symbol of national commitment.

86. Introduction to *'Arus al-janub* (Damascus: Dar Tlas, 1985).

87. Katherine Verdery describes the mixed messages concerning women's roles in the Rumanian context. Party literature presented women as capable of doing everything that men did while also emphasizing the gendered specificity of women's roles as mothers. See "From Parent-State to Family Patriarchs: Gender and Nation in Contemporary Eastern Europe," *East European Politics and Societies* 8, no. 2 (spring 1994): 234. Socialist regimes in Eastern Europe, like their counterparts in the Arab world, tended to devise industrialization programs that were labor-intensive and capital poor, thereby requiring the labor power of women as well as of men.

88. Marriage is also suggestive, in any context, of certain constraints. In the case of Syria, personal status laws prevent wives from divorcing their husbands without the latter's consent, deprive divorced women of their children when the children reach a certain age, and deny the children of a Syrian woman Syrian citizenship if the father is not Syrian.

89. M. E. Combs-Schilling, in her book about ritual sacrifice in Morocco, argues that the bride's blood "consummates the rite of passage, confirms proper male and female roles in creation, and initiates both bride and groom into adulthood." See *Sacred Performances: Islam, Sexuality, and Sacrifice* (New York: Columbia University Press, 1989), p. 207.

90. From *Sabah al-khayr,* 13 April 1985, cited in *Sana' Muhaydli: 'arus al-janub,* compiled by Riyad al-'Abd Allah, n.p., p. 39.

91. From *Sabah al-khayr,* 20 April 1985, cited in *Sana' Muhaydli: 'Arus al-janub,* compiled by Riyad al-'Abd Allah, n.p., p. 25. Her "chaste body" is reiterated in the same article, p. 28.

92. Henry Safir, cited in *Sana' Muhaydli: 'Arus al-janub,* n.p., p. 11.

93. The adjective *tahir,* which means "pure," is often used in descriptions of Muhaydli's exploding body.

94. *Sana' Muhaydli: 'Arus al-janub,* n.p., p. 12.

Chapter Three

1. M's story was told to me by a close friend of M's, one of my most reliable sources for information about Syrian politics, during the course of my field research in Syria.

2. See Human Rights Watch/Middle East Report, "Syria's Tadmor Prison" (April 1996).

3. For a discussion of corruption in Syria, see Yahya M. Sadowski, "Ba'thist Ethics and the Spirit of State Capitalism: Patronage and the Party in Contemporary Syria," in *Ideology and Power in the Middle East* (Durham: Duke University Press, 1988), pp. 160–84. See also Sadowski, "Guns, Cadres and Money," *Middle East Research and Information Project Reports*, no. 134 (July–August 1985): 3–8.

4. *Midaq Alley* is one well-known, compelling example.

5. Roger Caillois, "Logical and Philosophical Problems of the Dream," in *The Dream and Human Societies*, ed. G. E. von Grunebaum and Roger Caillois (Berkeley and Los Angeles: University of California Press, 1966), p. 51.

6. Slavoj Žižek, *The Sublime Object of Ideology* (London: Verso, 1989), p. 37.

7. Stephen Greenblatt, *Renaissance Self-Fashioning: From More to Shakespeare* (Chicago: University of Chicago Press, 1980), p. 13. For a discussion of the "theatricality" of politics in ancient Rome, the ways in which emperors required their audiences to "play a role they did not feel," and thereby to "validate the fictions of power," see Shadi Bartsch, *Actors in the Audience: Theatricality and Doublespeak from Nero to Hadrian* (Cambridge: Harvard University Press, 1994), pp. 10, 16. Economist Timur Kuran coined the term "preference falsification" to describe situations in which people express public "preferences" that diverge from their private ones. See Timur Kuran, "Now Out of Never: The Element of Surprise in the East European Revolution of 1989," *World Politics* 44 (October 1991): 7–48; id., *Private Truths, Public Lies: The Social Consequences of Preference Falsification* (Cambridge: Harvard University Press, 1995).

8. Václav Havel, "The Power of the Powerless," in *Living in Truth* (London: Faber and Faber, 1986), p. 41.

9. Ibid., p. 52.

10. Author's interview, 1996.

11. Author's interview, 1996. The person quoted used the word

raqaba, which means "control, supervision, or censorship," and in colloquial Arabic sometimes refers to the institution of censorship and to any persons whose job it is to be watchful. The French verb *surveillir,* for which there is no English equivalent, probably best captures the activities evoked by *raqaba.*

12. I am grateful to John Mark Hansen for this insight.

13. Havel, "The Power of the Powerless," p. 52.

14. Ibid.

15. Ibid.

16. Ibid., p. 53.

17. Ibid., p. 45.

18. Havel was writing at a time when it was clear that the Soviet Union would not intervene, no matter what the Czechoslovakians did.

19. Havel, "The Power of the Powerless," p. 53.

20. Of course there are instances in Syria, as elsewhere, in which people choose fulfillment over safety.

21. Kanan Makiya (Samir Al-Khalil), *Republic of Fear: The Politics of Modern Iraq* (Berkeley and Los Angeles: University of California Press, 1989), p. 72.

22. Ibid.

23. Hannah Arendt, *Eichmann in Jerusalem: A Report on the Banality of Evil,* rev. and enl. (New York: Penguin Books, 1976), p. 24.

24. Ibid.

25. Richard Rorty, *Contingency, Irony, and Solidarity* (Cambridge: Cambridge University Press, 1989), p. 178.

26. Ibid.

27. Elaine Scarry, *The Body in Pain: The Making and Unmaking of the World* (New York: Oxford University Press, 1985). Scarry's analysis is brilliant, provocative, but ultimately problematic because, among other reasons, it fails to account for those tortured prisoners who refuse to reveal information. According to my own interviews with victims of torture in Jordan, some victims refuse to disclose, or give incomplete information, enduring the punishment instead. The description of the self-extending torturer and the self-contracting victim fails to address this possibility of refusing to comply. Scarry's account of the torturers is also problematic. She assumes that the torturers are completely coincident with the state and share in its power, its expanding "self." But torturers are not necessarily, in political, economic, and therefore surely even psychological terms, particularly powerful: they may be

mere functionaries of the regime and subject, like any other functionaries, to the consequences of failing to obey the orders and even whims of their "superiors." Moreover, Scarry, in positing a metaphysical "self," does not consider the embeddedness of people in their environments. The dynamics of torture, its effect on the "voice" (itself a problematic category, which seems for Scarry to mean "the will") may vary according to a specific cultural construction of "will," "voice," or "self."

28. From *1984* quoted in Rorty, *Contingency, Irony, and Solidarity*, p. 177.

29. Author's interviews, 1989–1990, 1992, 1996.

30. Havel, "The Power of the Powerless," p. 37.

31. Oleg Kharkhordin, "Reveal and Dissimulate: A Genealogy of Public and Private in Soviet Russia," unpublished paper.

32. Usama Sa'id, "Qabr Sakran" (Drunken grave), in *Alef*, no. 5 (1991): 58–62. I have added the numbers to help readers distinguish voices.

33. The phrase "work the weakness" is from Judith Butler, *Bodies That Matter: On the Discursive Limits of "Sex"* (New York and London: Routledge, 1993), p. 237.

34. Thanks to Laura Green for drawing my attention to this aspect of M's response.

35. Tejumola Olaniyan, "Narrativizing Postcoloniality: Responsibilities," *Public Culture* 5, no. 1 (fall 1992): 50. His essay is one of a number of responses to Achille Mbembe, "The Banality of Power and the Aesthetics of Vulgarity in the Postcolony," *Public Culture* 4, no. 2 (spring 1992): 1–30. See also Mbembe's reply, "Prosaics of Servitude and Authoritarian Civilities," *Public Culture* 5, no. 1 (fall 1992).

36. Douglas Haynes and Gyan Prakash, introduction to *Contesting Power: Resistance and Everyday Social Relations in South Asia* (Berkeley and Los Angeles: University of California Press, 1992).

Chapter Four

1. Scott makes this point especially in chapters 6 through 8 of *Domination and the Arts of Resistance: Hidden Transcripts* (New Haven: Yale University Press, 1990). Scott's use of Havel and of examples from the former Soviet Union and Poland further underscore his message to political scientists who look only at official institutions: had

political scientists been analyzing the "hidden transcripts" they might have been able to predict the political upheavals of the 1980s. As Scott says in relation to Poland: "Behind 1980, then, lay a long prehistory, one comprising songs, popular poetry, jokes, street wisdom, political satire" (p. 212). Recently, works by anthropologists, social historians, and some political scientists have begun to emphasize the everyday and nonritual contexts in which relationships between dominance and resistance are observable. These studies may at times exaggerate the prevalence or significance of everyday infractions, but they nevertheless question assumptions about what resistance is. See, for instance, James C. Scott, *Weapons of the Weak: Everyday Forms of Peasant Resistance* (New Haven: Yale University Press, 1985); Michel de Certeau, *The Practice of Everyday Life* (Berkeley and Los Angeles: University of California Press, 1984); Pierre Bourdieu, *Outline of a Theory of Practice*, trans. Richard Nice (Cambridge: Cambridge University Press, 1982); Jean Comaroff, *Body of Power, Spirit of Resistance* (Chicago: University of Chicago Press, 1985). Comaroff's study also works with rituals. The *Subaltern Studies* series edited by Ranajit Guha is devoted to exploring a wide range of collective actions hitherto neglected as forms of popular protest in South East Asia. Most of the scholars contributing to the series, however, examine events such as grain riots and communal uprisings that, although useful to discuss because previously ignored, do not call into question conventional understandings of resistance as collective action.

2. Douglas Haynes and Gyan Prakash, introduction to *Contesting Power: Resistance and Everyday Social Relations in South Asia* (Berkeley and Los Angeles: University of California Press, 1992), p. 12.

3. Scott, *Domination*, pp. 191–92.

4. Interview with Adib Ghannam, Deputy Minister of Information, fall 1992.

5. Middle East Watch, *Syria Unmasked: The Suppression of Human Rights by the Asad Regime* (New Haven: Yale University Press, 1991), p. 116.

6. Film directors, actors, and scholars all articulated a general understanding of the prohibitions, which are not explicitly recorded anywhere.

7. Scott uses the term "hidden transcript," to refer to the discourse that occurs "'offstage,' beyond the direct observation of powerholders." Scott, *Domination*, p. 5. See also id., *Weapons of the Weak*, pp. 48, 287–

88, 329. The repeated invocation of this theatrical metaphor in studies of resistance, although helpful in alerting readers to the discrepancy between public expressions of loyalty and privately held beliefs, does tend to be problematic, for as Timothy Mitchell points out, the metaphor is often used to juxtapose visible, power-infused public behavior with a "contrasting sense of something unproblematically authentic," the "voice of an 'author' . . . a collective self that is the author of its own cultural constructions and actions, constituting a 'beginning' or point of originality that is embryonic, initially autonomous, and genuine." See Timothy Mitchell, "Everyday Metaphors of Power," *Theory and Society* 19 (1990): 563–64. For another critique of Scott which especially examines his arguments against hegemony, see Susan C. Stokes, "Hegemony, Consciousness, and Political Change in Peru," *Politics and Society* 19, no. 3 (1991): 265–90. Stokes rightly questions Scott's formulation of power: "Is 'power' really to be thought of as like the shade: either you are in it or you are out of it?" (p. 269). See also Susan Gal, "Language and 'the Arts of Resistance,'" *Cultural Anthropology* 10, no. 3 (1995): 407–24.

8. The word "conscript" is Scott's from *Domination*, p. 15. But an understanding of citizens' reluctant "conscription" as a source of potential power for the regime is my own.

9. See, for instance, Ranajit Guha, *Elementary Aspects of Peasant Insurgency* (Delhi: Oxford University Press, 1983), pp. 18–76; Michael Adas, "South Asian Resistance in Comparative Perspective," in *Contesting Power*, p. 301.

10. Bakhtin argues that in medieval Europe, the marketplace was a privileged site for the cultivation of counter-hegemonic discourses, the most dramatic expression of which was the carnival. Carnivals were the occasion for inverting hierarchies and subverting official standards; they enabled people to come together and parody, ridicule, and blaspheme the conventional. Carnivals typically invoked the grotesque, the scatological, and the obscene. Bakhtin both celebrates the "more or less oppositional character" of carnivals and also recognizes their possible 'authorizing' effects. See Mikhail Bakhtin, *Rabelais and His World*, trans. Helene Iswolsky (Bloomington: Indiana University Press, 1984). For a remarkably nuanced application of Bakhtin and French critical theory, see Peter Stallybrass and Allon White, *The Politics and Poetics of Transgression* (Ithaca: Cornell University Press, 1986), which argues that for long periods carnival can be a stable and

cyclical ritual with "no noticeable politically transformative effects, but that, given the presence of sharpened political antagonism, it may often act as *catalyst* and *site of actual and symbolic struggle*" (p. 14) (emphasis in the original). Furthermore, it may be that the terms of the safety-valve debate in recent years have been distorted by scholarly attention to carnivals and relative inattention to other forms of discursive resistance, as Nicholas Dirks points out in "Ritual and Resistance: Subversion as a Social Fact," in Haynes and Prakash, *Contesting Power*, p. 217.

11. Judith Butler makes a similar point concerning the subversive implications of cross-dressing. She writes: "Although many readers understood *Gender Trouble* to be arguing for the proliferation of drag performances as a way of subverting dominant gender norms, I want to underscore that there is no necessary relation between drag and subversion, and that drag may well be used in the service of both naturalization and reidealization of hyperbolic heterosexual norms." Judith Butler, *Bodies That Matter: On the Discursive Limits of "Sex"* (New York and London: Routledge, 1993), p. 125.

12. Censors at the Ministry of Information recognize that television serials poking fun at the regime are popular because they are critical, but this does not mean that they function solely or primarily as safety valves. Interview with Adib Ghannam, Deputy Minister of Information, 1992.

13. Scott points out that the functionalist account of safety-valve theory is problematic because it (1) confuses the "intentions of elites with the results they are able to achieve," (2) "ascribes a unique agency to elites," (3) dismisses the historical and cultural circumstances which, if considered, would suggest that the effects of carnival vary and evolve over time, and (4) ignores the actual history of carnivals in which carnivals were perceived by church and secular elites as potentially threatening. See Scott, *Domination*, pp. 178–82. For historical accounts of revolts occasioned by carnivals, see Emmanuel Le Roy Ladurie's account of the bloody carnival of 1580 in *Carnival in Romans*, trans. Mary Feeney (New York: George Braziller, 1979). See also Peter Burke, *Popular Culture in Early Modern Europe* (New York: Harper and Row, 1978), p. 203.

14. Scott makes a similar point in reference to the "hidden transcript": "the social spaces where the hidden transcript grows are them-

selves an achievement of resistance; they are won and defended in the teeth of power" (*Domination,* p. 119). Scott's perhaps overly simplistic bifurcation of the "hidden" and "public transcripts" becomes problematic when he argues that to the extent that criticisms evident in public are also made in private, then they remain "opaque" to officials: if analysts and Syrian citizens can "read" and interpret resistance in public, then it is reasonable to assume (indeed interviews with Ministry of Information officials affirm) that officials too are able to acknowledge that the success of these comedy skits, cartoons, and films is due to their critical orientation.

15. Interviews with artists in 1996 revealed that increased possibilities for travel and exposure to Western liberal democracies did not produce Syrians enamored with the West, but international recognition did make many feel safer and more protected than they had previously.

16. For a brief history of Syrian television, see Salam Kawakibi, "Le Rôle de la television dans la relecture de l'histoire," in *Monde arabe Maghreb Machrek,* no. 158 (October–December 1997): 47–49. Kawakibi's article is devoted primarily to a discussion of *Ikhwat al-Turab* (Brothers of the soil), an extremely popular television series aired in 1996 during the month-long holiday of Ramadan. Produced by the private company, Sham International, which belongs, in part, to a son-in-law of Syrian Vice President 'Abd al-Halim Khaddam, the serial was purchased by Middle East Broadcasting Channel in England and by channels in Dubai and Kuwait. The production quality and aesthetic sensibility of the series resembled American epic films, such as *Glory* (1989). The serial focused on the years 1915–1918, at the end of Ottoman rule, and depicted graphically the abuses of Ottoman "occupation" and the Armenian massacre. The serial angered the Turkish government, with whom relations were already strained, while basically conforming to regime formulations of Syria's harmonious unity against the injustices of external enemies.

17. This is, of course, a different explanation than the safety-valve one, but it is nevertheless "functionalist."

18. Scott, *Domination,* p. 92. See also Barrington Moore, *Injustice: The Social Bases of Obedience and Revolt* (White Plains, N.Y.: M.E. Sharpe, 1987), p. 84.

19. Barbara Harlow, introduction to *The Colonial Harem,* by Malek

Alloula (Minneapolis: University of Minnesota Press, 1986), p. xi. The expression "challenge and riposte" is borrowed from Pierre Bourdieu's discussion of Kabylian society in *Outline of a Theory of Practice,* trans. Richard Nice (Cambridge: Cambridge University Press, 1977), p. 12.

20. Barrington Moore observes, "in any stratified society there is a set of limits on what . . . dominant and subordinate groups can do. . . . What takes place, however, is a kind of continual probing to find out what they can get away with and discover the limits of obedience and disobedience." Moore, *Injustice: The Social Bases of Obedience and Revolt,* cited in Scott, *Domination,* p. 192. See also Scott's discussion of "probing" the "limits of the possible" on pp. 192–201.

21. Anthropologists who study the Middle East have recently done some important work on television and film that has tried to grapple with the difficulties of audience "reception." See Lila Abu-Lughod, "The Interpretation of Culture(s) after Television," *Representations* 59 (summer 1997): 109–34; and "The Objects of Soap Opera: Egyptian Television and the Cultural Politics of Modernity," *Worlds Apart: Modernity through the Prism of the Local,* ed. Daniel Miller (London: Routledge, 1995). See also Walter Armbrust, *Mass Culture and Modernism in Egypt* (Cambridge: Cambridge University Press, 1996). It is difficult to know exactly how people make sense of what they see on television, in plays and in films, but many popular Syrian plays are filmed live and reproduced on video, which allows subsequent viewers to know when audiences laughed. Sometimes I watched television with families, and particularly one friend drew my attention to the parts she thought were funny in the serial *Maraya* (Mirror). She liked the show especially when it was explicitly political because she was "surprised" that the actor could say such "dangerous" lines.

22. For a history of Syrian theater covering the years 1873–1982, see Wasfi al-Malih, *Tarikh al-masrah al-suri* (Damascus: Dar al-Fikr, 1984). For his discussion of Durayd Lahham, see pp. 215–18. In Durayd Lahham's work, the protagonist Ghawwar al-Tusha is often depicted as negligent, stingy, lazy, and a prankster—in short, a classic fool. He wears a *tarbush* (fez hat), *shirwal* (baggy, traditional pants), and clogs, which identify him (in exaggerated, knave-like form) as a son of Damascus. (See the chapter entitled "Durayd Lahham," in Samir ʿAbduh's *al-Tahlil al-nafsi lil-fannanin al-ʿArab,* Matbaʿat al-Ajluni, s.l. [1988], pp. 111–19). Lahham's early television serials as Ghawwar steer clear of political themes, but in 1969, in the aftermath

of the 1967 Arab-Israeli War, Lahham begins to act publicly in pieces that criticize political life. For a discussion of prevalent themes in Syrian political theater, see Ghassan Ghanim, *al-Masrah al-siyasi fi Suriya, 1967–1990* (Damascus: Dar 'Ala' al-Din, 1996).

23. In an interview, Lahham argued that "the writer and the artist must engage in self-censorship . . . because the circumstances of the country are more important than his freedom of thought." *al-Tadamun,* 9 June 1984.

24. In my interview with Durayd Lahham, he argued that the "nation" has a lot of capabilities, but values associated with consumerism have become more important than patriotism. September, 1992.

25. The 1955 Bandung conference was a meeting of Afro-Asian countries from which key leaders of the nonaligned bloc, such as Nkrumah, Nehru, and Nasir, emerged.

26. The *Mirror's* episodes have been rerun frequently, sometimes during the month-long Muslim holiday of Ramadan, when Syrian families tend to gather at dusk to break fast and watch television together. Even the Deputy Minister of Information acknowledged the popularity of the show and explained that it was popular because it was critical. Author's interview, 1992.

27. Interview with Yasir al-'Azma, June 1992. Al-'Azma describes the process by which he comes up with story ideas: he puts a piece of "carbon paper" on people and copies the details of their lives. The *Mirror* refers to television mini-serials produced in 1981, 1984, 1986, 1988, and 1996.

28. Indeed, the two men's personal biographies are instructive here. Yasir al-'Azma comes from a family of religious Sunni judges. Durayd Lahham is a Shi'i; the Shi'a constitute about 1 percent of the population in Syria and tend to be Arab nationalists.

29. Interview with Yasir al-'Azma, June 1992.

30. *Kishk* is a dough made of bulgar and sour milk, cut into small pieces, dried, and used for the preparation of other dishes.

31. The word for street vendors, *tanabir,* evokes men selling food and goods in pushcarts. The occupation of the *tanabir* is generally considered a lowly position, similar to that of collecting trash. By declaring that even the street vendors have paper tissues, Sa'id is claiming extremely high levels of refinement in Syria's streets or an extreme oversupply of paper tissues.

32. The noun *al-siyasa,* "politics," in Syrian colloquial is pro-

nounced *assiyaseh*, and sounds just like the adjective "political" or "clever."

33. Abu Saʿid likens the habit to that of Juhaʾs donkey going to the mill. Juha is a legendary Arab figure.

34. Bourdieu, *Outline of a Theory of Practice*, p. 164.

35. Interview with ʿAli Farzat, 1992.

36. Many of the Syrian intellectuals I interviewed during the course of my field work in 1992 spoke of their "internal censors," which affected how and what they wrote, and also how and what they read. See also Robert Darnton, "Censorship, a Comparative View: France 1789–East Germany 1989," in *Representations* 49 (winter 1995): 54. East German censors "insisted that they wielded their blue pencils lightly, because most of the effective censorship had already occurred—in the planning process and in the authors' heads." Darnton found that "censorship affected everyone involved with literature, not just the censors. It influenced the way writers wrote and readers read. It determined the relationship between writer and reader, and reader and text" (p. 58).

37. Interviews with ʿAli Farzat, 1992, 1996.

38. Middle East Watch, *Syria Unmasked: The Suppression of Human Rights by the Asad Regime* (New Haven: Yale University Press, 1991), p. 116.

39. Interview with ʿAli Farzat, 1992. Other intellectuals who must remain anonymous also invoked this explanation.

40. For a discussion of the material conditions, history, role, and problems of the Arab intelligentsia as a distinct class, see *al-Wahda*, no. 40, January 1988, especially: Muhammad Ahmad Ismaʿil ʿAli, "al-Muthaqqaf al-ʿArabi bayn al-taghrib wa al-asala," pp. 6–17; Ahmad Majdi Hijazi, "al-Muthaqqaf al-ʿArabi wa al-iltizam al-idyuluji," pp. 19–32; Jamal ʿAli Zahran, "Taʾthir al-awdaʿ al-mujtamaʿiyya ʿala dawr al-muthaqqaf al-ʿArabi," pp. 33–47; Muʿin Khalil ʿUmar, "Namadhij min al-muthaqqafin fi al-mujtamaʿ al-ʿarabi," pp. 48–54; George Tarabishi, "Min al-muthaqqafin ila al-intilijinsya," pp. 62–73; and al-Tahir Labib, "al-ʿAlam wa al-muthaqqaf wa al-intilijinsya," pp. 99–111.

41. One film director suggested that only three hundred people can sit in any one theater. At the most, 140,000 people can see a film in twenty weeks in Damascus. Moreover, film producers in the private sector have moved to television. Television serials are easier to distrib-

ute and sell for fixed prices, which make them less financially risky than films. Saudi Arabia is a major client for Syrian television, and Syrian producers can calculate costs and profits before going into production. Author's interview, 1996.

42. Syrian film production dates back to the 1920s. In the late 1940s, encouraged by Lebanese financing and distribution, Syrian filmmakers began to produce several films a year, predominantly light comedies and musicals. A new Syrian army studio also produced some serious films, and during the union with Egypt from 1958 until 1961, the government set up a short-lived state film studio within the new Ministry of Culture.

43. Muhammad Malas won first prize at the festivals of Valencia and Carthage for his first feature film, *Ahlam al-Madina* (Dreams of the city, 1984). His second feature film, *al-Layl* (The night, 1992), also won international recognition and appeared at the San Francisco Film Festival in 1994. Both of these films situate their narrative in the pre-Ba'thist era, but whereas *Ahlam al-Madina* managed to win the censor's approval in Syria, *al-Layl* was only shown to general Syrian audiences in 1996. Two other politically relevant films appeared in the late eighties: *Layali Ibn Awa* (Nights of the jackal) by 'Abd al-Latif 'Abd al-Hamid, and *Nujum al-Nahar* (Stars of the day) by Usama Muhammad, completed in 1988.

44. Interviews with Usama Muhammad, 1996.

45. For a discussion of Muhammad's views on the role of cinema, see Usama Muhammad, "al-Karasi kharij salat al-'ard," in *al-Hayat*, 21 March 1995, p. 18. In this article he likens cinema to a medical scope, penetrating the difficult and decisive areas of our lives. It is both the "stripping of the soul" and the "beauty and awfulness of this stripping."

46. Muhammad Malas's film *al-Layl*, for example, was recently shown in Syria, after years of postponement. For the most part *al-Layl* does not offend official historical understandings of the loss of Palestine and the creation of the state of Israel, but it does use the context of Syrian military coups in the 1940s to criticize the pomp and pretense of martial rule more generally. The film centers on a family in the Golan Heights town of Quneitra, and it weaves complex interrelationships among political events, neighborhood quarrels, and personal sensibilities to produce a textured, aesthetically appealing portrait of what Malas calls "the generation of the fathers," of pre- and

post-independent Syria. Malas's film does take some political risks. Most notably, his depiction of sacrifice suggests explicitly that citizens' sacrifices will be appropriated by military men whose bogus ceremonies overwhelm people's actual political commitments. As the main protagonist says, "The fear is that we'll sacrifice and die, and afterwards some bastards will come to negotiate over our corpses"—a line that has been cut from Syrian versions of the film. A shot of a military officer saluting while standing between two gigantic rams' horns, which opens and closes the film's narrative, reiterates this theme of appropriation and futility.

47. Author's interview, 1996.

48. Video cover blurb written by Malih.

49. Ibid.

50. See Samir Zikra's *The Half Meter Incident* for a description of the ways in which Syrian media announcements deceived Syrians during the 1967 War.

51. The verbal description of this dream is my own.

52. Sigmund Freud, *Jokes and Their Relation to the Unconscious*, trans. James Strachey (New York: W. W. Norton, 1960), pp. 118–20, 134–38.

53. The joke has a variation: **A man named Hafiz al-Khara' goes to the court to change his name. The judge asks, what would you like to change Khara' to? The man replies: no, I don't want to change Khara', it's Hafiz I want to change.** (1988; 1989). Dates in parentheses indicate the year or years a joke was related to me.

54. The point that transgressive practices seem often to redress hierarchical imbalances by inverting conventional understandings of high and low, exalted and base, is beholden to Stallybrass and White's discussion in *The Politics and Poetics of Transgression*.

55. See Freud, *Jokes*, p. 143 for the public nature of the joke. For a discussion of the joke's requirements of psychical accord and conformity, see ibid., p. 151.

56. Jokes about Asad and his political mythology are not the only jokes to be told in Syria, but they are the most political and dangerous. The speaker will generally know and trust everyone in the room. If someone informs on the joker, the joker may go to prison for insulting Asad or the regime he personifies. Those who recounted jokes to me either in the context of my research or at parties I attended did so at considerable risk to themselves. The jokes collected were from men and women, mostly between the ages of eighteen and sixty; Christian,

Sunni, and 'Alawi; and representative of varying class backgrounds. All of the jokes were told to me in Syrian dialect.

57. The comparison of an Arab leader with Western leaders is not, of course, unique to Syria. For other political jokes that compare Arab leaders with Western ones, see Ibrahim Muhawi, "The Metalinguistic Joke: Sociolinguistic Dimensions of Arabic Folk Genre," in *Arabic Sociolinguistics: Issues and Perspectives*, ed. Yasir Suleiman (Surrey, England, 1994), pp. 155–76. Ibrahim Muhawi is currently writing a book focusing on political jokes about Arab leaders.

58. For variations on this joke in Eastern bloc countries, see C. Banc and A. Dundes, *First Prize, Fifteen Years! An Annotated Collection of Romanian Political Jokes* (London: Associated University Presses, 1986), p. 170.

59. Although it is generally not permitted to criticize the party, one can sometimes suggest that the party is not worthy of its leader, Asad. Therefore, a joke about the party does not involve the same danger as a joke about Asad. For example: **A person wants to buy two chickens so he finds a store, which is named** *al-Ba'th* **[after the Ba'th Party] Chickens. He tells the shopkeeper: "Give me two fried comrades."** (1992; 1989). There are also a wide range of sexual jokes and jokes that poke fun at the people of Homs, Syria's fourth largest city. The only other jokes about Asad in print, to my knowledge, are found in Khalid Kishtainy, *Arab Political Humour* (London: Quartet Books, 1985). See especially pp. 176–77. Kishtainy has also written a book in Arabic that deals primarily, but not exclusively, with Western humor. See Kishtainy (Qishtayni), *'Alam Dahik: Fukahat, Shu'ub wa Nikatuha* (Beirut: Dar al-Hamra', 1991).

60. This joke has a number of variations that occur in diverse countries and refer to various leaders. According to some scholars, the joke was first told about Charles de Gaulle and later adapted to fit other cases. For an Egyptian version, see Afaf Lutfi al-Sayyid Marsot, "Humor: The Two-Edged Sword," in *Middle East Studies Association Bulletin* 14, no. 1 (July 1980): 9. For Russian versions, see Banc and Dundes, *First Prize*, p. 157.

61. The line outside the American consulate usually starts to form at 5:30 in the morning. The consulate opens at 8:30 A.M.

62. See Michel Foucault's essay, "Maurice Blanchot: The Thought from Outside," in *Foucault/Blanchot* (New York: Zone Books, 1987).

63. I take this point from Lila Abu-Lughod, who also argues that studies of resistance can be used as a "diagnostic of power." Lila Abu-

Lughod, "The Romance of Resistance: Tracing Transformations of Power through Bedouin Women," *American Ethnologist* 17 (February 1990): 41, 42, 48.

CHAPTER FIVE

1. Edouard Saab, *La Syrie ou la revolution dans la rancoeur* (Paris: Julliard, 1968), p. 92.

2. For a recent book in political science that focuses on pan-Arab initiatives, see Malik Mufti, *Sovereign Creations* (Ithaca: Cornell University Press, 1996). On the tumultuous events leading up to the U.A.R., see ibid., chap. 6.

3. Thomas Michael Callaghy, *State Formation and Absolutism in Comparative Perspective: Seventeenth-Century France and Mobutu Sese Seko's Zaire* (Ph.D. diss., U.C. Berkeley, December 1979), p. 33. Callaghy's categories are a succinct formulation of Amitai Etzioni, *A Comparative Analysis of Complex Organizations* (New York: Free Press, 1961), chap. 1, and id., "Power and Alienation in Comparative Perspective," *Comparative Perspectives: Theories and Methods,* ed. Amitai Etzioni and F. L. DuBow (Boston: Little, Brown, 1970), pp. 137–61. Studies of ways in which states generate compliance, as Joel Migdal has noted, tend to focus on "the degree to which the state's institutions can expect voluntary compliance with their rules (legitimacy) or need to resort to coercion." See Joel S. Migdal, "The State in Society: An Approach to Struggles for Domination," in *State Power and Social Forces: Domination and Transformation in the Third World,* ed. Joel S. Migdal, Atul Kohli, and Vivienne Shue (Cambridge: Cambridge University Press, 1994), p. 11.

4. Louis Marin, *Portrait of the King* (Minneapolis: University of Minnesota Press, 1988), p. 7.

5. James C. Scott, *Domination and the Arts of Resistance: Hidden Transcripts* (New Haven: Yale University Press, 1990), p. 48.

6. T. Fujitani, *Splendid Monarchy: Power and Pageantry in Modern Japan* (Berkeley and Los Angeles: University of California Press, 1996), p. 25.

7. Author's interview, 1996. Among the various security forces, the Presidential Guard, the Special Forces, and the Third Armored Division constitute the essential elite militias responsible for protecting the regime and its capital. Prior to 1984, Rif'at's Defense Com-

panies, whose numbers reached about 50,000, were also key to the regime's security. Asad balances these elite units and intelligence networks against one another, thereby attempting to ensure that no single group imperils his rule.

8. Interestingly, even the discourses of leftist opposition are often as tired and slogan-like as the Ba'th Party's. One scholar of Syria, Hans Gunter Lobmeyer, observes the failure of Leftist opposition to inspire an alternative politics among ordinary Syrians:

> In their pamphlets, highly abstract and sometimes even purely theoretical topics prevail, which have little or nothing to do with what is going on in Syria. The majority of these articles deal with problems that may stimulate the interest of academics and the slogans may sound revolutionary, but none of this affects the ordinary Syrian who tries hard to surmount the difficulties of everyday life and who is tired of political slogans.

See "*Al-dimuqratiyya hiyya [sic] al-hall?* The Syrian Opposition at the End of the Asad Era," in *Contemporary Syria: Liberalization between Cold War and Cold Peace*, ed. Eberhard Kienle (London: I.B. Taurus, 1994), p. 95.

9. Andrei Plesu, "Intellectual Life under Dictatorship," in *Representations* 49 (winter 1995): 62.

10. Ibid.

11. Robert Darnton, "Censorship, a Comparative View: France, 1789–East Germany 1989," *Representations* 49 (winter 1995): 56.

12. Cited in Alan Riding, *New York Times*, 3 August 1997, sec. 2, p. 1.

13. Ibid.

14. One might also recall the "absolutist" state in France in which Louis XIV ruled over the "court society" but was also dependent on his courtiers to sustain his rule. Courtiers monitored each other and themselves, deciphering the king and one another's gestures in terms of changing power relationships in court. But the king was also enmeshed in the system of power relations he had created, having to orchestrate his own movements and to make sure his signals were properly regulated and interpreted. The king, moreover, had to assess constantly the changing dynamics among his courtiers, managing tensions to his advantage. See Norbert Elias, *The Court Society* (New York: Random House, 1984).

15. Cited in Plesu, "Intellectual Life," p. 62.

16. See Lauren Berlant, *The Queen of America Goes to Washington City: Essays on Sex and Citizenship* (Durham: Duke University Press, 1997), p. 223.

17. As Plesu notes, "the reduced possibility of a normal intellectual life enables its irruptive force, its capacity to profit from all the cracks of the system, to be enormous." There is always a "space for play," a chance for maneuvering. See Plesu, "Intellectual Life," p. 63.

18. See also Marlon T. Riggs's essay, "Unleash the Queen," in Michele Wallace, *Black Popular Culture*, ed. Gina Dent (Seattle: Bay Press, 1992), pp. 99–105.

19. David Laitin, *Identity in Formation: The Russian-Speaking Populations in the Near Abroad* (Ithaca: Cornell University Press, 1998), p. 21. Laitin relies on Thomas Schelling's tipping model. See Thomas Schelling, *Micromotives and Macrobehavior* (New York: Norton, 1978).

20. I have in mind a range of disciplinary effects produced by liberal markets, from cultivating desires for commodities, to firing employees who fail to perform efficiently, to introducing incentives that foster competition among people who otherwise might collectively organize in opposition. See Michael Burawoy, *Manufacturing Consent: Changes in the Labor Process under Monopoly Capitalism* (Chicago: University of Chicago Press, 1979). Burawoy argues that in contemporary capitalist contexts the wage has become increasingly independent of the individual's expenditure of effort, and therefore coercion has been "supplemented by the organization of consent." The basis of this consent "lies in the organization of activities as though they presented the worker with real choices, however narrowly confined those choices might be. It is participation in choosing that generates consent" (p. 27). For Adam Przeworski, by contrast, democratic political participation by workers who believe that they profit from the system of capitalism and that they will continue to do so, produces consent. Adam Przeworski, *Capitalism and Social Democracy* (Cambridge: Cambridge University Press, 1985). Two recent studies in rational choice theory have explained aspects of citizen compliance in democratic systems by invoking "contingent consent." In John T. Scholz and Neil Pinney, "Duty, Fear, and Tax Compliance: The Heuristic Basis of Citizenship Behavior," *American Journal of Political Science* 39, no. 2 (May 1995): 490–512, the authors argue that citizens rely on their sense of duty to assess whether they are likely to get

caught if they were to cheat on their taxes. They argue that duty enhances compliance not only by providing a direct motivation to comply but also by indirectly biasing assessments of the likelihood of getting caught. The authors, it seems to me, exaggerate citizens' sense of duty and underestimate the "objective risks" because they focus on the risk of not getting caught in one year, whereas most would-be cheaters probably attempt to calculate the likelihood of getting audited over time. See also Margaret Levi's *Consent, Dissent, and Patriotism* (Cambridge: Cambridge University Press, 1997), which examines the concept of "contingent consent" in depth. For Levi, "contingent consent is a citizen's decision to comply or volunteer in response to demands from a government only if she perceives government as trustworthy and she is satisfied other citizens are also engaging in ethical reciprocity" (p. 19). Both studies focus on citizen motivations for compliance rather than on regime activities and their effects.

21. Michel Foucault, "Politics and the Study of Discourse," in *The Foucault Effect: Studies in Governmentality*, ed. Graham Burchell, Colin Gordon, and Peter Miller (London: Harvester Wheatsheaf, 1991), p. 60. I am thankful to Christina Tarnopolsky who drew my attention to this passage.

22. Václav Havel, "The Power of the Powerless," in *Living in Truth* (London: Faber and Faber, 1986), p. 54.

23. Slavoj Žižek, *Enjoy Your Symptom: Jacques Lacan in Hollywood and Out* (New York: Routledge, 1992), p. x.

24. Slavoj Žižek, *The Sublime Object of Ideology* (London: Verso, 1992), p. 33. This discussion is inspired by Peter Sloterdijk, *Critique of Cynical Reason* (Minnesota: University of Minnesota Press, 1988).

25. Max Weber, "Politics as a Vocation," in *From Max Weber: Essays in Sociology*, ed. H. H. Gerth and C. Wright Mills (New York: Oxford University Press, 1946), p. 78.

26. Paul Veyne makes this distinction in his discussion of public homage paid to the Roman emperor. See *Bread and Circuses: Historical Sociology and Political Pluralism*, trans. Brian Pearce, abridged with an introduction by Oswyn Murray (London and New York: Penguin Books, 1990), p. 381.

27. The similarities between Syria and East European examples were not lost on Syrian citizens. In 1990 on a wall in Damascus graffiti appeared which read, "Shamceascu" (*Sham* means Damascus, and sometimes Syria, in Arabic). This act of defiance ran counter to the

official narrative, which claimed that it was Asad's Corrective Move-
ment in 1970 that initiated the first perestroika, and that the events in
Eastern Europe were nothing but the "introduction of the Corrective
Movement in the socialist camp." See *Tishrin*, 4 March 1990.

28. Veyne, *Bread and Circuses*, p. 315.

Bibliography

Bibliography

Archives

Ministère des Affaires Étrangères, Paris
Ministère de la Défense, Vincennes
Maktabat al-Asad, Damascus

Newspapers and Magazines

al-Baʿth
Awraq min Tishrin
al-Hayat
al-Hadaf
al-ʿIraq al-dimuqrati
Jil al-thawra
al-Kifah al-ʿarabi
al-Ladhiqiyya 87
al-Nahar al-ʿarabi al-dawli
al-Sharq al-awsat
al-Silsila al-ʿilmiyya al-mubassata
Sawt al-shaʿb
al-Thawra
Tishrin
Urubba wa al-ʿarab
Usama

Published Speech of Hafiz Al-Asad

Majmuʿat khutab al-fariq al-qaʾid Hafiz al-Asad

FEDERATIONS PUBLISHING PAMPHLETS

al-Ittihad al-ʿAmm al-Nisaʾi
al-Ittihad al-Riyadi al-ʿAmm
Ittihad Shabibat al-Thawra
Talaʾiʿ al-Baʿth

BOOKS AND ARTICLES

al-ʿAbd Allah, Riyad, ed. *Sanaʾ Muhaydli: ʿarus al-janub.* n.p., n.d.

ʿAbduh, Samir. *al-Tahlil al-nafsi lil-fannanin al-ʿArab.* Matbaʿat al-Ajluni, s.l., 1988, pp. 111–19.

Abélès, Marc. "Modern Political Ritual: Ethnography of an Inauguration and a Pilgrimage by President Mitterand." *Current Anthropology* 29, no. 3 (June 1988): 391–404.

Abrahamian, Ervand. *Khomeinism: Essays on the Islamic Republic.* Berkeley and Los Angeles: University of California Press, 1993.

Abukhalil, Asʿad. "Arab Intellectuals on Trial." *Middle East Journal* 47, no. 4 (autumn 1993): 695–706.

Abu-Lughod, Lila. "The Interpretation of Culture(s) after Television." *Representations* 59 (summer 1997): 109–34.

———. "The Objects of Soap Opera: Egyptian Television and the Cultural Politics of Modernity." In *Worlds Apart: Modernity through the Prism of the Local,* edited by Daniel Miller. London: Routledge, 1995.

———. "The Romance of Resistance: Tracing Transformations of Power through Bedouin Women." *American Ethnologist* 17 (February 1990): 41–55.

Adams, John. "A Dissertation on the Canon and Feudal Law." In *The Political Writings of John Adams,* edited by George A. Peek, Jr. Indianapolis: Bobbs-Merrill Educational Publishing, 1954.

Adas, Michael. "South Asian Resistance in Comparative Perspective." In *Contesting Power: Resistance and Everyday Social Relations in South Asia,* edited by Douglas Haynes and Gyan Prakash. Berkeley and Los Angeles: University of California Press, 1992.

Adonis. *Kitab al-tahawwulat wa al-hijra fi aqalim al-nahar wa al-layl.* Beirut: Dar al-Adab, 1988.

Adorno, Theodor W. "Freudian Theory and the Pattern of Fascist Propaganda." In *The Essential Frankfurt School Reader.* New York: Urizen Books, 1978.

Agulhon, Maurice. *Marianne into Battle: Republican Imagery and Symbolism in France, 1789–1880.* Cambridge: Cambridge University Press, 1979.

ʿAli, Muhammad Ahmad Ismaʿil. "Al-muthaqqaf al-ʿarabi bayn al-taghrib wa al-asala." *al-Wahda* 40 (January 1988): 6–17.

Almond, Gabriel A., and Sidney Verba. *The Civic Culture: Political Attitudes and Democracy in Five Nations.* Princeton: Princeton University Press, 1963.

Althusser, Louis. "Ideology and Ideological State Apparatuses (Notes towards an Investigation)." In *Lenin and Philosophy and Other Essays by Louis Althusser.* New York: Monthly Review Press, 1971.

Anderson, Benedict. *Imagined Communities.* London: Verso, 1991.

Anderson, Perry. *Lineages of the Absolutist State.* London: Verso, 1979.

Antonius, George. *The Arab Awakening: The Story of the Arab National Movement.* London: H. Hamilton, 1938.

Apter, David E., and Tony Saich. *Revolutionary Discourse in Mao's Republic.* Cambridge: Harvard University Press, 1994.

Arendt, Hannah. *Eichmann in Jerusalem: A Report on the Banality of Evil.* Rev. and enl. New York: Penguin Books, 1976.

———. *The Origins of Totalitarianism.* New York: Harcourt, Brace, 1968.

———. "Truth and Politics." In *Between Past and Future.* New York: Viking Press, 1968.

Arjomand, Said. *The Shadow of God and the Hidden Imam: Religion, Political Order, and Societal Change in Shiite Iran from the Beginning to 1890.* Chicago: University of Chicago Press, 1984.

Armbrust, Walter. *Mass Culture and Modernism in Egypt.* Cambridge: Cambridge University Press, 1996.

al-Arsuzi, Zaki. *al-Muʾallafat al-kamila,* vol. 2. Damascus: Matabiʿ al-Idara al-Siyasiyya lil-Jaysh wa al-Quwwat al-Musallaha, 1973.

ʿArus al-janub. Damascus: Dar Tlas, 1985.

al-ʿAsha, Fuʾad. *Hafiz al-Asad: qaʾid wa risala.* Damascus: Dar al-ʿIlm, 1992.

al-ʿAttar, Najah. "Ummuna allati rahalat." *Tishrin.* 29 July 1992.

Bahout, Joseph. "The Syrian Business Community, Its Politics and Prospects." In *Contemporary Syria: Liberalization between Cold War and Cold Peace,* edited by Eberhard Kienle. London: I.B. Taurus, 1994.

Bakhtin, Mikhail. *Rabelais and His World*. Translated by Helene Iswolsky. Bloomington: Indiana University Press, 1984.

Banc, C., and A. Dundes. *First Prize, Fifteen Years! An Annotated Collection of Romanian Political Jokes*. London: Associated University Presses, 1986.

Barakat, Halim. "The Arab Family and the Challenge of Social Transformation." In *Women and the Family in the Middle East: New Voices of Change*, edited by Elizabeth Warnock Fernea. Austin: University of Texas Press, 1985.

———. *The Arab World: Society, Culture and State*. Berkeley and Los Angeles: University of California Press, 1993.

Barakat, Salim. *Al-fikr al-qawmi wa ususuhu al-falsafiyya 'inda Zaki al-Arsuzi*. Damascus: Matba' Mu'assasat al-Wahda lil-Sihafa wa al-Tiba'a wa al-Nashr, 1979.

Bartsch, Shadi. *Actors in the Audience: Theatricality and Doublespeak from Nero to Hadrian*. Cambridge: Harvard University Press, 1994.

Batatu, Hanna. "Some Observations on the Social Roots of Syria's Ruling Military Group and the Cause for its Dominance." *Middle East Journal* 35 (summer 1982): 331–44.

———. "Syria's Muslim Brethren." *Middle East Report* 12, no. 9 (November–December 1982): 12–20, 34, 36.

———. *The Old Social Classes and the Revolutionary Movements of Iraq*. Princeton: Princeton University Press, 1978.

The Ba'th Training Bureau. *al-Ikhwan al-Muslimun: nash'a mashbuha wa tarikh aswad*. Damascus: Maktab al-I'dad, 1985.

Ben-Dor, Gabriel. "Political Culture Approach to Middle East Politics." *International Journal of Middle East Studies* 8 (1977): 43–63.

Berlant, Lauren. *The Queen of America Goes to Washington City: Essays on Sex and Citizenship*. Durham: Duke University Press, 1997.

Bonnell, Victoria E. "The Representation of Women in Early Soviet Political Art." *Russian Review* (July 1991): 267–88.

Bourdieu, Pierre. *Outline of a Theory of Practice*. Translated by Richard Nice. Cambridge: Cambridge University Press, 1982.

Brenner, Neil. "Foucault's New Functionalism." *Theory and Society* 23 (1994): pp. 679–709.

Brubaker, Rogers. *Nationalism Reframed: Nationhood and the National Question in the New Europe*. Cambridge: Cambridge University Press, 1996.

Burawoy, Michael. *Manufacturing Consent.* Chicago: University of Chicago Press, 1979.

Burke, Peter. *Popular Culture in Early Modern Europe.* New York: Harper and Row, 1978.

Buruma, Ian. "Playing for Keeps." *New York Review of Books,* 10 November 1988, 44–50.

Butler, Judith. *Bodies That Matter: On the Discursive Limits of "Sex."* New York: Routledge, 1993.

————. *Gender Trouble.* New York: Routledge, 1990.

————. "Mbembe's Extravagant Power." *Public Culture* 5, no. 1 (fall 1992): 67–74.

Callaghy, Thomas Michael. *State Formation and Absolutism in Comparative Perspective: Seventeenth-Century France and Mobutu Sese Seko's Zaire.* Ph.D. diss., University of California, Berkeley, December 1979.

Callois, Roger. "Logical and Philosophical Problems of the Dream." In *The Dream and Human Societies,* edited by G. E. von Grunebaum and Roger Caillois. Berkeley and Los Angeles: University of California Press, 1966.

Clark, Katerina. *The Soviet Novel: History as Ritual.* Chicago: University of Chicago Press, 1981.

————. "Utopian Anthropology as a Context for Stalinist Literature." In *Stalinism,* edited by Robert Tucker. New York: W. W. Norton and Company, 1977.

Cohen, David William. "The Banalities of Interpretation." *Public Culture* 5, no. 1 (fall 1992): 57–60.

Collier, David, ed. *The New Authoritarianism in Latin America.* Princeton: Princeton University Press, 1979.

Comaroff, Jean. *Body of Power, Spirit of Resistance.* Chicago: University of Chicago Press, 1985.

Comaroff, Jean, and John Comaroff. *Of Revelation and Revolution.* Vol. 1, *Christianity, Colonialism, and Consciousness in South Africa.* Chicago: University of Chicago Press, 1991.

Combs-Schilling, M. E. *Sacred Performances: Islam, Sexuality, and Sacrifice.* New York: Columbia University Press, 1989.

Crystal, Jill. "Authoritarianism and Its Adversaries in the Arab World." *World Politics* 46, no. 2 (January 1994): 262–89.

Dallal, Ahmad. Book review of Kanan Makiya's *Cruelty and Silence: War, Tyranny, Uprising, and the Arab World. al-Hayat,* 23 May 1993.

Darnton, Robert. "Censorship, a Comparative View: France 1789–East Germany 1989." *Representations* 49 (winter 1995): 40–60.

Davis, Eric. "The Museum and the Politics of Social Control in Modern Iraq." In *Commemorations: The Politics of National Identity*, edited by John R. Gillis. Princeton: Princeton University Press, 1994.

Dawn, C. Ernest. *From Ottomanism to Arabism: Essays on the Origins of Arab Nationalism.* Urbana: University of Illinois Press, 1973.

Debord, Guy. *Society of the Spectacle.* Detroit: Black and Red, 1983.

de Certeau, Michel. *The Practice of Everyday Life.* Berkeley and Los Angeles: University of California Press, 1984.

Dirks, Nicholas. "Ritual and Resistance: Subversion as a Social Fact." In *Contesting Power: Resistance and Everyday Social Relations in South Asia.* Berkeley and Los Angeles: University of California Press, 1992.

Domhoff, G. William. *The Mystique of Dreams: A Search for Utopia through Senoi Dream Theory.* Berkeley and Los Angeles: University of California Press, 1985.

Douglas, Allen and Fedwa Malti-Douglas. *Arab Comic Strips: Politics of an Emerging Mass Culture.* Bloomington: Indiana University Press, 1994.

Dreyfus, Hubert L., and Paul Rabinow. *Michel Foucault: Beyond Structuralism and Hermeneutics,* 2d ed. Chicago: University of Chicago Press, 1983.

Drysdale, Alasdair. "Ethnicity in the Syrian Officer Corps." *Civilisations* 29 (1979): 359–74.

——— and Raymond Hinnebusch. *Syria and the Middle East Peace Process.* New York: Council on Foreign Relations Press, 1991.

Dwyer, Kevin. *Arab Voices: The Human Rights Debate in the Middle East.* Berkeley and Los Angeles: University of California Press, 1991.

Eagleton, Terry. *Walter Benjamin: Towards a Revolutionary Criticism.* London: Verso, 1981.

Edelman, Murray. *Constructing the Political Spectacle.* Chicago: University of Chicago Press, 1988.

———. *From Art to Politics: How Artistic Creations Shape Political Conceptions.* Chicago: University of Chicago Press, 1995.

Ehrenreich, Barbara. "Beatlemania: Girls Just Want to Have Fun." In *Remaking Love: The Feminization of Sex.* New York: Anchor Press/Doubleday, 1986.

Eliade, Mircea. *The Sacred and the Profane: The Nature of Religion.* New York: Harper and Row, 1961.

Elias, Norbert. *The Civilizing Process.* Translated by Edmund Jephcott. Vol. 2, *Power and Civility.* New York: Random House, 1982.

———. *The Court Society.* Translated by Edmund Jephcott. New York: Pantheon Books, 1983.

"Entretien avec Omar Amiralay." *Cahiers du cinema* 290–91 (July–August 1979): 79–89.

Etzioni, Amitai. *A Comparative Analysis of Complex Organizations.* New York: Free Press, 1961.

———. "Power and Alienation in Comparative Perspective." In *Comparative Perspectives: Theories and Methods,* edited by A. Etzioni and F. L. DuBow. Boston: Little, Brown, 1970.

Evans, Peter B. et al., eds. *Bringing the State Back In.* New York: Cambridge University Press, 1985.

Fahd, Toufic. "The Dream in Medieval Islamic Society." In *The Dream and Human Societies,* edited by G. E. von Grunebaum and Roger Caillois. Berkeley and Los Angeles: University of California Press, 1966.

Foucault, Michel. *Discipline and Punish: The Birth of the Prison.* Translated by Alan Sheridan. New York: Vintage Books, 1979.

———. *The History of Sexuality, Volume One: An Introduction.* Translated by Robert Hurley. New York: Pantheon Books, 1978.

———. "Maurice Blanchot: The Thought from Outside." In *Foucault/Blanchot.* New York: Zone Books, 1987.

———. "Politics and the Study of Discourse." In *The Foucault Effect: Studies in Governmentality,* edited by Graham Burchell, Colin Gordon, and Peter Miller. London: Harvester Wheatsheaf, 1991.

———. *Power/Knowledge: Selected Interviews and Other Writings 1972–1977.* Edited by Colin Gordon. Translated by Colin Gordon et al. New York: Pantheon Books, 1980.

Freitag, Ulrike. *Geschichtsschreibung in Syrie 1920–1990.* Hamburg: Deutsche Orient Institut, 1991.

Freud, Sigmund. "Family Romances." In *Standard Edition of the Complete Psychological Works of Sigmund Freud.* Translated by James Strachey. London: Hogarth Press, 1959.

———. *Group Psychology and the Analysis of the Ego.* Translated by James Strachey. London: Hogarth Press, 1949.

———. *Jokes and Their Relation to the Unconscious.* Translated by James Strachey. New York: W. W. Norton, 1960.

Freud, Sigmund, and Josef Breuer. *Studies on Hysteria*. New York: Basic Books, 1957.

Friedrich, Carl. *Totalitarianism*. Cambridge: Harvard University Press, 1954.

Fujitani, T. *Splendid Monarchy: Power and Pageantry in Modern Japan*. Berkeley and Los Angeles: University of California Press, 1996.

Gal, Susan. "Language and 'the Arts of Resistance.'" In *Cultural Anthropology* 10, no. 3 (1995): 407–24.

Gaventa, John. *Power and Powerlessness: Quiescence and Rebellion in an Appalachian Valley*. Urbana: University of Illinois Press, 1980.

Geertz, Clifford. "Deep Play: Notes on the Balinese Cockfight." In *Interpretive Social Science: A Second Look*, edited by Paul Rabinow and William M. Sullivan. Berkeley and Los Angeles: University of California Press, 1987.

———. *Local Knowledge: Further Essays in Interpretive Anthropology*. New York: Basic Books, 1983.

———. *Negara: The Theatre State in Nineteenth Century Bali*. Princeton: Princeton University Press, 1980.

———. *The Interpretation of Cultures*. New York: Basic Books, 1973.

Gellner, Ernest. *Nations and Nationalism*. Oxford: Basil Blackwell, 1983.

Gelvin, James L. *Popular Mobilization and the Foundations of Mass Politics in Syria, 1918–1920*. Ph.D. diss., Harvard University, September 1992.

———. "The Social Origins of Popular Nationalism in Syria: Evidence for a New Framework." *International Journal of Middle East Studies* 26 (1994): 645–51.

Gerschenkron, Alexander. *Economic Backwardness in Historical Perspective*. Cambridge: Belknap Press of Harvard University Press, 1962.

Ghalioun, Burhan. *Le Malaise arabe: L'état contre la nation*. Paris: Éditions La Découverte, 1991.

Ghanim, Ghassan. *al-Masrah al-siyasi fi Suriya, 1967–1990*. Damascus: Dar 'Ala' al-Din, 1996.

Girard, Rene. *Violence and the Sacred*. Translated by Patrick Gregory. Baltimore: Johns Hopkins University Press, 1972.

Gluckman, Max. *Order and Rebellion in Tribal Africa*. London: Allen Lane, 1970.

Goody, Jack. *The Development of the Family and Marriage in Europe*. Cambridge: Cambridge University Press, 1983.

Gramsci, Antonio. *Selections from the Prison Notebooks.* Edited by Quintin Hoare and Geoffrey Nowell-Smith. London: Lawrence and Wishart, 1971.

Greenblatt, Stephen. *Renaissance Self-Fashioning: From More to Shakespeare.* Chicago: University of Chicago Press, 1980.

Greenfeld, Liah. *Nationalism: Five Roads to Modernity.* Cambridge: Harvard University Press, 1992.

———. "Transcending the Nation's Worth." *Daedalus* 122, no. 3 (summer 1993): 47–62.

Greif, Avner. "Cultural Beliefs and the Organization of Society: A Historical and Theoretical Reflection on Collectivist and Individualist Societies." *Journal of Political Economy* 102, no. 5 (1989): 912–50.

"Group Think, For North Koreans Mass Games Are Sport and Indoctrination." *Wall Street Journal,* 15 August 1989, 1.

Guha, Ranajit. *Elementary Aspects of Peasant Insurgency.* Delhi: Oxford University Press, 1983.

Haim, Sylvia. *Arab Nationalism: An Anthology.* Berkeley and Los Angeles: University of California Press, 1962.

Hall, Stuart. "Signification, Representation, Ideology: Althusser and the Post-Structuralist Debates." In *Critical Studies in Mass Communication* 2, no. 2 (June 1985).

———. "The Toad in the Garden: Thatcherism among the Theorists." In *Marxism and the Interpretation of Culture,* edited by Cary Nelson and Lawrence Grossberg. Urbana and Chicago: University of Illinois Press.

Hammoudi, Abdellah. *Master and Disciple: The Cultural Foundations of Moroccan Authoritarianism.* Chicago: University of Chicago Press, 1997.

Harlow, Barbara. Introduction to *The Colonial Harem,* by Malek Alloula. Minneapolis: University of Minnesota Press, 1986.

Hatem, Mervat F. "Economic and Political Liberation in Egypt and the Demise of State Feminism." *International Journal of Middle East Studies* 24 (1992): 231–32.

Havel, Václav. "The Power of the Powerless." In *Living in Truth.* Boston: Faber and Faber, 1989.

Haynes, Douglas, and Gyan Prakash. Introduction to *Contesting Power: Resistance and Everyday Social Relations in South Asia.* Berkeley and Los Angeles: University of California Press, 1992.

Heydemann, Steven. *Successful Authoritarianism: The Social and*

Structural Origins of Populist Authoritarian Rule in Syria, 1946–1963. Ph.D. diss., University of Chicago, January 1992.

———. "Taxation without Representation." In *Rules and Rights in the Middle East,* edited by Ellis Goldberg, Resat Kasaba, and Joel Migdal. Seattle: University of Washington Press, 1993.

Hijazi, Ahmad Majdi. "al-Muthaqqaf al-ʿArabi wa al-iltizam al-idyuluji." *al-Wahda* 40 (January 1988): 19–32.

Hinnebusch, Raymond. *Authoritarian Power and State Formation in Syria: Army, Party, and Peasant.* Boulder: Westview Press, 1990.

———. "Does Syria Want Peace?" *Journal of Palestine Studies* (autumn 1996): 42–57.

———. *Peasant and Bureaucracy in Baʿthist Syria: The Political Economy of Rural Development.* Boulder: Westview Press, 1989.

———. "Political Recruitment and Socialization in Syria: The Case of the Revolutionary Youth Federation." *International Journal of Middle East Studies* 11 (1980): 143–74.

———. "State and Civil Society in Syria." *Middle East Journal* 47, no. 2 (spring 1993): 243–57.

Hobsbawm, Eric. *Nations and Nationalism since 1780.* Cambridge: Cambridge University Press, 1990.

———. *The Age of Empire, 1875–1914.* New York: Random House, 1987.

Hobsbawm, Eric, and Terence Ranger. *The Invention of Tradition.* Cambridge: Cambridge University Press, 1983.

Hopkins, Nicholas, and Saad Eddin Ibrahim, eds. *Arab Society: Social Science Perspectives.* Cairo: AUC Press, 1985.

Hourani, Albert. *Arabic Thought in the Liberal Age: 1798–1939.* London: Oxford University Press, 1962.

Hunt, Lynn. *The Family Romance in the French Revolution.* Berkeley and Los Angeles: University of California Press, 1992.

———. *Politics, Culture, and Class in the French Revolution.* Berkeley and Los Angeles: University of California Press, 1984.

Huntington, Samuel P. *The Third Wave: Democratization in the Late Twentieth Century.* Norman: University of Oklahoma Press, 1991.

Huntington, Samuel P., and Clement Henry Moore, eds. *Authoritarian Politics in Modern Society.* New York: Basic Books, 1970.

Ibn Khaldun. *The Muqaddimah: An Introduction to History.* Translated by Franz Rosenthal. Edited by N. J. Dawood. Princeton: Princeton University Press, 1967.

Ibn Sirin, Muhammad. *Tafsir al-ahlam al-kabir.* Cairo: Maktabat wa Matbuʿat Muhammad ʿAli Subayh wa Awladih, 1963.

Inden, Ronald. *Imagining India.* Cambridge: Blackwell, 1990.

Jaridat al-Baʿth fi sabʿa wa thalathin ʿaman. Damascus: Dar al-Baʿth, 1983.

Joseph, Suad. "Gender and Rationality among Arab Families in Lebanon." *Feminist Studies* 19, no. 3 (fall 1993): 465–86.

Jowitt, Ken. *New World Disorder: The Leninist Extinction.* Berkeley and Los Angeles: University of California Press, 1992.

al-Jundi, Sami. *al-Baʿth.* Beirut: Dar al-Nahar, 1969.

Kanafani, Ghassan. *Rijal fi al-shams.* In *al-Athar al-kamila: al-riwayat,* 3d ed., 1:29–152. Beirut: Muʾassasat al-Abhath al-ʿArabiyya, 1986.

Kantorowicz, Ernst H. *The King's Two Bodies: A Study of Medieval Political Theology.* Princeton: Princeton University Press, 1957.

Kawakibi, Salam. "Le Rôle de la télévision dans la relecture de l'histoire." *Monde arabe Maghreb Machrek,* no. 158 (October–December 1997): 47–55.

al-Khafaji, ʿIsam. "State Terror and the Degradation of Politics in Iraq." *Middle East Report* 22, no. 3 (May–June 1992): 15–21.

Khalidi, Rashid, ed. *The Origins of Arab Nationalism.* New York: St. Martin's Press, 1979.

al-Khalidi, Tarif, ed. *Land Tenure and Social Transformation in the Middle East.* Beirut, 1984.

al-Khalil, Hani. *Hafiz al-Asad: al-idyulujiyya al-thawriyya wa al-fikr al-siyasi.* Damascus: Dar Tlas, 1986.

———. *Hafiz al-Asad: al-dawla al-dimuqratiyya al-shaʿbiyya.* Damascus: Dar Tlas, 1987.

Kharkhordin, Oleg. "Reveal and Dissimulate: A Genealogy of Public and Private in Soviet Russia." Unpublished.

Khoury, Philip S. *Urban Notables and Arab Nationalism.* New York: Columbia University Press, 1991.

Kishtainy (Qishtayni), Khalid. *ʿAlam dahik: fukahat, shuʿub wa nikatuha.* Beirut: Dar al-Hamraʾ, 1991.

———. *Arab Political Humour.* London: Quartet Books, 1985.

Kuran, Timur. "Now Out of Never: The Element of Surprise in the East European Revolution of 1989." *World Politics* 44 (October 1991): 7–48.

———. *Private Truths, Public Lies: The Social Consequences of Preference Falsification.* Cambridge: Harvard University Press, 1995.

Labib, al-Tahir. "al-ʿAlam wa al-muthaqqaf wa al-intilijinsya." *al-Wahda* 40 (January 1988): 99–111.

Ladurie, Emmanuel Le Roy. *Carnival in Romans.* Translated by Mary Feeney. New York: George Braziller, 1979.

Laitin, David D. *Hegemony and Culture: Politics and Religious Change among the Yoruba.* Chicago: University of Chicago Press, 1986.

———. *Identity in Formation: The Russian-Speaking Populations in the Near Abroad* (Ithaca: Cornell University Press, 1998).

Laqueur, Thomas. "Crowds, Carnival and the State in English Executions, 1604–1868." In *The First Modern Society,* edited by A. L. Beier, David Cannadine, and James M. Rosenheim. Cambridge: Cambridge University Press, 1989.

———. *Making Sex: Body and Gender from the Greeks to Freud.* Cambridge: Harvard University Press, 1990.

———. "Orgasm, Generation, and the Politics of Reproductive Biology." *Representations* 14 (spring 1986): 1–41.

Lawson, Fred H. *Bahrain: The Modernization of Autocracy.* Boulder: Westview Press, 1989.

———. "Private Capital and the State in Contemporary Syria." *Middle East Report* 27, no. 2 (spring 1997): 8–13; 30.

———. "Social Bases for the Hamah Revolt." *Middle East Report* 12, no. 9 (November–December 1982): 24–28.

Layoun, Mary. "Telling Spaces: Palestinian Women and the Engendering of National Narratives." In *Nationalisms and Sexualities.* New York: Routledge, 1992.

LeFranc, Yannick, and Samir Tahhan. "Comment le Langage Ordinaire Joue Avec le Metalangage Des Grammairiens." *Bulletin d'Études Orientales* 43 (1991): 47–75.

Le Gac, Daniel. *La Syrie du General Assad.* Brussels: Éditions Complexe, 1991.

Levi, Margaret. *Consent, Dissent, and Patriotism.* Cambridge: Cambridge University Press, 1997.

Linz, Juan. "Totalitarian and Authoritarian Regimes." In *Handbook of Political Science,* edited by Fred Greenstein and Nelson Polsby. Vol. 3, *Macropolitical Theory.* Reading, Mass.: Addison-Wesley, 1975.

Lipset, Seymour Martin. *Political Man.* New York: Doubleday, 1960.

Lobmeyer, Hans Gunter. "*Al-dimuqratiyya hiyya* [*sic*] *al-hall?* The

Syrian Opposition at the End of the Asad Era." In *Contemporary Syria: Liberalization between Cold War and Cold Peace*, edited by Eberhard Kienle. London: I.B. Taurus, 1994.

Longuenesse, Elisabeth. "Bourgeoisie, petite bourgeoisie et couches moyennes en Syrie: Contribution à une analyse de la nature de classe de L'état." *Peuples Mediterraneens* (July–September 1978): 21–42.

———. "The Class Nature of the State in Syria." *Middle East Research and Information Project Reports*, no. 77 (May 1979): 3–11.

Luqa, Iskandar. *Hafiz al-Asad: qiyam fikriyya insaniyya.* Damascus: Dar Tlas, 1986.

Macciocchi, Maria-Antonietta. "Sexualité feminine dans l'idéologie fasciste." In *Sexualité et politique: Documents du congrès international de psychanalyse*, Milan, 25 –28 November 1975, edited by Armando Verdiglione. Paris: Union Générale d'Éditions, 1977.

Machiavelli, Niccolò. *The Prince and the Discourses*. New York: Random House, 1950.

Mahfouz, Nagib. *Midaq Alley.* Translated by Trevor Le Gassick. New York: Anchor Books, 1992.

Makiya, Kanan (Samir al-Khalil). *Cruelty and Silence: War, Tyranny, Uprising and the Arab World.* New York: W. W. Norton and Co., 1993.

———. *The Monument: Art, Vulgarity and Responsibility in Iraq.* Berkeley and Los Angeles: University of California Press, 1991.

———. *Republic of Fear: The Politics of Modern Iraq.* Berkeley and Los Angeles: University of California Press, 1989.

al-Malih, Wasfi. *Tarikh al-masrah al-suri.* Damascus: Dar al-Fikr, 1984.

Malik, George 'Ayn, and Anwar Salim Sallum. *Hafiz al-Asad: al-qiyada wa al-tarikh.* Damascus: Dar Ibn Hani, 1985.

Makarim, Hamdan and Tawfiq Kuttab. *Masirat al-wafa' wa al-'ata'.* N.p., 1988.

Maoz, Moshe. *The Sphinx of Damascus.* New York: Weidenfeld and Nicolson, 1988.

Marin, Louis. *Portrait of the King.* Translated by Martha M. Houle. Theory and History of Literature, vol. 57. Minneapolis: University of Minnesota Press, 1988.

Marsot, 'Afaf Lutfi al-Sayyid. "Humor: The Two-Edged Sword." *Middle East Studies Bulletin* 14, no. 1 (July 1980): 1–9.

Marx, Karl. *The Eighteenth Brumaire of Louis Bonaparte.* New York: International Publishers, 1963.

Mason, Robert Scott. "Government and Politics." In *Syria: A Country Study.* Washington, D.C.: Department of the Army, 1988.

Mayer, Ann Elizabeth. *Islam and Human Rights: Tradition and Politics.* Boulder: Westview Press, 1991.

Mbembe, Achille. "The Banality of Power and the Aesthetics of Vulgarity in the Postcolony." *Public Culture* 4, no. 2 (spring 1992): 1–30.

———. "Domaines de la nuit et autorité onirique dans les maquis du Sud-Cameroun (1955–1958)." *Journal of African History* 31 (1991).

———. "Prosaics of Servitude and Authoritarian Civilities." *Public Culture* 5, no. 1 (fall 1992): 123–49.

———. "Provisional Notes on the Postcolony." *Africa* (London) 62, no. 1 (1992): 3–37.

Melhem, Hisham. "Syria between Two Transitions." *Middle East Report* 27, no. 2 (spring 1997): 2–7.

Merrick, Jeffrey. "Patriarchalism and Constitutionalism in Eighteenth-Century Parlementary Discourse." *Studies in Eighteenth Century Culture* 20 (1990).

Messick, Brinkley. *The Calligraphic State: Textual Domination and History in Muslim Society.* Berkeley and Los Angeles: University of California Press, 1993.

Middle East Watch. *Syria Unmasked: The Suppression of Human Rights by the Asad Regime.* New Haven: Yale University Press, Human Rights Watch, 1991.

Migdal, Joel S. "The State in Society: An Approach to Struggles for Domination." In *State Power and Social Forces: Domination and Transformation in the Third World,* edited by Joel S. Migdal, Atul Kohli, and Vivienne Shue. Cambridge: Cambridge University Press, 1994.

Mitchell, Timothy. *Colonising Egypt.* Berkeley and Los Angeles: University of California Press, 1991.

———. "Everyday Metaphors of Power." *Theory and Society* 19 (1990): 545–77.

———. "The Limits of the State: Beyond Statist Approaches and Their Critics." *American Political Science Review* 85, no. 1 (March 1991): 77–96.

Montrose, Louis Adrian. "'Eliza, Queene of Shepheardes' and the

Pastoral of Power." In *The New Historicism Reader,* edited by
H. Aram Veeser. New York: Routledge, 1994.

Moore, Barrington. *Injustice: The Social Bases of Obedience.* White
Plains, N.Y.: M.E. Sharpe, 1987.

Mosse, George L. *The Nationalization of the Masses: Political Symbolism and Mass Movements in Germany from the Napoleonic Wars
through the Third Reich.* New York: New American Library, 1975.

Mufti, Malik. *Sovereign Creations.* Ithaca: Cornell University Press,
1996.

Muhammad, Usama. "Al-karasi kharij salat al-'ard." *al-Hayat,*
21 March 1995.

———. "Sadiq al-kadhdhab, sadiq al-munafiq." *al-Hayat,* June 1996.

Muhawi, Ibrahim. "The Metalinguistic Joke: Sociolinguistic Dimensions of Arabic Folk Genre." In *Arabic Sociolinguistics: Issues and
Perspectives,* edited by Yasir Suleiman. Surrey, England, 1994.

al-Naqeeb, Khaldoun. *Society and State in the Gulf and Arab Penin-
sula: A Different Perspective.* London: Routledge, 1990.

"Notes from the Annual Meetings: Culture and Rational Choice."
*American Political Science Association-Comparative Politics News-
letter* (summer 1997): 5–21.

Oh, Kong Dan. *Leadership Change in North Korean Politics: The Succession to Kim Il Sung.* Santa Monica: Rand Corporation, 1988.

Olaniyan, Tejumola. "Narrativizing Postcoloniality: Responsibilities." *Public Culture* 5, no. 1 (fall 1992): 47–55.

Ortner, Sherry B. "Introduction." In *Representations* 59 (summer
1997): 1–13.

———. *Making Gender: The Politics and Erotics of Culture.* Boston:
Beacon Press, 1996.

Ozouf, Mona. *Festivals and the French Revolution.* Translated by
Alan Sheridan. Cambridge: Harvard University Press, 1988.

Pascal, Blaise. *Pensées.* Harmondsworth: Penguin Books, 1966.

Perthes, Volker. *The Political Economy of Syria under Asad.* London:
I.B. Taurus, 1995.

———. "Syria's Parliamentary Elections: Remodeling Asad's Political Base." *Middle East Report* 22, no. 1 (January–February 1992):
15–18.

Peukert, Detlev J. K. *Inside Nazi Germany: Conformity, Opposition,
and Racism in Everyday Life.* Translated by Richard Deveson.
New Haven: Yale University Press, 1982.

Picard, Elizabeth. "Arab Military in Politics: From Revolutionary

Plot to Authoritarian Regime." In *The Arab State*, edited by Giacomo Luciani. London: Routledge, 1990.

———. "Clans militaires et pouvoir ba'thiste en Syrie." *Orient* (1979): 49–62.

Pitkin, Hanna Fenichel. *Fortune Is a Woman*. Berkeley and Los Angeles: University of California Press, 1984.

———. *Wittgenstein and Justice*. Berkeley and Los Angeles: University of California Press, 1972.

Plesu, Andrei. "Intellectual Life under Dictatorship." *Representations* 49 (winter 1995): 61–71.

Poggi, Gianfranco. *The Development of the Modern State: A Sociological Introduction*. Stanford: Stanford University Press, 1978.

Przeworski, Adam. *Capitalism and Social Democracy*. Cambridge: Cambridge University Press, 1985.

Putnam, Robert D. (with Robert Leonardi and Raffaella Y. Nanetti). *Making Democracy Work: Civic Traditions in Modern Italy*. Princeton: Princeton University Press, 1993.

Qudsi, Safwan. *al-Batal wa al-tarikh: qira'a fi fikr Hafiz al-Asad al-siyasi*. Damascus: Dar Tlas, 1984.

Rabinow, Paul, and William M. Sullivan, eds. *Interpretive Social Science: A Second Look*. Berkeley and Los Angeles: University of California Press, 1987.

Reid, Donald Malcolm. "The Postage Stamp: A Window on Saddam Hussein's Iraq." *Middle East Journal* 47, no. 1 (winter 1993): 77–89.

Ricoeur, Paul. "The Metaphorical Process as Cognition, Imagination, and Feeling." In *On Metaphor*, edited by Sheldon Sacks. Chicago: University of Chicago Press, 1979.

Riggs, Marlon T. "Unleash the Queen." In *Black Popular Culture*. A project by Michele Wallace, edited by Gina Dent. Seattle: Bay Press, 1992.

Rogin, Michael. *Fathers and Children: Andrew Jackson and the Subjugation of the American Indian*. New York: Alfred A. Knopf, 1975.

———. "Kiss Me Deadly: Communism, Motherhood, and Cold War Movies." *Representations* 6 (spring 1984): 1–36.

———. "'Make My Day!': Spectacle as Amnesia in Imperial Politics." In *The New Historicism Reader*, edited by H. Aram Veeser. New York: Routledge, 1994.

———. *Ronald Reagan, The Movie, and Other Episodes in Political*

Demonology. Berkeley and Los Angeles: University of California Press: 1987.

Rorty, Richard. *Contingency, Irony, and Solidarity.* Cambridge: Cambridge University Press, 1989.

Rugh, William A. *The Arab Press: News Media and Political Process in the Arab World.* 2d ed. Syracuse: Syracuse University Press, 1987.

Saab, Edouard. *La Syrie ou la révolution dans la rancoeur.* Paris: Julliard, 1968.

al-Saʿdani, ʾIzzat. *Basil fi ʿuyun al-Misriyyin.* Cairo: al-Ahram, 1995.

Sadowski, Yahya. "Baʿthist Ethics and the Spirit of State Capitalism: Patronage and the Party in Contemporary Syria." In *Ideology and Power in the Middle East: Studies in Honor of George Lenczowski,* edited by Peter Chelkowski and Robert J. Pranger. Durham: Duke University Press, 1988.

———. "Guns, Cadres and Money." *Middle East Research and Information Project Reports,* no. 134 (July–August 1985): 3–8.

Said, Edward W. *Orientalism.* New York: Vintage Books, 1978.

———. "The Intellectuals and the War," *Middle East Research and Information Project Reports,* no. 171 (July–August 1991): 15–20.

Saʿid, Usama. "Qabr Sakran." *Alef* 5 (1991): 58–62.

Salamé, Ghassan, ed. *The Foundations of the Arab State.* New York: Croom Helm, 1987.

Salih, al-Tayyib. *Mawsim al-hijra ila al-shamal.* Beirut: Dar al-ʿAwda, 1987.

Scarry, Elaine. *The Body in Pain: The Making and Unmaking of the World.* New York: Oxford University Press, 1985.

Schaar, John H. *Legitimacy in the Modern State.* New Brunswick: Transaction Publishers, 1989.

Schelling, Thomas. *Micromotives and Macrobehavior* (New York: Norton, 1978).

Scholz, John T., and Neil Pinney, "Duty, Fear, and Tax Compliance: The Heuristic Basis of Citizenship Behavior." *American Journal of Political Science* 39, no. 2 (May 1995): 490–512.

Scott, James C. *Domination and the Arts of Resistance: Hidden Transcripts.* New Haven: Yale University Press, 1990.

———. *Weapons of the Weak: Everyday Forms of Peasant Resistance.* New Haven: Yale University Press, 1985.

Seale, Patrick. *Asad: The Struggle for the Middle East.* Berkeley and Los Angeles: University of California Press, 1988.

————. *The Struggle for Syria: A Study of Post-War Arab Politics.* New Haven: Yale University Press, 1965.

Sewell, William H., Jr. "The Concept(s) of Culture." In *Beyond the Cultural Turn: History and Sociology in the Age of Paradigm Breakdown,* edited by Victoria Bonnell and Lynn Hunt. Berkeley and Los Angeles: University of California Press, forthcoming.

————. "The French Revolution and the Emergence of the Nation Form." Unpublished.

Sha'ban, Bouthaina. *Both Right and Left-Handed: Arab Women Talk about Their Lives.* Bloomington: Indiana University Press, 1991.

Sharabi, Hisham. *Neopatriarchy: A Theory of Distorted Change in Arab Society.* New York: Oxford University Press, 1988.

Sloterdijk, Peter. *Critique of Cynical Reason.* Minnesota: University of Minnesota Press, 1988.

Springborg, Robert. "Baathism in Practice: Agriculture, Politics, and Political Culture in Syria and Iraq." *Middle Eastern Studies* 17, no. 2 (April 1981): 191–209.

————. *Family, Power, and Politics in Egypt.* Philadelphia: University of Pennsylvania Press, 1982.

Stallybrass, Peter, and Allon White. *The Politics and Poetics of Transgression.* Ithaca: Cornell University Press, 1986.

Stokes, Susan C. "Hegemony, Consciousness, and Political Change in Peru." *Politics and Society* 19, no. 3 (1991): 265–90.

Strong, Roy. *The Cult of Elizabeth: Elizabethan Portraiture and Pageantry.* Berkeley and Los Angeles: University of California Press, 1977.

"Syria's Tadmor Prison." *Human Rights Watch/Middle East* 8, no. 2 (April 1996).

"Syria: The Price of Dissent." *Human Rights Watch/Middle East* 7, no. 4 (July 1995).

Tarabishi, George. "Min al-muthaqqafin ila al-intilijinsya." *al-Wahda* 40 (January 1988): 62–73.

Theweleit, Klaus. *Male Fantasies.* Minneapolis: University of Minnesota Press, 1987.

Tilly, Charles. "On the History of European State-Making." *The Formation of National States in Western Europe.* Princeton: Princeton University Press, 1975.

Tucker, Robert. "The Dictator and Totalitarianism." *World Politics* 27 (1974–75): 555–83.

Turner, Victor. *The Ritual Process: Structure and Anti-Structure.* Chicago: Aldine, 1969.

ʿUmar, Muʿin Khalil. "Namadhij min al-muthaqqafin fi al-mujtamaʿ al-ʿarabi." *al-Wahda* 40 (January 1988): 48–54.

van Dam, Nikolaos. *The Struggle for Power in Syria: Sectarianism, Regionalism, and Tribalism in Politics, 1961–1978.* New York: St. Martin's Press, 1979.

Verdery, Katherine. "From Parent-State to Family Patriarchs: Gender and Nation in Contemporary Eastern Europe." *East European Politics and Societies* 8, no. 2 (spring 1994): 225–55.

Veyne, Paul. *Bread and Circuses: Historical Sociology and Political Pluralism.* Translated by Brian Pearce. New York: Penguin Books, 1992.

Von Geldern, James. *Bolshevik Festivals 1917–1921.* Berkeley and Los Angeles: University of California Press, 1993.

Von Grunebaum, G. E. "The Cultural Function of the Dream as Illustrated by Classical Islam." In *The Dream and Human Societies,* edited by G. E. von Grunebaum and Roger Caillois. Berkeley and Los Angeles: University of California Press, 1966.

Watkins, Susan Cotts. *From Provinces into Nations.* Princeton: Princeton University Press, 1991.

Weber, Eugen. *Peasants into Frenchmen.* London: Chatto and Windus, 1979.

Weber, Max. *Economy and Society.* Edited by Guenther Roth and Claus Wittich. Berkeley and Los Angeles: University of California Press, 1978.

———. "Politics as a Vocation." In *From Max Weber: Essays in Sociology,* edited by H. H. Gerth and C. Wright Mills. New York: Oxford University Press, 1946.

Williams, Raymond. *Marxism and Literature.* London: Oxford University Press, 1977.

Yang, Mayfair. *Gifts, Favors, and Banquets: The Art of Social Relationships in China.* Ithaca: Cornell University Press, 1994.

Yates, Frances A. *Astraea: The Imperial Theme in the Sixteenth Century.* Boston: Ark Paperbacks, 1975.

Zahran, Jamal ʿAli. "Taʾthir al-awdaʿ al-mujtamaʿiyya ʿala dawr al-muthaqqaf al-ʿArabi." *al-Wahda* 40 (January 1988): 33–47.

Zerubavel, Yael. "The Historic, the Legendary, and the Incredible: Invented Tradition and Collective Memory in Israel." In *Com-*

memorations: The Politics of National Identity. Princeton: Princeton University Press, 1994.

———. *Recovered Roots: Collective Memory and the Making of Israeli National Tradition.* Chicago and London: The University of Chicago Press, 1995.

Žižek, Slavoj. *Enjoy Your Symptom: Jacques Lacan in Hollywood and Out.* New York: Routledge, 1992.

———. *The Sublime Object of Ideology.* New York: Verso, 1991.